Bangladesh at 50

'Bangladesh succeeded in making an enviable journey from a "bottomless basket" to a developing country; but there have been challenges as well. This book will certainly help to understand this journey as well as some of the challenges that Bangladesh needs to be wary about.'

—Imtiaz Ahmed
Professor of International Relations, Director, Centre for Genocide Studies
University of Dhaka, Dhaka, Bangladesh

'Datta and Narayan bring together incisive contributions to unpack the story of Bangladesh that remains understudied and poorly appreciated.'

—Raja Mohan
Director, Institute of South Asian Studies, National University of Singapore

Bangladesh at 50

Development and Challenges

Edited by

S. Narayan

Sreeradha Datta

with a Foreword by

Rehman Sobhan

Orient BlackSwan

BANGLADESH AT 50: DEVELOPMENT AND CHALLENGES

ORIENT BLACKSWAN PRIVATE LIMITED

Registered Office
3-6-752 Himayatnagar, Hyderabad 500 029, Telangana, India
e-mail: centraloffice@orientblackswan.com

Other Offices
Bengaluru, Chennai, Guwahati, Hyderabad, Kolkata,
Mumbai, New Delhi, Noida, Patna

First published by Orient Blackswan Pvt. Ltd. 2020

ISBN 978-93-90122-60-8

Cover design: Mishta Roy.

Front cover: Eighth March Rally in Dhaka, Jatiyo Nari Shramik Trade Union Kendra (National Women Workers' Trade Union Centre); photograph by Soman.

Back cover: Balaka Cinema Hall, Dhaka New Market; photograph by Ragib Hasan for Wikipedia, Bangladesh, 9 September 2007.

Typeset in New Baskerville 10/12.5 by
Shine Graphics, Delhi

038370

Printed in India at
Thomson Press, New Delhi 110 020

Published by
Orient Blackswan Private Limited
3-6-752 Himayatnagar, Hyderabad 500 029, Telangana, India
e-mail: info@orientblackswan.com

Contents

Tables and Figures

Tables

Figures

Abbreviations

ABB	Association of Bankers, Bangladesh
ACC	Anti-Corruption Commission
ACFTA	African Continental Free Trade Area
ADB	Asian Development Bank
AGOA	African Growth and Opportunities Act
AIIB	Asian Infrastructure Investment Bank
AML	Anti-Money Laundering
APTA	Asia-Pacific Trade Agreement
AQIS	Al Qaeda in the Indian Sub-continent
ASA	Association for Social Development
ASEAN	Association of Southeast Asian Nations
ATM	Automated Teller Machine
AUSAID	Australian Aid
BAB	Bangladesh Association of Bankers
BAEC	Bangladesh Atomic Energy Commission
BAKSAL	Bangladesh Krishak Sramik Awami League
BAPEX	Bangladesh Petroleum Exploration and Production Company Limited
BBIN	Bangladesh–Bhutan–India–Nepal
BBS	Bangladesh Bureau of Statistics
BBT	Billion Bangladeshi Taka
BCCSAP	Bangladesh Climate Change Strategy and Action Plan
BCCT	Bangladesh Climate Change Trust
BCIM	Bangladesh–China–India–Myanmar
BDR	Bangladesh Rifles
BFIU	Bangladesh Financial Intelligence Unit
BFTA	Bilateral Free Trade Agreement
BIMSTEC	Bay of Bengal Initiative for Multi-Sectoral Technical and Economic Cooperation
BIMSTEC-FTA	Bay of Bengal Initiative for Multi-Sectoral Technical and Economic Cooperation-Free Trade Agreement
BJI	Bangladesh Jamaat-e-Islami
BJP	Bharatiya Janata Party

BNP	Bangladesh Nationalist Party
BoE	Bank of England
BPL	Below Poverty Line
BRAC	Bangladesh Rural Advancement Committee
BRI	Belt and Road Initiative
BSEC	Bangladesh Security Exchange Commission
BSF	Border Security Force
CAMELS	Capital adequacy, Assets, Management capability, Earnings, Liquidity, Sensitivity
CDP	Committee for Development Policy
CEDAW	Convention on Elimination of all Forms of Discrimination against Women
CEOs	Chief Executive Officers
CEPA	Comprehensive Economic Partnership Agreement
CTF	Combating Terrorist Finance
CG	Caretaker Government
CHT	Chittagong Hill Tracts
CIDA	Canadian International Development Agency
CIF-SREP	Climate Investment Funds Scaling Up Renewable Energy Program
CNG	Compressed Natural Gas
CPD	Centre for Policy Dialogue
CPI	Consumer Price Index
CPTPP	Comprehensive and Progressive Trans-Pacific Partnership
CRS	Congressional Research Service
CSE	Chittagong Stock Exchange
CSR	Corporate Social Responsibility
CTTC	Counter-Terrorism and Transnational Crime
DC	Developing Country
DFID	Department for International Development
DFQF	Duty-Free Quota-Free
DSE	Dhaka Stock Exchange
DSM	Dispute-Settlement Mechanism
EBA	Everything But Arms
EIF	Enhanced Integration Framework
EPB	Export Promotion Bureau
EPZs	Export Processing Zones

ERD	Economic Relations Division
ESCAP	Economic and Social Commission for Asia and Pacific
ESP	Essential Services Package
EU	European Union
EVI	Economic Vulnerability Index
EWS	Early Warning System
FCA	Financial Conduct Authority
FCBs	Foreign Commercial Banks
FDI	Foreign Direct Investment
FIs	Financial Institutions
FP	Family Planning
FRC	Financial Reporting Council
FSRP	Financial Sector Reform Program
FSRU	Floating Storage Regasification Unit
FTAs	Free Trade Agreements
FY	Fiscal Year/Financial Year
GATT	General Agreement on Tariffs and Trade
GDI	Gross Domestic Income
GDP	Gross Domestic Product
GII	Gender Inequality Index
GIZ	Gesellschaft für Internationale Zusammenarbeit
GNI	Gross National Income
GSP	Generalised System of Preferences
GSS	Gano Shahajjo Sangstha
GWH	Gigawatt Hours
HAI	Human Asset Index
HDI	Human Development Index
HIC	High-Income Country
HIESs	Household Income and Expenditure Surveys
HNPSP	Health, Nutrition and Population Sector Programme
HR	Human Resources
IBBL	Islami Bank Bangladesh Ltd
ICT	International Criminal Tribunals
IDA	International Development Association
IDRA	Insurance Development and Regulatory Authority
IEA	International Energy Agency

IFAD	International Fund for Agricultural Development
ILO	International Labour Organization
ILO-SANEM	International Labour Organization-South Asian Network of Economic Modelling
IMF	International Monetary Fund
IPCC	Intergovernmental Panel on Climate Change
IPO	Initial Public Offering
IPoA	Istanbul Programme of Action
IS	Islamic State
ISMs	International Support Measures
JBIC	Japan Bank for International Cooperation
JICA	Japan International Cooperation Agency
JMJB	Jagrata Muslim Janata Bangladesh
JMB	Jama'atul Mujahideen Bangladesh
JS	Jatiya Sangsad
KPIs	Key Performance Indicators
Ktoe	Kilotonnes of Oil Equivalent
KWF	Kreditanstalt für Wiederaufbau
KWH	Kilowatt Hours
L/Cs	Letter of Credits
LBA	Land Boundary Agreement
LDC	Least Developed Country
LIC	Low-Income Country
LMIC	Lower Middle-Income Country
LNG	Liquefied Natural Gas
LOCs	Lines of Credit
LPG	Liquefied Petroleum Gas
LTTE	Liberation Tigers of Tamil Eelam
MCR	Minimum Capital Requirements
MDGs	Millennium Development Goals
MDs	Managing Directors
MFA	Multi-Fibre Arrangement
MFIs	Micro-Finance Institutions
MIC	Middle-Income Country
MMSCFD	Million Million Standard Cubic Feet Per Day
MoEF	Ministry of Environment and Forests
MoHFW	Ministry of Health and Family Welfare
MoUs	Memorandums of Understanding

MPs	Members of Parliament
MPI	Multidimensional Poverty Index
MPS	Monetary Policy Statement
MRA	Microcredit Regulatory Authority
MSMEs	Micro, Small and Medium Enterprises
MT	Metric Tonnes
Mtoe	Millions of Tonnes of Oil Equivalent
MVA	Motor Vehicles Agreement
MW	Megawatt
NAM	Non-Aligned Movement
NBFIs	Non-Bank Financial Institutions
NDB	New Development Bank
NDC	Nationally Determined Contribution
NFPE	Non-Formal Primary Education
NGOs	Non-Governmental Organisations
NPLs	Non-Performing Loans
NRR	Net Reproduction Rate
NTJ	National Towheeth Jamath
ODA	Official Development Assistance
ODA	Overseas Development Agency
OECD	Organisation for Economic Cooperation and Development
OIC	Organisation of Islamic Cooperation
OXFAM	Oxford Committee for Famine Relief
PCA	Permanent Court of Arbitration
PCBs	Private Commercial Banks
PEC	Primary Education Completion
PEOC	Primary Education for Older Children
POL	Petroleum, Oil and Lubricants
PPP	Purchasing Power Parity
PRA	Prudential Regulation Authority
PSMP	Power and Energy Sector Master Plan
PTI	Press Trust of India
PV	Photovoltaic
RCEP	Regional Comprehensive Economic Partnership
RMG	Readymade Garment
RNDC	Royal Norwegian Development Cooperation
ROO	Rules of Origin

RTAs	Regional Trade Agreements
RTI	Right to Information
RWA	Risk Weighted Asset
S&D	Special and Differential
SAARC	South Asian Association for Regional Cooperation
SAFTA	South Asia Free Trade Agreement
SAP	Structural Adjustment Programs
SBs	Specialised Banks
SCBs	State-owned Commercial Banks
SDGs	Sustainable Development Goals
SEZs	Special Economic Zones
SIBL	Social Islami Bank Ltd
SIDA	Swedish International Development Agency
SMEs	Small and Medium-sized Entrepreneurs
SREDA	Sustainable and Renewable Energy Development Authority
STEM	Science, Technology, Engineering and Mathematics
SWIFT	Society for Worldwide Inter-bank Financial Telecommunication
tcf	Trillion Cubic Feet
TFA	Trade Facilitation Agreement
TICFA	Trade and Investment Cooperation Forum Agreement
ToRs	Terms of Reference
TRIMS	Trade-Related Investment Measures
TRIPS	Trade-Related Intellectual Property Rights
UAE	United Arab Emirates
UIC	Upper-Income Country
ULFA	United Liberation Front of Assam
UMIC	Upper Middle-Income Country
UN	United Nations
UNCAC	United Nations Convention against Corruption
UNDP	United Nations Development Programme
UN-ECOSOC	Economic and Social Council of the UN
UNESCO	United Nations Educational, Scientific and Cultural Organization
UNFPA	United Nations Population Fund

UNSC	United Nations Security Council
US	United States
USAID	United States Agency for International Development
USTR	US Trade Representative
WDI	World Development Indicators
WEF	World Economic Forum
WTO	World Trade Organization
XPB	Export Performance Benefit

Foreword

Any volume commemorating the fiftieth anniversary of Bangladesh independence would have to retail an interesting but complex narrative of notable progress in the area of development and regression in the sphere of governance. Interestingly enough, a similar polarised narrative was projected in a publication on Bangladesh to commemorate its twenty-fifth anniversary, *Bangladesh: Promise and Performance* (Jahan 2000). The chapters contributed to this volume were presented at a conference convened by the Southern Asian Institute, School of International and Public Affairs, at Columbia University, in December 1996. Comparing the tone and context of these two studies, separated by a quarter of a century, what is notable is the significant improvement in economic performance and the further deterioration in the state of governance. The polarised trajectory between development and governance has become sufficiently noticeable to earn conceptual recognition as the Bangladesh development paradox. This paradox originates in Bangladesh's challenge to the conventional wisdom popularised in contemporary development literature, that good governance is a precondition for strong development. The chapters presented in this volume do attempt to address this paradox, but at the end of the day, the readers will have to judge whether they emerge as appreciably better equipped to unravel this contradiction in Bangladesh's journey over the last quarter of a century.

A careful reading of the chapters on economic development, trade, industry, environment and energy spell out some of the positive outcomes registered in areas such as macroeconomic growth, export dynamism, poverty reduction and improved human development indicators. In all the areas, Bangladesh has surpassed Pakistan, which, in 1971, and for some years after, was well-ahead of Bangladesh. Not only have we surpassed Pakistan in terms of human development indicators, including reducing levels of poverty, but robust growth rates have also enabled us to surpass Pakistan in terms of per capita income and export volume. In recent years, Bangladesh has even surpassed India in a number of human development indicators such as life expectancy, infant mortality, and reducing gender inequality.

Bangladesh's high Gross Domestic Product (GDP) growth rate has been an important driving force in reducing poverty. Some of the important drivers of growth, such as the expansion in agricultural output, growth and diversification of the non-farm economy, export growth driven by readymade garments (RMGs), high migrant remittances, growth of the construction sector, all have strong labour-intensive characteristics, which have contributed to poverty reduction.

Successive governments, particularly in the democratic era from 1991 onwards, have substantially increased investment in human development. These public efforts have been greatly augmented by a variety of programmes initiated by NGOs in education, health and population control. In recent years, the private sector has also emerged as a major investor in education and healthcare services. However, our human development/GDP ratios still remain below many developing countries, which lag behind Bangladesh's development performance. Such increases in expenditure contributing to improved quantitative indices are unfortunately not backed up by a strong governance of the human development sector, so that quality of service in the sector tends to be inequitably distributed and exposed to unacceptable levels of rent extraction.

The Bangladesh government's major contribution to the growth of the economy, particularly in the last decade, has been through massive investments in infrastructure, mostly in the area of power and communications. The recent deceleration in private investment, which has stabilised at around 21/22 per cent of GDP, has been compensated for by the expansion in public sector investment, which is now in the range of 8 per cent GDP. High levels of public investment have been sustained by growth in revenue generation. Compared to other developing and neighbouring countries, Bangladesh's revenue/GDP ratio remains low and well below its recoverable potential. The growth in revenues has thus originated largely in high rates of GDP growth. The burgeoning of revenue collection has made it possible for the government to invest heavily in the construction of mega projects such as the Padma Bridge, drawing largely on domestic budgetary resources. However, as with the human development sector, the governance of public infrastructure projects has been weak and exposed again to rent extraction, reflected in substantial cost and time overruns.

The developmental dynamism registered by the economy has enabled Bangladesh to cross two thresholds: graduation from the UN-defined category of a least developed country (LDC), and also graduation from the status of a low-income country (LIC) as categorised by the World Bank. The challenge before the country is to sustain this trajectory of growth so that Bangladesh can attain the level of an upper middle-income country (UMIC), and eventually an upper-income country (UIC) by the target dates set by the present government for 2041.

The chapters in this volume indicate that there are strong objective reasons to be optimistic about attaining these targets, but important concerns, mostly associated with the deteriorating quality of governance, remain. Some encouragement may be derived from the experience of the past 25 years, where concerns registered over the quality of governance, recorded in the twenty-fifth anniversary commemorative volume, have persisted, and in some areas, have aggravated; but this has not arrested the upward trajectory of the development process. I have argued in a recent public address (Sobhan 2017) that some of the key drivers of growth have managed, over the years, to transcend the liability of malgovernance, which could have depreciated their entrepreneurial energies. Some of these drivers of growth are identified below:

- The dynamism of small holder peasant agriculture, which has quadrupled food production since 1972 while greatly diversifying the rural economy through crop diversification, rising investments in fisheries, poultry-farming, animal husbandry and non-farm economic activity in the rural area;
- The dynamism of an emergent entrepreneurial class, which has not only driven Bangladesh's RMG export growth, but has also greatly diversified the industrial economy into areas such as high-rise construction, pharmaceuticals, steel manufacture, shipbuilding, and many other new areas that have served both the export sector and a growing domestic market;
- The gender revolution, which has transitioned rural women from living out their lives in low-income households into

the urban labour force, particularly in the RMG sector, and has drawn them into household-based economic activities through their creditworthy engagement with the micro-credit revolution. The gender revolution has further encouraged rural families to fully exploit opportunities created by both the government and NGOs to educate girls, which has further encouraged their participation in the market economy;

- The enterprise and risk-taking capacity of Bangladeshis, drawn largely from the lower-income households, to travel to every corner of the world in search of their livelihood, has ensured a growing stream of remittances that has not only strengthened the balance of payments of the country, but has also enhanced the level of gross national savings;
- Bangladesh's energetic and creative NGOs, which have served as the conduit linking an educated, urban middle class with the rural society for the provision of public services to the less privileged households.

All these above drivers of growth remain active today. They have, over the years, expanded the stream and scope of their activities, gained from experience, and have established an autonomous capacity for regeneration and growth independent of access to public resources. The operational issue governing the sustainability of these autonomously driven agents of growth is the extent to which the state retains the ability to inhibit, even frustrate their growth, or can be supportive in enhancing their dynamism.

While accelerated economic growth and poverty reduction remain a commendable achievement of successive regimes, particularly the present incumbents, over the last quarter of a century, income inequalities and social disparities have also significantly widened. An elite class has graduated from the ranks of our fast-growing business community into a strong political force that has captured various tiers of representative offices as well as enhanced their influence on the major political parties. Such interest groups have, as a result, been able to expand their influence over the policymaking process as well as their interventions in the regulatory process. Within this empowered business elite, a narrower, politically more privileged elite has begun to demonstrate a capacity for interfering with the competitive process and to use their influence to extract rents from major business transactions, particularly those associated with the rising volume of public expenditure. This state patronage directed towards a politically privileged business elite, drawing on public resources, including bank financing, has further contributed to the widening of inequalities.

This trend in widening inequalities may originate in some measure from the dynamics of the growth process, but much of the rise in such disparities in recent years may also be attributed to a conspicuous regression in the quality of governance. The source of this deterioration lies in the progressive weakening of the institutions of democracy. Twenty-five years ago, Bangladesh could celebrate its emergence from a decade-and-a-half of cantonment rule where the electoral process had remained unfree and the parliament was subordinated to an all-powerful executive presidency. Between 1991 and 2001, Bangladesh experienced the luxury of three relatively free and fair elections presided over by a non-partisan Caretaker Government (CG), which permitted on each occasion the transfer of power from an incumbent government to a party from the opposition.

The main lament of democrats at the time of our twenty-fifth anniversary was the confrontational nature of a two-party political system and the consequential dysfunctional nature of the parliamentary process. The weakness of the parliament accentuated the lack of transparency and accountability in the administrative process and enhanced the opportunities for corruption. The trend towards the capture of the electoral process by those with wealth and coercive power at their disposal was also becoming more evident, in spite of exposure to a decade of electoral democracy. In this renewed democratic era, we were already witness to the progressive erosion of inner party democracy and the emergence of absolutist tendencies in the exercise of leadership. This trend accentuated the process of transforming the Prime Minister's office into an all-powerful executive presidency.

Over the next 25 years, the positive gains of electoral democracy were progressively eroded. The Bangladesh electorate could continue to cast their vote with relative freedom over two further elections in 2001 and in 2009, under a CG. Unfortunately, the election of 2009 turned out to be the last such election which could be objectively categorised as free, fair and inclusive. The Awami League government, elected to office in 2009, moved to re-amend the Constitution to do away with the system of holding elections under a non-partisan CG. As a result, elections held under the incumbent Awami League government in 2014 were boycotted by the leading opposition parties. In the face of the violence unleashed by the opposition, the voter turnout was low, resulting in a parliament with weak representative credentials without any meaningful opposition.

This trend of organising a non-competitive election was repeated in the recent election held in January 2019, where the incumbent regime persuaded all political parties to participate, with the promise of a free and fair election. Unfortunately, the ruling party, which had performed sufficiently well to win a contested election, preferred to ensure its re-election through various forms of electoral malpractice. As a result, only six members could be elected from the opposition in a house of 350 members. The tenure of two parliaments, without any significant challenge from a credible opposition, has ensured that the government has remained largely unaccountable for most of their acts of omission and commission.

The end result of a decade of virtual one-party rule has been the weakening of the institutions of democratic governance and the institutionalisation of the 'winner takes all' culture. Without exposure to any form of electoral accountability, the executive has perpetuated the partisanisation of the administration as well as the law enforcement agencies, and has further compromised the independence of the judiciary. Within such an unaccountable regime, exposed to increasing elite capture where close to two-thirds of the members of parliament (MP) are self-declared businessmen, the crisis in governance has been aggravated. Such a captured legislature has been disinclined to address a range of governance issues of immediate relevance to the development process, such as the weakening of regulatory institutions. This has encouraged wilful bank default, weak enforcement of building codes and road safety rules, land grabbing, river erosion, and a variety of other such regulatory inadequacies.

It is arguable that such a regime, which remains indifferent to enforcing the rule of law or only enforces it for partisan or material gain, could constrain the path to upper-middle income status. Therefore, the challenge before both the government and people of Bangladesh is the need to enhance governance to a level that is consistent with the needs of our drivers of growth and the extensive opportunities opening up for us in the global economy. The first task will be to move towards a regime of accountability in governance through the return to a system of free, fair and inclusive elections that minimises the influence of money and muscle power so that people of modest means can freely participate in the political process. It would be expected that a more representative political process would allow for a more inclusive development process which democratises economic opportunity and narrows social disparities.

For meaningful, more inclusive elections to take place, we would need to restore full freedom to the media, permit the unfettered right of public assembly, and protect these freedoms through a genuinely independent judiciary. Institutions of good governance such as an independent Election Commission, a credible Anti-Corruption Commission (ACC), a strong Public Services Commission, and other empowered regulatory agencies should be appointed through a non-partisan process, and their integrity should be protected through an uncompromised judicial system.

Is there any credible expectation that such a transformation in the system and instruments of governance can be recreated in Bangladesh? Much will depend on the capacity and space available to the drivers of growth to maintain their dynamism. As in the period from 1996–2019, the Bangladesh paradox may continue to sustain our upward trajectory. But the upward journey to the higher ranks of the development community may demand rather higher standards of governance than those which elevated us out of the LDC ghetto. In such circumstances, within a system of weak democratic accountability, the commitment to and capacity for self-correction of the incumbent regime to address issues of governance will need more rigorous evaluation. In the absence of such a commitment, contradictions between the state and the drivers of change may emerge as one of the key challenges for the future. This will render the journey to the developed country status much more problematic, exposing a society faced with widening social disparities as well as growing inner contradictions, to mounting dangers of social and political instability. It is hoped that the chapters presented in this volume will encourage further debate on such challenges confronting Bangladesh in the days ahead.

Rehman Sobhan
Chairman, Centre for Policy Dialogue (CPD)
Dhaka, Bangladesh

May 2020

References

Jahan, Rounaq (ed.). 2000. *Bangladesh: Promise and Performance.* London: Zed Books.

Sobhan, Rehman, 'Bangladesh's Permanent Liberation Struggle: Constructing an Inclusive Democratic Society', Abdur Razzaq Memorial Lecture, Dhaka, January 2017.

Introduction

S. NARAYAN AND SREERADHA DATTA

The graduation of Bangladesh into a middle-income country is a story of remarkable economic development success. A country, which at the time of its independence in 1971, was considered too poor to succeed, has over the years, and through successive changes in its government, managed to achieve considerable progress in terms of development as well as social welfare parameters.

When it gained independence in December 1971, Mujibur Rahman's idea of the dream of *Sonar Bangla* (Golden Bengal) had inspired Bangladeshis to take their nation to a position where the twin pillars of freedom and democracy would lead Bangladesh to become a land of prosperity, progress and peace. Bangladesh would embody the reassertion of its Bengali identity, its political and cultural freedoms as well as liberty. Five decades later, Bangladesh stands strong and far more resilient than it was ever imagined during the early decades of the 1970s. Where does Bangladesh stand now? And how far has the country come towards fulfilling its dream? This volume is an attempt to understand this process and examine its many achievements and what lies ahead.

The accomplishments of Bangladesh are significant and substantial. While the country is now recognised as a multi-party democracy, in its early days, the nation faced several phases of turbulence. The assassination of *Bangabandhu* (Friend of Bengal) Mujibur Rahman, and series of coups and counter-coups led to a long spell of authoritarian/military rule. There was also an interregnum period of two years. Except for this phase of nearly two years, periodic elections, smooth transition of power and the successful completion of the governments' terms have lent strength to the democratic parliamentary system in Bangladesh. The Caretaker System (an interim government meant to oversee free and fair elections) essentially oversaw free and fair elections from 1991 onwards, and was widely accepted by all the political parties. Its removal through an Amendment in 2014 polarised the political environment. However, Bangladesh stayed the course by holding its periodic elections and it has been business as usual for the elected government, despite some intense rounds of street protests and demonstrations questioning the legitimacy of the electoral process.

Bangladeshi politics has largely been confrontational in nature, where ruling and opposition parties have clashed over several issues, especially those relating directly to the holding of elections. Several of these clashes have turned violent. Violence has been a tool for all political parties and groups in Bangladesh, and unfortunately, the political environment of neither the past nor the present has been able to revoke this trend. Despite this, Bangladesh has been able to govern through a civilian elected authority, successfully keeping the military behind the scenes. This reflects an inner strength and ethos that stands in stark contrast to the erstwhile Pakistan that it had broken away from.

The passing away of former military leader Hussain Muhammad Ershad, who played a key role in lending support to the party forming the government, left behind a legacy that grew around propping religion as a pillar in the political process, and a show of strength and power enabling wily manipulations. He personified the changing nature of Bangladeshi politics, which has been held hostage to political manoeuvring at the cost of the common good. While Bangladesh meanders through a political mosaic of largely four main political parties, namely the Awami League, Bangladesh Nationalist Party, Jatiya Party and Bangladesh Jamaat-e-Islami Party, towards what appears to be an Awami League-led coalition party consolidation, it seems poised for interesting times ahead.

More importantly, Bangladesh has been able to leverage its geographical position effectively, and is now being coveted by two Asian powers—India and China—for investments, aid and credit lines. Bangladesh's quest for regional influence and recognition was seen even under Ziaur Rahman, its first military leader who sought to establish the first regional organisation in the South Asian region. The formation of the South Asian Association for Regional Cooperation (SAARC) led to all the seven regional states coming together on a common platform. Bangladesh has pursued an independent foreign policy, and over the years, it has stabilised its ties with its neighbours, India, Nepal, Bhutan and Sri Lanka. Some recent developments have, however, led to tension vis-à-vis Myanmar and Pakistan, but Bangladesh has worked at strengthening regional and sub-regional cooperation. It has expanded its developmental cooperation with the developed countries, for instance, with the United States (US), European Union (EU), Japan and Canada, to form trade partnerships. In solidarity with the Muslim Ummah, and through economic cooperation within the framework of Organisation of Islamic Cooperation (OIC), Bangladesh has maintained a fraternal relationship with the countries of the Middle East. The foreign policy outreach of Bangladesh has helped to successfully develop and sustain bilateral ties with its neighbours as well as overseas.

Economically, Bangladesh's achievements have been tremendous, and the country has been described as a 'land of impossible attainments'. It has come a long way since the end of the War of Liberation that produced a very poor country, with its poverty exacerbated by months of conflict and deprivation. The nascent State's institutions were in disarray, its governance systems were strained, and it faced an enormous resource crunch. The ideology in the earlier years was close to being socialist, with a heavy reliance on the government as the instrument for development, and on the public sector as the vehicle of growth.

This changed after 1974, and successive governments moved away from a public-sector ideology to a greater acceptance of market-based development. The development of the garment industry and an export-oriented textile industry was due to the pragmatism displayed in opening the sector to foreign investment and technology, as well as leveraging the country's status as a Least Developed Country (LDC) to preferentially access developed markets. Today, Bangladesh is the largest exporter of readymade garments, second only to China, with its largest markets in the EU. The policy of export-led growth, a policy that has also served China so well, is at the heart of the economic development that has kept the exchange rate steady, provided employment to women, and has also improved technical capability and entrepreneurship. It has bred an elite class with close links to political parties and to international markets who, in fact, determine the course of economic policy today. The success of Bangladesh's foreign policy in protecting its market interests and creating access to employment opportunities for migrant workers has played an important role in ensuring healthy remittance flows that help to keep the currency stable.

The early plight of the economy brought in external donors, who met periodically to assess the ground conditions and to bring in help. Most multilateral agencies, for instance, the World Bank, Asian Development Bank (ADB) and Japan International Cooperation Agency (JICA), were willing to provide support. Initially, there was support in the form of help for relief and rehabilitation, and subsequently, for programmes and projects. Rather than budgetary assistance at the fiscal level, the aid agencies focused on specific programmes that had been identified as priorities by the government. The population programme was one of these, and it was given a very high priority by successive governments. The aid programme in population management has been a resounding success over the years, with state agencies and institutions cooperating with the multilaterals to make it a success. The population growth rate in Bangladesh was at 1 per cent in 2017. Female fertility, which was around 6.3 per cent in the 1970s, reduced to 2.1 per cent in 2018. One hundred per cent coverage in primary education is reported, and the participation of women in the work force is close to 34 per cent. Life expectancy is at 72.5 per cent and is higher than in India, where it is at 68 per cent. All the social indicators, therefore, have improved over the years.

There was yet another element to this growth-story. Government policy permitted non-governmental organisations (NGOs) to access foreign funds, as a result of which many NGOs came up in the country, with the most prominent among them being the Bangladesh Rural Advancement Committee (BRAC) and the Grameen Bank. BRAC has had a tremendous impact in the field of school education, especially with respect to girl children, while Grameen Bank has become internationally renowned for its concept of providing micro-credit to self-help groups, especially to the rural poor. The government ceded space to NGO-activity due to two main reasons. First, the focus of government policy and activity in the earlier years was very urban, concentrated on Dhaka and a few major towns, and there was little attention to the development of rural areas. Second, there was a severe constraint of resources in the early years. The government was willing to allow aid agencies access to rural areas for programmes and projects; and in the first decade after independence, aid constituted nearly 80 per cent of the total budget.

The common thread in the development-story is the *laissez-faire*, market-friendly approach of the government, through different regimes. State-sector banks provided the credit for expansions in business and they could, in turn, access capital from multifarious sources, including external sources. Entrepreneurs developed and even NGOs functioned like profit centres. The emergence of a privileged elite, which had the ears of the government and could mould government policy, marks one of the features of Bangladesh's growth.

The Gross Domestic Product (GDP) of Bangladesh grew by 7.3 per cent in 2017 and is expected to do better in the coming years. At this rate, its growth will overtake the numbers that India and China are expected to achieve. Per capita incomes are reported at $1,750, and the population below poverty line (BPL) has come down from 56 per cent in 1990–91 to 21.8 per cent in 2018. The currency in Bangladesh is stable, unlike in Pakistan, where there has been a significant erosion in the value of the local currency against the US dollar. This growth, however, has its own share of imperfections.

Most importantly, employment opportunities are limited to the garment sector, which accounts for close to 80 per cent of organised employment. There are several reports of Bangladeshis fleeing the country in search of employment in the EU countries, and risking their lives in illicit crossings of the Mediterranean. There is a big gap between rural and urban livelihoods, as well as between the privileged and the underprivileged. Infrastructure remains poor, and border crossings are a place for rent-seeking. There is prevalence of corruption in public services. Logistics are a challenge for the movement of goods, and not enough investment is being made in infrastructure.

One recurring issue that Bangladesh is forced to confront is that of rising sea levels and the resultant shrinking of habitable areas. Eighty per cent of the land in Bangladesh is less than 12 metres above sea level. According to one estimate, at the present level of population growth and global warming, by 2050, Bangladesh 'will have 300 million people to live in just about 120,000 square kilometre area', thereby increasing the country's population density to 2,500 or more per square kilometre (Ministry of Environment and Forests [MoEF] 2012: 114). This, in practical terms, would mean that at least 20 million or 7 per cent of the population would lose their inhabitations and become climate refugees.

As per some estimates, riverbank erosion displaces more than 1,00,000 people annually in Bangladesh. The country periodically faces severe flooding, and consequentially, the impact of climate change would unleash many challenges, including issues of relocation and internal migration, unemployment, poverty, and many more negatives emanating from this problem. The 2007 Sidr Cyclone had revealed the levels of devastation and consequences of such disasters. Given the impending threat, Bangladesh has in place the Bangladesh Climate Change Strategy and Action Plan (BCCSAP), identifying six pillars and over 40 actions. Also, the Bangladesh Climate Change Trust (BCCT) fund was created to fund the measures to tackle and counter the effects of climate change. These are included in the national, sectoral and local planning processes for achieving comprehensive results.

At the individual level, the government is engaged in creating awareness and preparedness among the public to reduce their susceptibility to the adverse effects of extreme climatic change. The measures adopted include forecasting and an early warning system, land-use planning, and improved relief and rehabilitation mechanisms. In recent times, measures were also taken to create a green belt along the coast of the Bay of Bengal, and to employ volunteers to offset the impact of natural disasters like cyclones and tidal surges.

Finally, Bangladesh is concerned about energy security. The country's natural gas reserves will be adequate only for a decade, and growing power consumption would need to be addressed through imports of gas, oil and coal. In the coming decades, this would put pressure on foreign-exchange resources.

The chapters in this volume are an attempt to examine the various aspects of this journey of Bangladesh, looking at the significant successes while commenting on the concerns and anxieties that societal, political and institutional structures will be facing on the way forward. It aims to objectively assess the positives and negatives of Bangladesh development-story.

Chapters 10 and 11 examine these developments in the context of Bangladesh's external relations with India and with the rest of the world, as well as its internal dynamics of institutional growth. The growth of textile exports is likely to be impacted by the graduation of Bangladesh to a middle-income country, as the concessions of LDCs will no longer be available. There is also a need to diversify manufacturing, as the textile sector alone would not be a guarantee to future prosperity. Chapters 2 and 3 examine the development of the garments industry and also the way forward. Interactions with the rest of the world have to be contextualised within the foreign policy framework of the country, and Chapters 10 and 11 examine the developments from a historical perspective. India–Bangladesh relations have had many ups and downs, and the reasons for and ramifications of the current positive relationship are analysed critically.

The development-story has to be looked at in terms of internal policies, institutions as well as implementers. Chapter 1 documents the parameters of development and the policies that enabled this development to take place. Chapter 4 looks at the role of multilateral funding agencies, their programmes, as well as the success of two major NGOs, the Grameen Bank and BRAC, to examine the causes of success, and the reasons why the Bangladesh development-story appears to be such an exceptional one.

There are serious worries as well. The democratic dispensation is heavily skewed in favour of one party, and there are concerns that free and fair liberal choice is not available. There are growing threats of Islamisation. And even though Islamisation and militancy are not synonymous, there is evidence of radicalisation within the country as well as among the migrant labour. Coercive measures to combat and curb this have had only limited success, and the country and society urgently needs a more inclusive approach to contain social unrest and extremism. Chapters 6 and 8 examine these aspects.

There are other concerns as well. Chapter 7 looks at the role of women in society and in the workplace, and concludes that while much has been achieved, much remains to be done. Finally, Chapter 9 looks at the concerns around energy security. With development, energy use increases. Bangladesh is running out of natural gas, and there is an accelerated development of coal-fired stations. Coal is also not produced adequately within the country. Energy security would be a serious issue in the near future.

The chapters attempt to present a balanced picture of the success of Bangladesh, the reasons for the success, and point out some serious concerns at the political and societal levels as well as in economic development paradigms. While attempting to encapsulate many of the core issues surrounding Bangladesh in its 50-year journey, we are aware of many aspects of new technologies, innovations and artificial intelligence that Bangladesh has taken important strides in; but were not able to consider them for this volume due to a variety of reasons.

This volume is the outcome of a project conducted by the Institute of South Asian Studies (ISAS), National University of Singapore. The project helped to bring all the contributors together for a workshop in Singapore in May 2019, where the format of the papers was discussed and finalised. The advice and guidance of Professor C. Raja Mohan, Director of ISAS, was of immeasurable value at all stages of this process.

Reference

'Second National Communication of Bangladesh to the United Nations Framework on Climate Change', MoEF, Government of the People's Republic of Bangladesh. Available at https://unfccc.int/resource/docs/natc/bgdnc2.pdf.

1

Bangladesh
A Journey of Dual Graduation and the Attendant Challenges

MUSTAFIZUR RAHMAN

Bangladesh's journey of four-and-a-half decades since its independence in 1971 can claim to be unique in many ways. One recalls that one of the very first books on Bangladesh, which was published in the mid-1970s by two well-known academics, J. Faaland and J. R. Parkinson, was given the title, *Bangladesh: The Test Case for Development*. In the Introduction to this book, the authors explained that they had chosen the sub-title, *The Test Case for Development* (and not *A Test Case for Development*), because they felt that this newly independent country was beset with so many difficulties that needed to be overcome, and so many challenges that needed to be addressed, that if economic development was possible in this country, it would be possible in any other developing country. There were those who had ventured to foretell the future of the country as one of a *perennial bottomless basket case*.

Given this backdrop, looking back from the vantage point of the present times, Bangladesh as a country and its citizens as a nation should take genuine pride in the road travelled, and in the fact, that those who took such a pessimistic view about the future of the country were proved wrong by the subsequent history. In spite of the significant challenges it faced in its journey, Bangladesh blazed an impressive track record of resilience, business, entrepreneurship development and economic growth, and socio-economic progress. Bangladesh's impressive score card is built on her success in terms of attaining a consistently high pace of economic growth and the impressive performance with regard to various developmental indicators, including those relating to the Millennium Development Goals (MDGs). In recent times, these cumulative achievements have led to the country's *dual graduation*—graduation from a Low-Income Country (LIC) to a Lower Middle-Income Country (LMIC) according to the World Bank criteria, attained in 2015, and eligibility for graduation from the group of Least Developed Country (LDC) to Developing Country (DC) status, in 2018, according to the United Nations (UN) criteria (UN 2015).

There is no doubt that supportive government policies and concrete measures have played a critical role in this remarkable journey. No less important was the entrepreneurial energy of Bangladesh's private sector, the efforts of its farmers, workers and migrant labourers. Low-cost solutions and micro-credit interventions innovated, championed and implemented by Bangladesh's non-governmental organisations (NGOs), and awareness-raising activism of social movements have also contributed to this success.

However, Bangladesh's dual graduation and its capacity to avoid the possible *middle-income trap*[1] entail addressing several challenges in going forward. There is an urgent need to design an appropriate graduation strategy, pursue policies and implement targetted actions if the journey is to be sustained and infused with momentum.

Following the introductory remarks, the next section captures Bangladesh's track record through some selected stylised facts and a number of the key drivers that propelled Bangladesh's journey towards dual graduation. The third section highlights several emerging challenges that need to be addressed through appropriate initiatives if the current momentum is to be continued in the post-graduation future. The fourth section concludes the discussion with some final remarks.

The Journey: Selected Stylised Facts and Drivers of the Narrative

Table 1.1 captures some of the key indicators that inform the Bangladesh development narrative, which some have termed as the Bangladesh *development paradox*.[2] The figures speak for themselves. Bangladesh has been able to post robust GDP growth rates for several decades now, with the pace accelerating by about ine per cent every few years, over successive decades. The GDP growth rate is expected to reach 8.13 per cent in the ongoing FY 2018–19.

Table 1.1 Bangladesh Economy: Selected Stylised Facts

Fiscal Year (FY) / *Indicators*	*FY 1991*	*FY 2001*	*FY 2011*	*FY 2018*
GDP (in billion Purchasing Power Parity [PPP]$)	94.50	184.00	395.68	638.43[a]
GDP growth (in percentage over preceding years)	3.49[1]	5.08	6.46	7.86 (8.13)[e]
Per Capita Gross National Income (GNI) per annum (in nominal US$)	—	427.92	927.97	1,751.39
Population below poverty line (in percentage)	58.8[b]	48.9[c]	31.5[d]	21.8
Share of agriculture (as percentage of GDP)	31.68	21.85	16.81	13.41[a]
Food grains production (in million metric tons)	19.32[b]	26.76	34.51	37.38
Export earnings (in billion US$)	1.72	6.47	22.93	36.67 (40.54)
Remittance earnings (in billion US$)	0.76	1.88	11.65	14.98 (16.42)
Export earnings (as percentage of import payments)	49.48	69.28	68.12	62.29
External debt servicing (as percentage of export and remittance earnings)	23.63	10.69	5.31	4.26

Note: [a]Data for 2017; [b]data for 1991–92; [c]data for 2000; [d]data for 2010; [e]data for 2018–19 (projected).

Source: Compiled from various sources: World Development Indicators (WDI), World Bank; Bangladesh Bureau of Statistics (BBS); Export Promotion Bureau (EPB); Bangladesh Economic Review; calculated from EPB and Bangladesh Bank data; calculated from Economic Relations Division (ERD), EPB and Bangladesh Economic Review data.

A distinctive feature of Bangladesh's growth has been not only the growth acceleration, but also the relatively low volatility of the achieved growth rate. A sustained GDP growth has contributed to a secularly rising per capita income over the years. Bangladesh's per capita GNI crossed $1,900 (about $4,000 in PPP terms) in 2018. Earnings from remittances sent by the diaspora stood at about $16.4 billion in FY 2019, and it has been contributing to the rising income of the households, particularly in the rural areas. The composition of the GDP shows a shift from agriculture (the share of which in the GDP has reduced from 55 per cent in the 1970s to 15 per cent in 2020) to manufacturing and services sectors. Food grains production has doubled since independence, to reach 35 million tonnes in 2017. Bangladesh's strength in the global market is manifested in the emergence of the competitive export-oriented sectors, with the creation of a large number of jobs. Export-oriented readymade garments, accounting for 83 per cent of Bangladesh's global export, employs about 3.5 million people (64 per cent of whom are women), which makes Bangladesh rank second in the export of readymade garments, globally, after China. This sector has been able to cope with the immediate adverse consequences originating from the Rana Plaza tragedy, although at present, it is having to address many challenges as it readjusts under the new circumstances (Rahman and Moazzem 2017).

It is to be noted that Bangladesh has recorded remarkable success in reducing poverty, from 56 per cent of the population living below the national poverty line in 1990–91 to 24 per cent in 2016.[3] According to the Multidimensional Poverty Index (MPI) Report (United Nations Development Programme [UNDP] 2019), Bangladesh was able to get 14.3 million people out of poverty between 2004 and 2014.[4] Indeed, this was the fastest reduction in MPI among the 101 countries that were reviewed as part of the aforesaid report.[5] In the context of the MDGs, Bangladesh's success is manifested in notable improvements in the access of its citizens to education and health services, the significant reduction in maternal and child mortality rate, the availability of safe drinking water, and rise in adult literacy. Average life expectancy at birth has risen from 64.0 years to 72.5 years between 2003 and 2018. Bangladesh has attained 100 per cent primary enrolment and gender parity in primary education. Extensive micro-credit programmes implemented by NGOs led to significant financial inclusion of the poor (Mahmud and Osmani 2017). According to the World Bank Report, Bangladesh is among the five fastest-growing economies of the world (World Bank 2019). The share of the population with access to electricity increased from 44.2 per cent in 2005 to

62.4 per cent in 2014, while mobile penetration jumped to from 6.3 per cent in 2005 to 81.9 per cent in 2015. At present, 14.4 per cent of the population has internet access, up from about 1 per cent in 2005.

In the early 1990s, Bangladesh made important policy shifts towards trade liberalisation, deregulation of the economy, export orientation and privatisation. The country has been able to successfully deal with the challenges posed by the market-focused reorientation of its erstwhile inward-looking and public sector-dependent economy. Over the years, Bangladesh has experienced an increasing global integration of its economy. The degree of openness of the economy[6] has risen to 32.8 per cent in FY2016–17, compared to 16.8 per cent in 1990–91 (Table 1.1).

Bangladesh became eligible for graduation from LIC to LMIC in 2015 when the country's per capita GNI crossed the World Bank graduation threshold of $1,045 (according to the Atlas method).[7] The journey to (lower) middle income graduation may be traced from Figure 1.1.

In 2018, the Committee for Development Policy (CDP) of the Economic and Social Council of the UN (UN-ECOSOC) recognised Bangladesh as eligible for graduation from the group of LDCs.[8]

Figure 1.1 LMIC Threshold Trends and Bangladesh's Middle-Income Journey

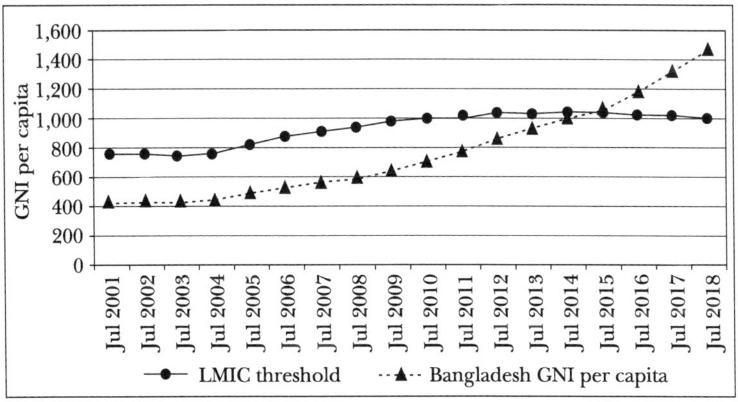

Note: In current US$, according to Atlas method.

Source: World Bank n.d.

It is to be noted that while for LDC-graduation, the LDC would need to graduate in two out of the three graduation criteria,[9] Bangladesh was one of the few LDCs that has been able to meet all three criteria.[10] According to the CDP timeline, countries are to finally graduate after two subsequent triennial reviews (for Bangladesh, in 2021 and 2024), subject to endorsement by the UN-ECOSOC, and to the final nod by the UN General Assembly in 2024. As Table 1.2 indicates, Bangladesh is expected to graduate out in 2024 with considerable *comfort zones*.[11] Indeed, if Bangladesh is able to maintain the current momentum, as projections made by Rahman and Bari (2019) testify, the comfort zones will continue to be further expanded as the country moves towards the final graduation year of 2024 (Table 1.2).

Table 1.2 LDC Eligibility Scenario and Projected Values of Per Capita GNI, Human Asset Index (HAI) and Economic Vulnerability Index (EVI) Developed as Rankings

	2018		*2021*		*2024*	
Indicators	*Threshold*	*Actual values*	*Threshold*	*Projected values*	*Threshold*	*Projected values*
GNI per capita ($)	1,230	1,274	1,245–1,270	1,730–1,780	1,345–1,375	2,260–2,500
HAI)	66 or above	73.2	66 or above	79.2	66 or above	86.3
EVI	32 or below	25.2	32 or below	24.8	32 or below	24.7

Source: Rahman and Bari (2019).

As a matter of fact, Bangladesh's graduation is a relatively more broad-based and balanced one compared to that of the other 15 candidate LDCs (for graduation).[12] If one examines the sub-indices and sub-sub-indices, both in the case of the HAI and the EVI, one cannot but appreciate Bangladesh's significant achievements in terms of some of the crucial socio-economic parameters. Mention may be made here of health (for example, reducing under-five infant mortality rate and maternal mortality ratios, curtailing under-nourishment, etc.); education (for example, enhancing gross secondary enrolment ratio and adult literacy rate); exposure to vulnerabilities (for example, reducing dependence on agriculture); and exposure to shocks (for example, overcoming agricultural instability, addressing adverse impacts of natural disasters, and maintaining stability of export earnings).

Another key distinctive feature that has informed Bangladesh's graduation pathway is the country's transition from a predominantly aid-receiving country to a trading economy. The economy adjusted well, following the opening up of policies of deregulation, trade liberalisation and market orientation initiated in the early 1990s. As Table 1.3 indicates, at present, two-fifths of the country's economy is integrated with the global economy through the export and import of goods and services, and financial and investment flows.

Table 1.3 Global Integration of Bangladesh

Fiscal Year (FY) / *Indicators*	*FY 1981*	*FY 1991*	*FY 1911*	*FY 1914*	*FY 1915*	*FY 1918*
Degree of Openness (Export + Import as per cent of GDP)	13.5	16.8	44	40.9	39.1	34.9
Extent of Global Integration (per cent)	21.2	24.9	55	51.7	49.5	43.1
X as per cent of M	37.1	49.5	68.1	74.3	69	62.3
(X+R) as per cent of M	56.5	71.5	102.7	109.3	102.9	87.7
Official Development Assistance (ODA) as per cent of GDP	5.8	5.6	1.4	1.7	1.6	2.2
ODA as per cent of export of goods	158.1	100.9	7.8	9.7	9.9	16.7
ODA as per cent of export of goods and services	103.8	69.8	5.1	6.6	6.7	11.9

Source: Author's calculations from various sources. Compiled and estimated from BBS, n.d.

The above indicators testify to the strength of the Bangladesh economy as it prepares for, and embarks upon, its graduation journey. However, there are formidable challenges lying ahead, which will need to be adequately addressed.

The Road Ahead: Attendant and Emerging Challenges

Three considerations are important in the context of LDC-graduation: 1) *smooth graduation*: to be able to move towards final graduation by maintaining an adequate comfort zone; 2) *graduation with momentum*: accelerating the pace of achievement in terms of the various graduation criteria to embed momentum in the graduation journey; and 3) *sustainable graduation:* harnessing the needed capacities to ensure that once graduated, the country is able to sustain the status in going forward (our emphases). Bangladesh will need to do the needful so that her graduation is smooth, sustainable, and is attained by embedding momentum. In view of this, it is reckoned that initiatives will be required in a number of areas on a priority basis.

Six Considerations in View of the Dual Graduation

While the dual graduation testifies to Bangladesh's significant achievements in the economic and social arena, six considerations need to be taken into cognisance, moving forward.

1. First, dual graduation refers to the performance of the country according to selected indicators and sub-indicators. A country's readiness for graduation is assessed and measured only against these. Important indicators such as competitive strength, domestic resource mobilisation capacity, distribution and inequality, state of governance and accountability, and environmental sustainability, to name a few, are not included among these criteria. However, these are critically important factors from the perspective of sustainable graduation and sustainable development.
2. Second, the two graduations will entail important implications in the areas of market access, the special and differential treatment enjoyed by Bangladesh as an LDC (originating from LDC graduation), and in terms of foreign borrowings (originating from the middle-income graduation). A graduating country will need to be cognisant of these factors and be ready to address the associated challenges.
3. Third, one will have to keep in mind how indices such as HAI and EVI are calculated. Although weights are assigned to the various sub-indices, the HAI and EVI sub-indices conceal diverse levels of attainment across the sub-indices.

Bangladesh's progression over the past one-and-a-half decades with respect to the three LDC-graduation criteria may be tracked from Table 1.4. While the progress with regard to HAI and per capita GNI are quite visible, some unevenness is observed with regard to EVI. If the sub-indices are considered (Table 1.5), one finds that it conceals some disquieting trends; for example, there has been a rise in export concentration index over the years. The percentage of the population who are victims of natural disasters, while showing some decreasing

Table 1.4 Bangladesh's Performance in View of the LDC-Graduation Criteria

Year	*EVI*	*HAI*	*GNI per capita, Atlas method (US$)*
2003	22.93	45.30	363.33
2006	25.78	50.11	403.33
2009	23.21	53.34	453.33
2012	32.41	54.68	636.67
2015	25.11	63.80	926.26
2018	25.22	73.15	1,274.08

Source: UN CDP Secretariat, n.d.

Table 1.5 Bangladesh's Performance in Selected Indicators of EVI and HAI

	EVI indicators		*HAI indicators*	
Year	*Export concentration*	*Victims of natural disasters (per cent)*	*Under-five mortality (per 1,000)*	*Prevalence of under-nourishment in total population (per cent)*
2003	0.32	N/A	92.26	N/A
2006	0.30	N/A	79.28	30.0
2009	0.40	N/A	83.15	27.0
2012	0.38	6.05	61.37	26.0
2015	0.37	4.65	41.10	16.7
2018	0.41	3.97	34.20	15.1

Note: The extreme left column, Export concentration, is expressed as the Herfindahl-Hirschman Index.

Source: UN CDP, n.d.

trend, by definition, has inherent uncertainties, which are informed by various factors, many of which are beyond the control of policymakers. The fact that Bangladesh is one of the countries most affected by adverse climate-related impacts is widely known and needs to be kept in mind. As regards HAI, the challenge of the last mile is clearly discernible from the data on undernourishment sub-index. For sustainable LDC-graduation, Bangladesh will need to pay special attention to the sub-indices where the comfort zone is relatively narrow, and where a gradual slowdown is becoming increasingly discernible in recent years.

4. Fourth, the graduation thresholds refer to only the average scenario, in terms of income level, indices and sub-indices. On the other hand, as it is known, the averages could conceal significant disparities across sub-groups. Also, many of the spatial dimensions of inequality could be hidden under the averages.
5. Fifth, countries will need to be cognisant of the last mile challenge, which means that further achievements become increasingly difficult and challenging as more marginalised areas and groups need to be reached to make further progress.
6. Sixth, the emerging global scenario, in the context of which the graduation journey is to be undertaken, is becoming increasingly uncertain and volatile.

Addressing the Higher Borrowing Costs

The middle-income graduation will entail important implications with regard to the cost of borrowings from international financial institutions such as the World Bank, the Asian Development Bank (ADB), and also bilateral development partners. The LMIC-graduation has resulted in Bangladesh's transition from International Development Association (IDA)-only type of highly concessional loans[13] to blended finance.[14] Once Bangladesh crosses the $1,905 per capita GNI,[15] which is expected in a few years, the cost of loans will rise significantly. Bangladesh will have to make a transition from grant to loan. Higher lending rates, shorter maturity terms and more stringent conditionalities will be the order of the day. More emphasis will need to be placed on negotiating loans on better terms and diversifying loan portfolio with new sources of finance.[16] Opportunities to take advantage of better creditworthiness (thanks to the middle-income transition) should also be explored more energetically.

It is to be noted that till now, Bangladesh's external debt–GDP ratio has been quite manageable, coming down from about 30 per cent in the early-2000s to about 14 per cent in recent times. However, attention to three points are called for in going forward: first, the debt–GDP ratio has started to rise in recent years (Figure 1.2). Second, the ratio is expected to rise further in view of the rising amount of debts being incurred in recent years. This is clearly visible from Table 1.6. Third, the growing amount of aid in the pipeline, and its use, are also expected to raise Bangladesh's future debt-servicing liability. No doubt the aid being incurred, a large part of which is going into building the much-needed infrastructure, should enable Bangladesh to attract more investment, and thereby accelerate economic growth, which, in turn, should raise her debt-servicing capability. What Bangladesh needs to ensure is quality and timely use of the aid and to be cognisant of the risk of possible exchange rate volatility and maturity mismatch. Negotiating aid on favourable terms and ensuring overall good governance in aid utilisation will be important to ensure that Bangladesh does not fall into a *debt trap*.[17]

Figure 1.2 External Debt–GDP Ratio of Bangladesh (in Per Cent)

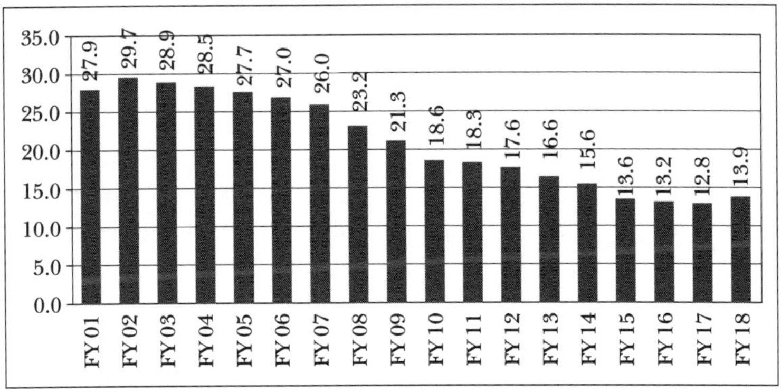

Source: Calculated from ERD and BBS data.

Table 1.6 Aid in Opening Pipeline (in Million US$)

Year	*Aid in opening pipeline (million US$)*
FY 2001	5,752
FY 2005	6,911
FY 2010	8,861
FY 2015	18,175
FY 2016	18,694
FY 2017	22,068
FY 2018	35,749

Source: Authors' calculations from ERD data 2018.

In view of the rising cost of borrowings, emphasis will have to be put on mobilising more domestic resources through fiscal initiatives and taxation. Bangladesh's current tax–GDP ratio of only about 10 per cent ought to be raised significantly by bringing more eligible people under the tax net and by raising the capacity of relevant institutions. Raising to even that of India and Pakistan (at about 17–18 per cent of the GDP) will help mobilise a significantly large amount of additional resources to underwrite developmental expenditure.

Addressing the Loss of ISMs

LDC-graduation will mean that Bangladesh will not be eligible for the international support measures (ISMs) in place for the LDCs. Opinions, however, vary regarding the extent to which the ISMs have been able to effectively address the challenges facing the LDCs. Bhattacharya (2019), for example, has criticised ISMs as being inefficient and insufficient. Nevertheless, to the extent that LDCs have been able to take advantage of the ISMS, they will no longer be available to these countries once they graduate. In the case of Bangladesh, this would mean loss of preferential and non-reciprocal duty-free, quota-free market access and non-eligibility of derogation from trade-related intellectual property rights (TRIPS) and trade-related investment measures (TRIMS) obligations;[18] flexibilities enjoyed under the World Trade Organization (WTO) decision on

TRIPS and pharmaceuticals;[19] aid for trade for the LDCs; and a host of other measures. Of crucial importance to Bangladesh is the adverse impact originating from loss of preferential market access. Rahman and Bari (2019) estimate that Bangladesh could lose about $2.7 billion worth of exports (8.7 per cent of the country's global export in FY 2015 terms) in the 40 countries where she currently enjoys preferential market access.[20]

The implications of LDC-graduation for the country's flagship readymade garment (RMG) sector, accounting for about 83 per cent of her export, will be quite significant. Preference erosion will also adversely affect the market access it enjoyed as an LDC as part of regional trading arrangements such as the South Asia Free Trade Agreement (SAFTA). In view of this, Bangladesh will need to undertake appropriate measures to raise export-competitiveness. Energetic steps will be required to be pursued to raise productivity, upgrade human resource capabilities and skills, attract more FDI to export-oriented sectors, improve the cost of doing business scenario, raise efficacy of trade logistics and trade facilitation, and take steps towards product and market diversification. The incentive structure currently in place and human resource development strategies must be revisited and recalibrated to make the transition to a higher productivity economy that is capable of translating Bangladesh's comparative advantages into competitive advantages.

A New Role in the WTO

In the context of the WTO, Bangladesh must pursue a proactive policy in view of LDC-graduation. The purpose has to be: (a) to ensure that ISMs favouring the LDCs are actually delivered to make the best use of time in the run up to 2024; (b) to negotiate a package of support for the graduating the LDCs; and (c) to pursue negotiations by taking cognisance of the country's future as a developing country.

It is important to keep in mind that a large number of LDCs are slated for graduation in the next few years. There is a strong case for putting in place a package of measures to incentivise sustainable graduation of the LDCs. As a matter of fact, there are a number of UN resolutions which urge UN members to extend support to graduating LDCs (Rahman and Bhattacharya 2019). Indeed, in view of this, the EU has offered an extension of its preferential scheme—the EBA—by an additional three years for the graduating LDCs.[21] As a leading LDC, Bangladesh should take the lead in negotiating similar initiatives with other preference-offering countries. Along with this, an extension of eligibility may be sought for enjoying time-bound flexibilities that are in place for the LDCs (for example, for pharmaceuticals), till the expiry of the current timeline of December 2032.

Graduating LDCs should also be able to take advantage of current negotiations in support of LDCs, such as the *services waiver.* The package for graduating LDCs could also include greater aid-related support under the Enhanced Integration Framework (EIF) of the WTO. Graduating LDCs could also seek extension of derogation/waivers/timelines for the implementation of obligations under the various agreements, including TRIMS and the trade facilitation agreement (TFA) of the WTO. At the same time, Bangladesh must make adequate preparations for its future in the WTO specifically, but also in general, as a *future developing country.* In view of the ongoing negotiations on *fisheries subsidies* and with respect to discussions on *new issues* such as e-commerce and micro, small and medium enterprises (MSMEs), Bangladesh's stance will need to be informed by the interests of the developing country members of the WTO.[22] New coalitions, some issue-specific, some (developing country) group-specific, will need to be forged to secure future interests in the WTO. Against this backdrop of multiple identities, Bangladesh's trade-related diplomacy must be significantly strengthened, and emphasis must be put on building adequate negotiating capacities in view of the emergent scenario.

Renewed Emphasis on Regional Cooperation

Bangladesh should do its best to take advantage of the emerging opportunities at the regional and sub-regional levels. These relate to recent developments concerning the Bangladesh–Bhutan–India–Nepal (BBIN) Motor Vehicles Agreement (MVA), Belt and Road Initiative (BRI), regional energy grid, and a joint exploration of hydro-resources of the Himalayan–Ganges–Brahmaputra basins and the potentials of the *blue economy.* Resources should be strategically allocated to promote transport, trade, logistics, investment and people-to-people connectivity to reap the potential benefits originating from these. If Bangladesh is to realise its potentials as a regional transport and production hub, and as a gateway to the Bay of Bengal, it will have to coordinate the development of seamless transport networks with its extensive hinterland. It will also need to proactively explore new sources of financing to underwrite the significant expenditures involved. Opportunities of public–private partnerships, issuance of sovereign bonds, and access to credit from the Asian Infrastructure Investment Bank (AIIB), New Development Bank (NDB) and other potential sources will have to be explored. In this context, Bangladesh should take the initiative to deepen and broaden cooperation in view of the SAFTA and The Bay of Bengal Initiative for Multi-Sectoral Technical and Economic Cooperation-Free Trade Agreement (BIMSTEC-FTA). More emphasis on South–South cooperation, and more particularly, integration with South and Southern Asian economies must be seen as critically important strategic options as Bangladesh moves forward in the twenty-first century.

Bangladesh remains one of the very few developing countries which is not a member of any Bilateral Free Trade Agreement (BFTA). In the absence of preferential market access as an LDC, Bangladesh should explore greater market access by negotiating BFTAs with important trading partners. This will call for a significant strengthening of analytical and negotiating capacities in relevant trade-negotiating institutions. Indeed, Bangladesh will have to think of negotiating not merely BFTAs, but also Comprehensive Economic Partnership Agreement (CEPA) type of bilateral agreements, which envisage cooperation not only in areas of trade in goods, but also trade in services in the areas of investment, technology, transport, logistics and finance, and undertaking joint initiatives to establish value chains and production networks.

Coping with the Emerging Global Scenario

Bangladesh's graduation journey is taking place at a time when the emerging global scenario is fraught with formidable challenges—the looming trade war between the US and China, uncertainties originating from Brexit, and the weakening of the rules-based multilateral trading system represented by the WTO, attempts to reform the WTO by questioning some of the key systemic issues,[23] the growing emphasis on regional trading arrangements and mega-regionals, to name only a few. Bangladesh must pursue an active policy of bilateral, regional and multilateral engagement, and domestic preparedness to mitigate the risks and address the challenges. These developments could slow down global growth with consequent adverse effects on Bangladesh's export earnings and remittance flows. Product and market diversification and search for new markets for migrant workers must be accorded the highest priority in view of the emerging uncertainties.

Indeed, the deepening of regional cooperation in Southern Asia ought to be seen as the next frontier as Bangladesh makes its journey in the twenty-first century. The potentials of closer cooperation in South Asia have, till now, remained largely untapped (Kathuria 2018). These must be realised through close collaboration aimed at integrating trade, investment, transport, logistics and people-to-people connectivity (De and Rahman 2017). The BBIN MVA projects, initiatives at land customs stations (particularly in Benapole and Petrapole at the border between Bangladesh and India), and proposed initiatives under the Bangladesh–China–India–Myanmar (BCIM) Economic Corridor and Energy trade with India are some of the ongoing initiatives that must be leveraged to attract higher investment to Bangladesh, create competitive supply-side capacities, and establish regional value chains and production networks. Without this, the target of higher exports from Bangladesh to South Asia and the global market will not be attained.[24]

Raising Productivity and Competitiveness

As was pointed out, LDC- and middle-income graduation do not include some key dimensions of development, including technological upgradation and preparedness for the *new economy* (in contrast to the *traditional economy*; our emphases). According to the World Economic Forum (WEF 2018), Bangladesh's position belongs to the lowest stage of the technological preparedness hierarchy, which is as follows: *Leading, High Potential, Legacy* and *Nascent* (our emphases). Bangladesh will need to design its policy incentive structure to promote technological upgradation, strengthen skills endowment, enhance productivity and raise competitiveness capacity towards a strengthened global integration of her economy. Successful operation of the special economic zones (SEZs),[25] which now constitutes the fulcrum of Bangladesh's industrialisation strategy, will also hinge on Bangladesh's capacity to undertake these initiatives.

Future competitiveness will depend on Bangladesh's ability to transform itself from a *factor-driven economy to a productivity-driven economy*. Low levels of productivity in the country undermine Bangladesh's competitiveness. Even in the case of the flagship apparels sector, according to a 2016 report by the International Institute for Labour Studies, Bangladesh's labour productivity was significantly lower than some of its major competitors in the global market. A key challenge for Bangladesh is to be able to make the transition by avoiding jobless growth. Bangladesh's policies must be geared towards diversification of the economy, creation of supply-side capacities, structural transformation of the economy, creation of decent jobs that pay living wages, and taking advantage of new market opportunities. Indeed, Bangladesh will need to run on two legs—by catering to the growing domestic demand and by taking advantage of the regional and global markets. Energetic steps will have to be taken in order to bring the benefits of the digital economy and e-governance to people and businesses. These will play an important role in improving the performance of enterprises, harnessing the competitiveness of the economy, and enhancing overall quality of service delivery in the country.

The challenges of the fourth industrial revolution are formidable and real. The government of Bangladesh has set a goal to attain the *digital transformation* of the economy by 2030. However, Bangladesh has a long way to go if its ambition of the *Digital Bangladesh* vision is to be fully realised. According to the World Bank data, internet penetration in the country currently stands at only 14.4 per cent, for example. There is a need to extend support to online businesses and services to help them scale up and be able to take advantage of the opportunities of the digital and data-driven economy. Facilitating the expansion of e-commerce-based businesses should be seen as an important strategy in going forward.

Addressing Rising Inequality

Addressing inequality remains a major concern for Bangladesh. Despite the country's robust economic growth and poverty reduction record, inequality has risen in recent times, as evidenced by data from Bangladesh's successive Household Income and Expenditure Surveys (HIESs). Income inequality in Bangladesh, measured by the Gini Coefficient, has risen from 0.35 in the mid-1980s, to 0.48 in 2016. In 2016, the country's wealthiest 10 per cent of the population had income which was 2.9 times higher than the bottom 40 per cent together; this was about 1.5 times higher in the mid-1980s (Centre for Policy Dialogue [CPD] 2019). Sobhan (2010) argues that the sources of structural injustice will need to be addressed head on if inequality is to be reduced. This injustice is rooted in unequal access to assets, unequal participation in the markets, unequal access to human development and unjust governance. Emphasis in policies ought to be put on ensuring distributive justice and promoting the cause of reducing inequality in all forms. A number of scholars, such as Harvard economist Dani Rodrik, have shown that countries which start with lower inequality tend to grow faster. As may be recalled, the Sustainable Development Goals (SDGs) call to *leave no one behind* in the development process. Fiscal–financial–institutional policies must be geared towards reducing inequality. Creation of more decent jobs and transitioning towards the formalisation of the labour market will be important in this connection. Moving from social safety-net to social security, a greater focus on gender-inclusive growth will be crucial for reducing inequality and for promoting the cause of upward social mobility of women. Since the relatively poor are particularly, and comparatively, more vulnerable to the impacts of climate change, environmentally sustainable development will be essential to ensure a more equitable growth in Bangladesh.

Reaping the Benefits of Demographic Dividend

Bangladesh stands at the cusp of a demographic dividend. According to the BBS, the population aged between 15 and 29 years constitutes about one-third of the country's working population of 62.1 million (as of 2016), while the median age of the population is just about

26 years. This offers Bangladesh a crucial window of opportunity to take advantage of the ongoing demographic dynamics. Indeed, the country's prospect of achieving the vision of transforming into a developed economy by 2041 will critically hinge on Bangladesh's ability to take full advantage of its youthful workforce and the potentially highly rewarding demographic dividend. In order to be able to do so, Bangladesh must invest significantly in its youth. Rehauling of the education system, emphasis on Science, Technology, Engineering and Mathematics (STEM) education, vocational training and skills upgradation must be accorded priority attention in this regard. The window of opportunity is estimated to last over the next three decades. Hence, it is important that adequate budgetary allocations are made to equip the human resources adequately to enable Bangladesh to reap the expected benefits.

Tackling Infrastructure Deficits

As Bangladesh strives to add momentum to its pace of development, infrastructure deficit presents a frontier that is yet to be conquered. According to estimates by the Bangladesh Planning Commission, an additional amount of $928 billion will be required if the goals and targets of the SDGs are to be attained. SDG implementation could play a critically important role in addressing the challenges of Bangladesh's dual graduation (Fahmida, Pervin and Rahman 2019). As is well-appreciated, infrastructure plays an important role in stimulating and crowding-in private sector investment. By some estimates, Bangladesh will need to make investments of well over $100 billion in the course of the next decade to build ports and roads, set up rail lines, establish power-generation capabilities, and provide utilities and services to meet the ever-increasing demands of the economy and the people.

To be true, the government has been making significant allocations towards addressing the attendant challenges by putting in place new power-generation capacities, improved port services, building transport infrastructure such as road and rail networks, and expanding mobile phones and internet services. However, in order to raise the competitive strength of the economy and cater to the growing needs of its producers, exporters and consumers, to reduce the cost of doing business, to improve efficiency at ports, and to be able to take full advantage of the digital economy, Bangladesh will need to make significant additional investments in its infrastructure. The Lines of Credit (LoCs) offered by India, China and other bilateral as well as international development partners will need to be appropriately utilised to ensure the expected returns, so that the rising debt-servicing liabilities can be adequately met. Projects will have to be implemented within the stipulated time frames, and with good governance.

Coping with Climate Impact

According to the Intergovernmental Panel on Climate Change (IPCC) (2014), Bangladesh is one of the most 'climate vulnerable' countries in the world. IPCC (2014) identifies Bangladesh as being at serious risk from climate change due to its exposure to sea-level rise and extreme events. Bangladesh's population at risk of sea-level rise is projected to grow to 27 million by 2050; and the World Bank Report mentions estimates of adaptation deficit to be to the tune of $25 billion (IPCC 2014; Pachauri and Meyer 2014). In the southern region of the country, 40 per cent of productive land could be lost if sea levels rise by about 65 centimetres, which could happen, according to a World Bank study, by the 2080s (Mani, Bandyopadhyay, Chunabayashi, et al. 2018). The report states that crop production is likely to be severely affected, with consequent adverse implications for food security and poverty. About 20 million people in the coastal areas are already affected by high salinity levels in drinking water. According to the report, the pace of salinity intrusion, river erosion and desertification was expected to significantly rise in future. Cropping practices will need to be calibrated according to the needs of climate change. Rapid urbanisation will add new challenges to the existing ones. Bangladesh will need to pursue environment-friendly policies and practices to mitigate and address the adverse effects that climate change will have on both its economy and society.

Bangladesh must put emphasis on the sustainable use of its resources, for example, by promoting the use of surface water instead of ground water for agriculture. This is particularly important as some specialists are of the opinion that Bangladesh has reached a technological frontier. Significant investment will need to be made to promote agricultural research to develop new technologies and innovate high-yield crop varieties that are resistant to salinity, flooding and cold. Policy support, zoning, fiscal incentives and other measures will have to be put in place to confront these challenges. In light of the activities envisaged under the Bangladesh Climate Change Trust Fund, initiatives will need to be taken to address food security, social protection, health emergencies, disaster management, climate resilient infrastructure, knowledge management, climate change mitigation, capacity-building and institutional strengthening. In this context, special efforts will need to be deployed to harness global support, including access to additional resources from the Global Climate Fund.

Better Governance as a Key Driver

The contrast between Bangladesh's robust macroeconomic performance and the weak state of governance has often been referred to as the *Bangladesh Paradox*. The question that also needs to be posed in this context is whether the Bangladesh economy is performing to its fullest potential or whether it is underperforming. If the current pace of growth is to be sustained and is to gain further momentum, which is indeed needed to address the challenges of dual graduation, Bangladesh will have to address the governance deficit and improve the functional quality of its institutions with due importance and urgency. Corruption, weak institutions and illicit financial flows combine to create a drag on the pace of performance of the economy. Going forward, these could give rise to not only economic inefficiencies, but also social tensions, which could induce new vulnerabilities and seriously undermine the country's future growth. Bangladesh's policymakers must be alert to these challenges and take appropriate measures to address and mitigate them. There ought to be zero tolerance of corruption and corrupt practices. In this connection, initiatives such as the National Integrity System, adopted by the government in 2012 to mainstream integrity and accountability within the government system, could play an important role. A key factor here will be the political will to promote good governance in all spheres of the economy.

Concluding Remarks

It is to Bangladesh's distinct credit that in spite of the doomsday prophecies voiced during her initial years, she has been able to make the two impressive graduations noted at the beginning of the chapter: LDC graduation and middle-income graduation. As the preceding sections have pointed out, while indicative of Bangladesh's past success, there are important implications of this dual graduation, going forward. Bangladesh's future journey will also coincide with the implementation of the SDGs, which call for a triangulation of economic development, social inclusiveness and environmental sustainability in the development process, leaving no one behind. Indeed, successful implementation of the SDGs could reinforce Bangladesh's efforts to address the challenges of dual graduation. No doubt, Bangladesh's past performance record and developmental achievements do provide a solid foundation to embark upon the new lap of her twenty-first century journey.

Fiscal–financial–institutional policies must be designed and coordinated in a way that addresses the prevailing structural weaknesses of the economy towards a structural transformation-enabled sustainable transition of the economy. As has been emphasised in the preceding sections, sound macroeconomic management, good governance, regulatory reforms, and transparency and accountability in the development process will be critically important as Bangladesh moves forward. Bangladesh's policymakers will need to design appropriate strategies, backed by the needed homework, if the emerging challenges of dual graduation are to be successfully addressed, and the potential opportunities originating from the post-graduation scenario are to be fully realised.

Notes

1. Middle-income trap refers to a situation where a country, after having made the transition from low-income to middle-income status, fails to sustain the pace of development, and is stuck in the middle-income group for a prolonged period of time, not being able to graduate to a developed country status.
2. The *development paradox* refers to Bangladesh's achievements in the socio-economic arena, some being unique at such low levels

of economic development, while the state of governance remained relatively weak.

3. The poverty rate is projected to stand at about 21 per cent in 2018.
4. Number of people in multidimensional poverty dropped from 93.7 million in 2004 to 74.4 million in 2014.
5. MPI uses 10 indicators to determine different dimensions of poverty: nutrition, child mortality, years of schooling, school attendance, cooking fuel, sanitation, drinking water, electricity, housing and assets.
6. Measured as a share of export and import in the GDP.
7. The World Bank identifies four categories of countries, which are identified primarily for purposes of operational lending activities, based on three-year average per capita GNI, estimated according to the Atlas method. The thresholds are shifting numbers, estimated annually. In 2018, the thresholds were as follows: for LICs: below $1,005; for LMICs: between $1,006 and $3,955; for upper middle-income country: between $3,956 and $12,235; and for developed country: $12,236 and above.
8. Bangladesh's dual graduation also reflects her track record of success in attaining the MDGs.
9. Or double the per capita GNI threshold.
10. For the income criteria threshold, the per capita GNI is fixed at 20 per cent higher than the World Bank threshold for LICs for the relevant year (estimated according to the Atlas method). The other two indices have been fixed in 1991; for HAI, at 66, and for EVI, at 32. Indeed, there is a fourth criteria as well, which stipulates that no new LDC will have a population exceeding 75 million people. Thus, for Bangladesh, graduation is an irreversible journey, with no possibility of falling back.
11. Defined as the difference between the actual scenario and the respective graduation thresholds.
12. Indeed, Bangladesh's graduation is being followed with keen interest by the global community for a number of reasons. It will be the first major LDC to graduate. If the 15 graduating LDCs are considered, Bangladesh accounted for 17.3 per cent of the combined population, 13.6 per cent of the exports and 18.3 per cent of the GDP.
13. IDA (which is the soft window of the World Bank) loans are given at an interest rate of 0.75 per cent per annum, with longer maturity and grace periods. These are for countries which have a per capita GNI of $1,165 (according to the Atlas method).

14. Mix of concessional and non-concessional loans.
15. Bangladesh's per capita GNI for 2018 was estimated to be $1,750 and for 2019, it was $1,909. However, this is in nominal US$, which is lower when re-estimated according to the Atlas method.
16. For example, blended finance, which is geared to mobilising private-sector finances with the help of concessional loans.
17. Debt trap refers to a situation where a country's accumulated debt is equivalent to a high percentage of its GDP and in this scenario, the country finds it either extremely difficult or is unable to service the debt (the principal and the interest amount).
18. LDCs enjoy waivers from many of the obligations stipulated under the TRIPS and TRIMS of the WTO.
19. This allows LDCs to produce pharmaceutical items without having to buy patents and pay for license fees. This has now been extended till December 2032. Bangladesh has been able to take good advantage of this, to reduce cost of production and increase exports. At present, Bangladesh exports more than $100 million worth of pharmaceutical items to about 130 countries. However, once graduated, Bangladesh will no longer be eligible to enjoy the preferential treatment.
20. After graduation, Bangladesh will also not be eligible for special considerations in terms of ceilings and waivers with regard to budgetary contributions to UN organisations, as well as for travel support to various international events. Same is the case of access to the Technological Fund set up following the Istanbul Programme of Action (IPoA) for the LDCs.
21. Under the Everything But Arms (EBA) scheme of the EU, the LDCs enjoy duty-free, quota-free market access in the 28 EU countries (including the UK) for all items, excepting arms. Thus, Bangladesh, a key beneficiary of the EBA, will continue to benefit from the preferential market access in the EU till 2027 (that is, after she graduates out of the LDC group in 2024).
22. This would mean that from now on, Bangladesh must take an active interest in the *special and differential* (S&D) provisions put in place for the developing countries (as against the LDCs, which was the case till now) in the various WTO negotiations.
23. For example, some powerful members have questioned the justification of the S&D provisions for developing countries, the single undertaking (*nothing is agreed unless everything is agreed*) principle of decision-making, the working of WTO's

dispute-settlement mechanism (DSM). Many LDCs and developing countries are apprehensive that some of the suggested reforms will weaken the rule-based multilateral system of the WTO and lead to dilution and erosion of the developmental dimensions of the WTO.

24. It is interesting to note here that Vietnam, a country of comparable economic size (nominal GDP of Vietnam was $240.3 billion as against $274.0 billion for Bangladesh in 2018), had an export of more than $220 billion against $36.7 billion for Bangladesh in 2018.
25. Bangladesh has planned to set up 100 SEZs to encourage and attract investment by domestic, joint venture and foreign investors. About 25 SEZs are currently being established on a priority basis. One million jobs and $40 billion worth of annual exports are envisaged when the SEZs come into full swing.

REFERENCES

Bangladesh Bank. *Annual Review of Import Payments 2013–14.* Available at https://www.bb.org.bd/econdata/openpdf.php?i=2.

———. *Export Trend of Bangladesh (1980–1981 to 2018–2019).* Available at https://bb.org.bd/pub/annual/expreceipt/exp1819/chap8.pdf.

———. *Total Import Payments by Countries/Territories 2002/03–2017/18,* Bangladesh Bank. Available at www.bb.org.bd/pub/annual/imppayment/imp1819/statable5.pdf.

Bangladesh Bureau of Statistics (BBS). n.d. Dhaka, Bangladesh.

———. 2015. *Poverty and Inequality in Bangladesh (2014–15),* Bangladesh Ministry of Finance. Available at https://mof.portal.gov.bd/sites/default/files/files/mof.portal.gov.bd/page/83ea3b2c_3a6e_4073_8261_c4da472536be/poverty14-15EN.pdf.

———. 2018a. '45 years Agriculture Statistics of Major Crops: Aus, Amon, Boro, Jute, Potato and Wheat', Statistics and Information Division, Ministry of Planning. Available at http://bbs.portal.gov.bd/sites/default/files/files/bbs.portal.gov.bd/page/16d38ef2_2163_4252_a28b_e65f60dab8a9/45%20years%20Major%20Crops.pdf.

———. 2018b. *Poverty and Extreme Poverty, 2017 and 2018,* Bangladesh Ministry of Finance. Available at http://bbs.portal.gov.bd/sites/default/files/files/bbs.portal.gov.bd/news/c40016e4_bfe1_4dba_bba2_a34146688700/Poverty_Estimates.pdf.

———. 2018c. 'Report on Quarterly Labour Force Survey 2016–17', Dhaka, Bangladesh.

Bhattacharya, D. 2019. 'The LDC Paradigm, Graduation and Bangladesh: Concepts, Comparison and Policy'. In D. Bhattacharya (ed.), *Bangladesh's Graduation from the Least Developed Countries Group: Pitfalls and Promises.* London: Routledge.

CPD. 2019. 'State of the Bangladesh Economy and National Elections 2018: Priorities for Electoral Debates. Dhaka: Centre for Policy Dialogue (CPD)'. Available at https://cpd.org.bd/state-of-the-bangladesh-economy-and-national-elections-2018-priorities-for-electoral-debates/.

De, Prabir, and M. Rahman (eds). 2017. *Regional Integration in South Asia: Essays in Honour of Dr M. Rahmatullah.* New Delhi: K. W. Publishers.

Faaland, J., and J. R. Parkinson. 1976. *Bangladesh: The Test Case for Development.* London: C. Hurst & Co.

Fahmida, K., S. Pervin, and M. M. Rahman. 2019. 'Bangladesh's Pursuit of the 2030 Agenda: Will it Facilitate Smooth Transition after LDC Graduation?' In Bhattacharya (ed.), *Bangladesh's Graduation from the Least Developed Countries Group.*

'Government of Summary of Aid Commitment and Disbursement, (1971/72–2017/18)', ERD, Government of the People's Republic of Bangladesh. Available at https://erd.ortal.gov.bd/sites/default/files/files/erd.portal.gov.bd/page/b09c0301 8d15 49e1 8af9 3231f08b8ad8/Tbl-9.0%20%281%29.pdf.

IPCC. 2014. 'Report on Bangladesh Launch of the Fifth Assessment Report (AR5) of the Intergovernmental Panel on Climate Change', Dhaka, Bangladesh, 6–8 August.

Kathuria, S. (ed.). 2018. *A Glass Half Full: The Promise of Regional Trade in South Asia.* Washington, D.C.: World Bank.

Mahmud, W., and S. R. Osmani. 2017. *The Theory and Practice of Microcredit.* Abingdon, Oxon; New York: Routledge.

Mani, M. S., S. Bandyopadhyay, S. Chunabayashi, et al. 2018. *South Asia's Hotspots: The Impact of Temperature and Precipitation Changes on Living Standards.* Washington, D.C.: World Bank.

Pachauri, R. K., and L. A. Meyer (eds). 2014. *Climate Change 2014: Synthesis Report. Contribution of Working Groups I, II and III Fifth Assessment Report of the Intergovernmental Panel on Climate Change.* Geneva, Switzerland: IPCC.

Rahman, M., and D. Bhattacharya. 2019. 'Graduating LDCs in an Evolving WTO: Options and Strategies', Dhaka, Bangladesh: Friedrich-Ebert-Stiftung; CPD.

Rahman, M., and E. Bari. 2019. 'Pathways to Bangladesh's Sustainable LDC Graduation: Prospects, Challenges and Strategies'.

In Bhattacharya (ed.), *Bangladesh's Graduation from the Least Developed Countries Group.*

Rahman, M., and K. G. Moazzem. 2017. 'The Legacy of Rana Plaza: Improving Labour and Social Standards in Bangladesh's Apparel Industry'. In A. Hira and M. Benson-Rea (eds), *Governing Corporate Social Responsibility in the Apparel Industry after Rana Plaza.* London: Palgrave-Macmillan.

Sobhan, R. 2010. *Challenging the Injustice of Poverty: Agendas for Inclusive Development in South Asia.* New Delhi: Sage Publications.

UN. 2015. 'Sustainable Development Goals (SDGs), Transforming Our World: The 2030 Agenda'. Available at https://sustainabledevelopment.un.org/post2015/transformingourworld.

UN CDP Secretariat. n.d. Triennial Review Dataset 2000–18.

UNDP. 2019. *Global Multidimensional Poverty Index (MPI).* Available at http://hdr.undp.org/en/2019-MPI.

WEF. 2018. Available at https://www.weforum.org/ (accessed 14 May 2019).

World Bank. 2019. 'Bangladesh Development Update: Towards Regulatory Predictability (English)'. Washington, D.C.: World Bank Group.

———. n.d. 'GNI Per Capita, Atlas Method (Current US$). Available at https://data.worldbank.org/indicator/NY.GNP.PCAP.CD?locations=BD.

Yearwise Statement of Debt Service Payments (1973/74–2016/2017), ERD, Bangladesh. Available at https://erd.portal.gov.bd/sites/default/files/files/erd.portal.gov.bd/page/b09c0301_8d15_49e1_8af9_3231f08b8ad8/Tbl-9.0%20%281%29.pdf.

2

Bangladesh's Future Export Challenges and the Need for an FTA Strategy*

AMITENDU PALIT

Bangladesh is on its way to graduate from its current status of a Least Developed Country (LDC) to a Middle-Income Country (MIC) by 2024. This graduation is testimony to Bangladesh's sustained improvement in terms of various economic and social indicators. One of the key factors behind Bangladesh's success has been its ability to effectively pursue an export-oriented strategy of industrial development. The strategy has enabled Bangladesh to emerge as one of the world's leading exporters of apparels and readymade garments. The achievement has been significantly facilitated by Bangladesh's effective use of the non-reciprocal preferential market access schemes offered to LDCs by various countries, and the Special and Differential (S&D) treatment for LDCs under the multilateral rules-based trade framework of the World Trade Organization (WTO). However, these benefits would cease to exist once Bangladesh graduates to an MIC. This means that the country has to deal with a new set of challenges, particularly relating to the expected loss in export earnings due to the loss of preferential access and the impact of the same on Bangladesh's economy. Therefore, in order to overcome the adverse impacts of the loss of preferential access, Bangladesh needs to pursue efforts aimed at obtaining 'new' preferential access from elsewhere.

---

* This chapter is an expanded version of an earlier paper prepared for the Cosmos Foundation, Dhaka, Bangladesh. The author is grateful to participants of the ISAS Workshop on 'Assessing the transformation of Bangladesh', organised at Singapore on 23 May 2019, for useful comments and suggestions on the chapter.

This chapter looks at the challenges that Bangladesh exports would encounter post-graduation; it also highlights the importance of Bangladesh making efforts to combine the non-reciprocal access it would continue to receive as a developing country in major developed country markets, with reciprocal preferential access obtained through new Free Trade Agreements (FTAs). Highlighting Bangladesh's current limited engagement in FTAs, the chapter further explores the broad characteristics and possible areas of emphasis in the FTA strategy that Bangladesh might aim at pursuing.

Non-Reciprocal Access: Features, Withdrawal and Further Contraction

This section examines the nature of preferential access currently available to Bangladesh's exports as an LDC, implications following such access from major export markets, and the developments narrowing the scope of preferential access in the global trade landscape.

Duty-Free Quota-Free (DFQF) Preferential Access and Everything But Arms (EBA)

Bangladesh's exports, like those from other LDCs, enjoy Duty-Free Quota-Free (DFQF) access to various major world markets. These preferences are deeper and wider than the more standard Generalised System of Preferences (GSP), offered by several developed countries to other developing countries. Emerging from the consultations held in the Doha and Hong Kong Ministerial meetings of the WTO in 2001 and 2005, respectively, the DFQF facilities offer special access to LDC exports, in addition to what they obtain through general GSP schemes, although both categories of access are non-reciprocal in nature. Furthermore, these facilities are not just offered by developed countries, but are also extended by some developing countries, such as China, India and Chile (Table 2.1).

A large part of Bangladesh's current exports is to destinations offering DFQF facilities. These include the EU, US, Canada, Japan and China. The EU accounts for around 55 per cent of Bangladesh's

Table 2.1 Existing Preferential Access Schemes for LDC Exports

Country	*Existing preferential access scheme*
1. Australia	GSP for LDCs and developing countries. One hundred and six duty-free tariff lines for 50 LDCs, including five for agriculture and 101 for non-agricultural items.
2. Canada	GSP for LDCs and developing countries; 1,518 duty-free tariff lines for 49 LDCs, out of which 411 are for agriculture and 1,107 are for non-agriculture exports.
3. Chile	Duty-free treatment for 48 LDCs. This includes 8,450 duty-free tariff lines, out of which 1,430 are for agricultural goods and 7,020 for non-agricultural goods.
4. China	Duty-free treatment for LDCs. Covers 38 LDCs and includes 7,527 duty-free tariff lines, with 1,004 for agricultural goods and 6,523 for non-agricultural goods. Bangladesh has a lower coverage of 4,437 duty-free tariff lines, out of which 571 are for agricultural and 3,866 are for non-agricultural exports (WTO, Preferential Trade Arrangements).
5. European Union (EU)	EBA duty-free scheme for 49 LDCs. Includes 6,967 duty-free lines, out of which 1,619 are for agricultural and 5,348 are for non-agricultural exports.
6. India	Unilateral Tariff Preference Scheme for 48 LDCs. Includes 10,949 preferential tariff lines, out of which 10,575 are duty-free, including 1,087 agricultural goods and 9,488 non-agricultural goods.
7. Japan	GSP for LDCs and developing countries. LDCs are offered 3,598 duty-free tariff lines, out of which 1,152 are for agriculture and 2,446 are for non-agricultural items.
8. New Zealand	GSP for LDCs and developing countries; 3,105 duty-free tariff lines only for LDCs, out of which 367 are for agriculture and 2,738 are for non-agriculture exports.
9. South Korea	Preferential Tariff for 48 LDCs; 8,972 duty-free tariff lines, out of which 931 are for agriculture and 8,041 are for non-agricultural exports.
10. United States (US)	GSP for LDCs and developing countries; 4,969 duty-free tariff lines only for LDCs, out of which 1,223 are for agriculture and 3,746 are for non-agriculture goods.

Source: Palit (2019).

total exports (WTO, Bangladesh Member Profile). More than 90 per cent of these exports comprise garments and clothing (European Commission [EU], Trade Policy). Bangladesh has been an important beneficiary of the EU's DFQF scheme for LDCs, popularly referred to as 'Everything But Arms' or the EBA.

The EBA has played a significant role in the growth of Bangladesh's exports, particularly garments, to Europe. The EBA was introduced by the European Parliament on 25 October 2012 (Official Journal of the European Union, Regulation No. 978/2012), marking a significant expansion in the scope of preferential market access for LDC exports. It was the third and the most exhaustive category of non-reciprocal preferential access offered by the EU, in addition to the standard GSP, and a further specialised version of the GSP, defined as GSP+, aiming to incentivise sustainable development and good governance in recipient countries.

The EBA will no longer be available once Bangladesh graduates. This would mean significant loss of preferential access for Bangladesh's most important export market. Bangladesh is seeking to obtain the GSP+ preferential benefits from the EU (*The Daily Star*, Star Business Report 2016). The GSP+ is another sub-scheme of preferential access offered by the EU to some non-LDC developing countries. Currently, the scheme includes eight beneficiaries: Armenia, Bolivia, Capo Verde, Kyrgyz Republic, Mongolia, Pakistan, Philippines and Sri Lanka (WTO, Preferential Trade Arrangements). It provides almost as much preferential access as the EBA. However, it is contingent upon beneficiaries successfully adhering to and maintaining a large number of international conventions on human rights, labour rights, environmental protection and good governance. While Bangladesh might well be able to fulfil these obligations, it will need to adjust to an era of strict monitoring by the EU, EU member states, European Parliament and civil society actors.

United States (US) GSP: Non-restoration

The implicit concern for Bangladesh, in its efforts to extract the GSP+ benefits from the EU, stems from its lack of success in restoring GSP benefits from the US. The US is the largest single market for Bangladesh exports, accounting for almost 20 per cent of its total exports. The US withdrew GSP access for Bangladeshi exports after major industrial accidents in the country in 2012 and 2013 (*bdnews24.com*, Special Correspondent 2019). The most serious of these incidents included the catastrophic developments at Rana Plaza in Dhaka, which led to the death of more than 1,000 garment workers. Thereafter, notwithstanding the signing of a bilateral Trade and Investment Cooperation Forum Agreement (TICFA) in November 2013, and multi-country efforts to build a framework on improving labour rights and industrial safety standards (Congressional Research Service [CRS] 2019), the GSP is yet to be renewed. If cynicism prevails on the progress made by Bangladesh in upgrading its industrial working conditions and labour rights, then, as with the US GSP, obtaining GSP+ from the EU might also be difficult.

Rising Demand for Curtailing S&D Flexibilities within the WTO

Bangladesh currently has a share of around 0.25 per cent in world merchandise trade and 0.1 per cent in global commercial services trade. Its proficiency in manufacturing exports, principally garments, and its greater integration in global value chains is expected to result in an expanding share of the country in future global trade. Paradoxically, however, a higher share in global trade might mean less eligibility for preferential access to major global markets. This possibility is significant, given the efforts by developed countries to limit preferential access, as available through S&D treatment for all developing country WTO members, to only those who are really 'needy'.

At the WTO, the US is leading efforts to restrict preferential access flexibilities available through the S&D provisions to a handful of poor countries by excluding those, for example, who have a share of 0.5 per cent or more in global trade, those that are part of the G20,[1] or are member countries of the Organisation for Economic Cooperation and Development (OECD) (Miles 2019). There are efforts by other OECD countries, such as Canada and Japan, to systematically exclude beneficiary countries from their GSP programmes once they achieve 1 per cent share in world exports

(*EveryCRSReport.com*, Generalised System of Preferences). There is no reason why such conditions would not be gradually adopted by other preference-offering countries, particularly for non-LDC GSP schemes. This is a situation that Bangladesh needs to take note of and prepare for.

Growth of Mega-Regional Trade Agreements (RTAs) and Preference Erosion

The emergence of several RTAs has been a major development in global trade in recent years. These RTAs, such as the Comprehensive and Progressive Trans-Pacific Partnership (CPTPP) and the ongoing Regional Comprehensive Economic Partnership (RCEP),[2] are humongous multi-country agreements carving out specific sets of reciprocal trade preferences for members. One of the concerns with respect to such agreements for many non-members, particularly for LDCs, is the erosion of trade preferences. From an LDC perspective, this implies that the preferential access-extending members of these mega-RTAs (for example, Australia, Canada, Japan and New Zealand for CPTPP; Australia, China, India, Japan, Korea and New Zealand for RCEP [see Tables 2.1 and 2.2]) offer the same access to non-LDC members of the RTAs by reducing the earlier applied tariffs on exports from the latter to zero, or much less than the current levels. Such erosion of existing tariff preferences can have adverse effects for several LDCs, including Bangladesh, as noted by empirical studies (Milner, Morrissey and Zgovu 2010).

Mega-RTAs pose other challenges, too. For instance, a mega-RTA, like the RCEP, is likely to retain flexibilities for its LDC members such as Cambodia, Lao and Myanmar. This is due to the RCEP being fashioned as an Association of Southeast Asian Nations (ASEAN)-style FTA, which has the tradition of providing flexibilities according to the economic circumstances of its members. Some from among these economies, such as Cambodia, compete with Bangladesh in textile and garment exports to major RCEP markets like Australia, Canada and Japan. As a non-signatory of RCEP, Bangladesh's garment exports will be rendered less competitive in these markets vis-à-vis exports from such member countries. Even as an LDC, Bangladesh garment exports will encounter comparative disadvantage since Cambodia, Lao and Myanmar are likely to have greater flexibilities within RCEP. These difficulties will be compounded by the country's graduation, as in the foreseeable future, Bangladeshi exports would receive only overall GSP benefits from developed RCEP member markets, while its LDC competitors would receive much deeper preferences. From the perspective of country competitiveness, both CPTPP and RCEP include Vietnam, which is a formidable competitor of Bangladesh in global textile and garment exports, and which would obtain deep preferential access in several major markets through both RTAs.

Mega-RTAs like the RCEP, the Pacific Alliance and the African Continental Free Trade Area (ACFTA)[3] pose greater challenges for Bangladesh. These are trade arrangements where several WTO members come together to carve out specific zones of reciprocal market access preferences over and above those available through the WTO. These RTAs do not comprise only developed countries, but also the emerging market in developing countries and LDCs. In addition to creating new chunks of preferential access among members in terms of zero or very low tariffs, these RTAs also create rules on several other important trade issues, including rules of origin, product standards, investment and services. Much of the current global conversation and movement on trade issues—both traditional issues like standards and trade in services, as well as more modern issues like ecommerce and environment rules—now happen within the RTAs, given the difficulty of achieving progress on all these subjects at the WTO. It is important for Bangladesh to stay abreast of these developments for maintaining its progress on its export-intensive strategy for economic growth.

Rationale for a New Preferential Access-seeking Strategy

Bangladesh is at a critical juncture in its path of economic development. Exports, particularly garment exports, have contributed significantly to the growth and expansion of the country's macroeconomy, and the rise in income and living standards. With a nominal GDP of almost $300 billion, Bangladesh currently ranks forty-first among world economies in economic size (International Monetary Fund [IMF],

World Economic Outlook Database). This economic expansion has substantially contributed to the rise in the country's per capita income,[4] enabling its graduation from the status of an LDC. The next phase of its journey on export-oriented industrialisation will need to overcome the challenge of the absence of deep preferential access in its major export markets. There are some concerns in this regard, with the apprehensions pointing towards adverse economic prospects. Various studies provide projected estimates of the decline in Bangladesh's exports—likely from the loss of preferential access—ranging from around $2.7 billion annually in export revenue to 5–7 per cent decline in overall exports (*The Economist* 2018).

In order to carefully assess the implications of the withdrawal of non-reciprocal preferential market access to Bangladesh's exports and to develop an alternative strategy for tackling the difficulties, it is important to take a close look at the current access that is available for Bangladesh. This is summarised in Table 2.2.

Bangladesh is currently a beneficiary of 12 non-reciprocal GSP benefit schemes and eight LDC-specific benefit programmes. These are in addition to the benefits of the EBA scheme of the EU. The larger context of the implications that follow from the withdrawal of non-reciprocal preferential market access is specifically with respect to the discontinuation of the eight LDC programmes and the EBA of the EU. Exports will continue to benefit from the GSPs that are being extended to Bangladesh now, unless the extending countries decide to review its eligibility as a beneficiary, similar to the way in which the US has been reviewing for a few years now.

Withdrawal of current non-reciprocal preferential access, specific to LDCs, after graduation, does not obviously mean that Bangladesh will cease receiving benefits of this access entirely, as long as the GSPs mentioned above continue. At one level, however, the change in the nature of non-reciprocal access limits the degree and depth of preferential access that Bangladesh receives now as an LDC, thereby affecting the competitiveness of its exports. It is hardly surprising that official estimates like those by the Ministry of Finance project close to a loss of $3 billion in annual expected earnings, inflicted by additional tariffs of around 6.7 per cent that would come up post-graduation. The impact of lower export competitiveness and

Table 2.2 Bangladesh's Preferential Access

Country	*Preferential Access*
1. Armenia	GSP
2. Australia	GSP
3. Canada	GSP
4. European Union	GSP
5. Iceland	GSP
6. Japan	GSP
7. Kazakhstan	GSP
8. New Zealand	GSP
9. Norway	GSP
10. Russian Federation	GSP
11. Switzerland	GSP
12. Turkey	GSP
13. India	LDC-specific
14. Chile	LDC-specific
15. China	LDC-specific
16. Chinese Taipei	LDC-specific
17. Kyrgyz Republic	LDC-specific
18. Montenegro	LDC-specific
19. Thailand	LDC-specific
20. Korea, Republic of	LDC-specific

Note: This table does not include the preferences extended by the EU under the EBA arrangement. It is also important to note that GSP benefits by the US to Bangladesh have remained suspended since 2013.

Source: WTO, Preferential Trade Arrangements.

concomitant lower export earnings could be significant over a period of time, unless Bangladesh can compensate the loss of access by obtaining broadly equivalent access from other markets.

Before reflecting on the possibilities of Bangladesh obtaining new access, it is important to note strenuous developments in global trade that might compound the adverse economic impact of the withdrawal of preferential access from multiple major markets on Bangladesh, as well as on other preference-receiving LDCs nearing graduation. These include a variety of factors that are working towards limiting the scope of non-reciprocal preferential access for beneficiary countries, both within the WTO as well as outside.

Conditionalities and 'Image'

For a newly 'graduating' economy like Bangladesh, the upcoming challenges will include stiffer conditions for obtaining 'substitute' preferential access in existing host country markets, such as the GSP+ scheme of the EU, and continuing with GSP programmes of other advanced economies like Canada and Japan. Given that the GSP+ scheme entails fairly strict conditionalities, including adherence to rules and standards specified by the EU, like sustainability and good governance, becoming 'eligible' for GSP+ would entail different challenges. As a beneficiary of the EBA, Bangladesh cannot expect an automatic transition to GSP+. Indeed, post-graduation and post-expiration of the transitional period, the withdrawal of EBA market access might not be substituted by the accommodation of Bangladesh in GSP+ at all, but it might just mean the continuation of benefits under the overall GSP, with several other beneficiary developing countries, including formidable large economies like China, India, Brazil and Indonesia. The usual GSP, while continuing to extend preferential access, albeit at a far lower scale and scope than the EBA, would put Bangladesh at par with beneficiary economies that are not only larger and faster-growing than itself, but also major competitors in garment exports. As of now, these economies—China, India, Vietnam—are the largest apparel exporters to the EU, with Bangladesh having rapidly closed its gap with China during the current decade. This would not have been possible without the EBA. However, sans the EBA and the resultant preference erosion, Bangladesh's ability to compete with other major apparel exporters in the European market might be significantly reduced. The concerns expressed in this regard do not appear to be misplaced.

For Bangladesh, contraction in competitiveness in Europe and other major markets, such as North America, vis-à-vis other major garment exporters, is not limited to the issue of erosion of preference. It is compounded by the adverse impression that

Bangladesh has acquired on labour safety and working conditions in industrial enterprises. The implications would be serious, if across-the-board preferential access available through GSP schemes get linked to overcoming 'image' perceptions that hinder such market access (see Table 2.2). The fact that the US has continued to deny the restoration of GSP preferences to Bangladesh, notwithstanding the US Trade Representative (USTR)'s official recognition of the 'progress' made by Bangladesh in improving workplace safety (Jha 2018), points to the prevalence of the 'image issue' that Bangladesh continues to be a victim of.[5] With the US in particular, the impression of Bangladesh as a country with unsafe working conditions and limited labour rights, works against one of the central principles of its GSP programme, which insists on beneficiaries complying with a variety of internationally recognised labour rights.[6] Whether the GSP will be eventually restored at a point in time in future is a subject of speculation. However, the US action might act as a precedent for complicating Bangladesh's eligibility for other non-reciprocal preferential access GSP programmes.

Concerns over Bangladesh's commitment to labour rights and safety issues will also be significant in determining its eligibility for the GSP+ programme of the EU post-graduation. The GSP+ conditions require the fulfilment of 15 core human and labour rights conventions of the UN, in addition to several other obligations on environment and governance. Commitment to these conventions is binding on the part of beneficiaries, and the market access benefits can be withdrawn if the latter are found to have fallen short of honouring the commitments, according to the monitoring mechanism of the EU (Regulation [EU] No. 978/2012). As opposed to the almost complete lack of monitoring for EBA beneficiary LDCs—a system that benefits Bangladesh exports considerably as of now—the GSP+ would be a different, and much more difficult, arrangement to comply with. The conditionalities become all the more critical in Bangladesh's potential efforts to lock in to GSP+, given the fact that the EU is already working with the US and Canada in improving labour rights and safety conditions in the garment industry.[7] The fact that the US has not agreed to restore GSP yet, will be hardly be lost upon the EU and other GSP providers like Canada, given that they would draw conclusions from the degree of progress on the same initiative that they are partners in.

Non-reciprocal Turns Reciprocal

Post-graduation challenges of obtaining new preferential access for Bangladesh's exports, produced by the above possibilities, can be compounded by some other factors mentioned earlier, such as more far-reaching efforts by developed countries to reduce the scope of S&D treatment of developing countries within the WTO, and the forceful emergence of mega-RTAs on the global trade landscape. The multilateral rules-based framework of the WTO enables developing countries to benefit from several flexibilities, including longer periods for implementing member commitments to market access liberalisation, such as in the Trade-Related Intellectual Property Rights (TRIPS) framework. The S&D provisions, backed up by the 'Enabling Cause' for developing countries, are also the basis for institutionalising non-reciprocal GSP preferences for developing country members, as extended by their developed counterparts (WTO, Development: Trade and Development Committee).

There is, however, a growing effort within the global trade community, pioneered primarily by the US, to limit the S&D flexibilities to only low-income 'deserving' LDCs. This intention stems largely from the US disapproval of the system where a member is permitted to self-declare itself as a 'developing' country at the WTO and stake 'rightful' claims to S&D flexibilities thereafter. The deeper intent of the US, by raising objections to the process, is to deny larger developing countries S&D flexibilities. The most pertinent example of this intent is visible in the US withdrawal of GSP benefits from large developing countries like India and Turkey in the recent past. These actions mark US efforts to restrict non-reciprocal preferential access to only LDCs, which Bangladesh will no longer remain after a few years. Indeed, the recent withdrawal of GSP preferences from India by the US underscores the fact that non-reciprocal preferences such as GSP might increasingly be linked by extending countries to reciprocal market access provided by beneficiaries.[8] This would, therefore, point to such preferences becoming more 'reciprocal' in character than 'non-reciprocal' over time, particularly for non-LDC developing country beneficiaries. It is likely that more GSP-extending OECD countries will begin following the US example by insisting on reciprocity and by drawing a sharp distinction between 'developing' and 'LDC' economies in targeting their preferences. Bangladesh might suffer as a result.

The larger context beginning to dominate the global trade landscape and the greater space for preferential market access is that of non-reciprocal preferential access getting increasingly replaced by reciprocal access. Nothing reflects this more than the emergence of mega-RTAs. These large trade agreements, such as the RCEP, comprising both developed and large developing countries, are increasingly beginning to confine market access to well-defined trade blocs on an entirely reciprocal basis. The possibility of preferential access being made available through these RTAs by increasingly substituting those available on a non-reciprocal basis is markedly high. Such an eventuality would greatly impact the export competitiveness of various countries, particularly those like Bangladesh, which need to develop strategies for sustaining exports in a global trading order undergoing rapid changes in the distribution of market access preferences.

This context and the discussion leave little doubt about the fact that Bangladesh needs to prioritise a broad and multi-faceted external trade and economic engagement strategy to enable its exports to continue obtaining as much preferential access as possible. The character of this access would require changing from the current exclusive LDC-specific non-reciprocal access to one that is a combination of non-reciprocal 'general' access provided by GSPs, and most importantly, reciprocal preferential access obtained through trade agreements. With the prospects of benefitting from even straightforward non-reciprocal access like the GSP schemes likely to get more difficult over time, the pursuit of reciprocal preferential access needs to be prioritised. It is clear that Bangladesh will need to gradually prepare for a phase where it will need to 'give' access in its domestic market, in order to obtain similar access in other markets. This will entail a robust strategy for engaging in FTAs. The next section will attempt to provide some broad perspectives in this regard.

Current Engagement and Broad Tenets of a Prospective FTA Strategy

Till now, Bangladesh has had limited experience of engaging in FTAs. Apart from being a member of the WTO, it is part of the South Asian Free Trade Area (SAFTA) and the Asia-Pacific Trade Agreement (APTA). The former includes all eight economies of the South Asian region, that is, Afghanistan, Bangladesh, Bhutan, India, Maldives, Nepal, Pakistan and Sri Lanka. The SAFTA, an outcome of the regional trade architecture formalisation efforts of the South Asian Association for Regional Cooperation (SAARC), has been effective since 2006 (UN LDC Portal). On the other hand, the APTA, earlier known as the Bangkok Agreement, comprises Bangladesh, China, India, Lao, Korea and Sri Lanka (APTA, UN Economic and Social Commission for Asia and Pacific [ESCAP], 2018), and it has a broader Asia-Pacific orientation. The agreement came into force in its current form since September 2013.

Both SAFTA and APTA, despite their great potential for regional and cross-regional integration, respectively, have failed to produce expected results. The scope of these agreements remains narrow, mostly confined to preferential tariffs across a range of goods, with limited progress on trade facilitation, investments and services. Between the two agreements, APTA is relatively more wide-ranging in scope. Even then, it has failed to achieve significant progress in market access. Its limited success is evident from the fact that notwithstanding APTA being open for accession to all developing country members of the ESCAP, it has failed to pick up membership. SAFTA, of course, remains handicapped by the conspicuous lack of progress in economic integration within South Asia, attributable largely to the difficult relations between India and Pakistan, the two largest economies of the region.

Bangladesh benefits as an LDC contracting party from both the agreements. With respect to SAFTA, it benefits from the flexibilities offered to LDC contracting members of the agreement, in terms of longer concession periods on relaxation of tariffs and continuation of quantitative restrictions on imports (Agreement on SAFTA). Within the APTA, Bangladesh benefits from more flexible provisions in the Rules of Origin (ROO) for LDCs (Rahman

2014). Notwithstanding these benefits, the market access obtained by Bangladesh exports through these FTAs are hardly comparable to the deep and wide access available through the EBA of EU, other LDC-specific DFQF schemes, and the non-reciprocal GSPs (Tables 2.1 and 2.2). With most of the latter expected to cease from 2024, Bangladesh needs to compensate the loss by extracting preferences elsewhere by exploring engagements through FTAs with other markets. In this regard, till now, it is reportedly considering prospective FTAs with Sri Lanka, Thailand, Argentina and Brazil, although there has hardly been any major progress on any of these. Bangladesh is also part of the cross-regional grouping comprising several countries from South and Southeast Asia around the Bay of Bengal rim, described as the Bay of Bengal Initiative for Multi-Sectoral Technical and Economic Cooperation (BIMSTEC).[9] The BIMSTEC is negotiating a regional FTA, although it is yet to get close to the formalisation of a specific architecture.

A meaningful FTA policy must work on obtaining extensive preferential access in major markets for leading exports from Bangladesh. Over time, such access should also enable Bangladesh to diversify exports by reducing the excessive dependence on garments, and broaden the domestic manufacturing base. The FTA policy should also enable Bangladesh to pursue outward-integration strategies in a wider spectrum of areas, including trade in services, investment, intellectual property, e-commerce and competition policy. The FTAs proposed with other countries should be conceived as comprehensive economic cooperation or partnership agreements, and should not be limited to a narrow range of subjects like tariffs and trade in goods.

How can these objectives be achieved? The first step is to identify potential FTA partners. Bangladesh's exports currently show a rather unbalanced share among major destinations. Around 80 per cent of Bangladesh's goods exports are accounted for by the EU, USA, Canada and Japan. Among these, the EU and the US account for almost 75 per cent of the exports. As mentioned earlier, DFQF preferences from these markets are either going to cease—as they already have for the US GSP—or are going to be contracted to a domain of hard monitoring and conditions, such as the GSP+ in EU, or closely monitored GSPs in different providing countries.

On the other hand, the main sources of Bangladesh's imports are quite different from its exports. Bangladesh imports extensively from China, India and Singapore, who, together comprise more than 40 per cent of its total imports. As a starter, and with the greater objective of pursuing balanced trade relations through deeper market access for its exports, Bangladesh will be well-off pursuing FTAs with all three countries. With China and India, it already enjoys preferential access through the APTA, SAFTA (India only) and the DFQF schemes that both the countries allow for LDCs. The latter would go once Bangladesh graduates. Bangladesh can hope to ride on the momentum of the good external relations it enjoys with both these countries to retain much of the preferences through bilateral FTAs. This would enable it to optimally exploit the benefits of regional connectivity projects in which it partners China and India.[10]

Singapore should be an important country in Bangladesh's future FTA strategy. It is a country with consumer tastes and preferences fashioned by high per capita income, and can be a substitute market for high-end garments and other final product exports from Bangladesh, once non-reciprocal preferential access gets limited in the European and North American markets. An FTA with Singapore will also pave the way for Bangladesh's greater integration with the ASEAN economic region. Such integration includes the possibility of Bangladesh becoming a member of RCEP in future, as and when the agreement seeks to expand membership. An FTA with Singapore is expected to be a modern twenty-first century trade agreement, inclusive of a wide focus beyond goods and covering services and investment (Aggarwal 2019). Bangladesh needs to be a part of such FTAs to enable greater expansion of its upcoming sectors, particularly those that are knowledge-intensive and technology-driven, for securing greater global market access.

Beyond China, India and Singapore, Bangladesh's FTA strategy must focus on greater engagement with the Middle East and Africa. Formal trade agreements with countries from these regions would help it in obtaining new export markets. By physically relocating to Africa, Bangladesh garment manufacturers can hope to exploit the benefits of the common African market of the ACFTA, and also export to the US through the preferential scheme available for African countries through the African Growth and Opportunities Act (AGOA) scheme.

Concluding Remarks

Bangladesh has displayed commendable resilience in graduating from the status of an LDC. The next phase in its economic development journey, however, needs to adapt to circumstances that are bereft of typical 'handholding' conditions that LDCs benefit from. From the perspective of non-reciprocal preferential access, Bangladesh needs to accelerate efforts to compensate the lack of such access by obtaining equivalent access elsewhere. This, however, will require it to engage in extensive consultations with other country partners or trade blocs—an engagement that it has limited experience of, as it was not required to engage so. The importance of a forward-looking FTA strategy with Asian and African markets cannot be overemphasised in this regard. However, for the successful progress of such a strategy, Bangladesh needs to realise the importance of granting reciprocal access—a concession that till now it has not been required to make in sufficient measure. Overcoming lack of experience in negotiating FTAs, and convincing sceptical and often cynical domestic constituencies about the benefits of engaging in FTAs, are the major challenges the country would need to overcome.

Notes

1. G20 comprises both developed and large developing countries and includes Argentina, Australia, Brazil, Canada, China, European Union, France, Germany, India, Indonesia, Italy, Japan, Mexico, Russia, Saudi Arabia, South Africa, South Korea, Turkey, the UK and the US.
2. Both the CPTPP and RCEP are pan-continental RTAs spanning various countries of the Asia-Pacific. CPTPP includes Australia, Brunei Darussalam, Canada, Chile, Japan, Malaysia, Mexico, New Zealand, Peru, Singapore and Vietnam. It has become effective from 30 December 2018. The RCEP includes Australia, Brunei

Darussalam, Cambodia, China, India, Indonesia, Japan, Lao PDR, Malaysia, Myanmar, New Zealand, Philippines, Singapore, South Korea, Thailand and Vietnam. It is being negotiated for seven years and is likely to be concluded soon.

3. The Pacific Alliance includes Chile, Columbia, Mexico and Peru. The ACFTA includes 49 African countries.
4. Bangladesh's per capita income was $1,745 in 2018. With this income, it was globally ranked at 144, following India, the largest economy in South Asia, whose per capita income is $2,036.
5. Bangladesh Commerce Minister Tipu Munshi described the non-restoration of GSP as an 'image issue' and claimed that it would be corrected once the benefits are restored.
6. Under 19 U.S.C §2462(b)(2) of the GSP statute, mandatory criteria for a country's eligibility under GSP include:

   > A GSP beneficiary must have taken or is taking steps to afford internationally recognized worker rights, including 1) the right of association, 2) the right to organize and bargain collectively, 3) a prohibition on the use of any form of forced or compulsory labor, 4) a minimum age for the employment of children, and a prohibition on the worst forms of child labor, and 5) acceptable conditions of work with respect to minimum wages, hours of work and occupational safety and health (US GSP Guidebook 2018).

7. The EU, US and Canada are working with the International Labour Organization (ILO) and the government of Bangladesh on the 'Sustainability Compact' for ensuring labour rights and worker safety (Bangladesh, European Commission website).
8. The Presidential Proclamation terminating GSP benefits for India mentions ' ... India has not assured the United States that India will provide equitable and reasonable access to its markets. Accordingly, it is appropriate to terminate India's designation as a beneficiary developing country effective June 5, 2019' (Federal Register, Presidential Documents 2019).
9. BIMSTEC includes Bangladesh, Bhutan, India, Nepal, Maldives and Sri Lanka from South Asia, and Myanmar and Thailand from Southeast Asia.
10. These include the Bangladesh–Bhutan–India–Nepal (BBIN), Bangladesh–China–India–Myanmar (BCIM), and the BIMSTEC programme apart from the China-led Belt and Road Initiative (BRI).

References

Aggarwal, Narendra, 'Bangladesh's Big Draws for Business', *The Business Times*, 26 March 2019. Available at https://www.busiesstimes.com.sg/hub-projects/bangladesh-national-day/bangladeshs-big-draws-for-business.

Agreement on SAFTA. Available at https://commerce.gov.in/writereaddata/trade/safta.pdf (accessed 1 July 2019).

APTA, UN ESCAP. Brochure, November 2018. Available at https://www.unescap.org/sites/default/files/Brochure-of-the-APTA_Nov-2018.pdf (accessed 20 May 2019).

CRS, 'Co-Generalized System of Preferences: Overview and Issues for Congress', 8 January 2019. Available at https://fas.org/sgp/crs/misc/RL33663.pdf (accessed 19 May 2019).

EU, Trade Policy. Available at http://ec.europa.eu/trade/policy/countries-and-regions/countries/bangladesh/ (accessed 17 May 2019).

EU Website, Bangladesh. Available at http://ec.europa.eu/trade/policy/countries-and-regions/countries/bangladesh/ (accessed 19 July 2019).

Federal Register, Presidential Documents, 'To Modify the List of Beneficiary Developing Countries Under the Trade Act of 1974', Proclamation 9902 of May 31, 2019, By the President of the United States of America, Vol. 84, No. 108/Wednesday, 5 June 2019/. Available at https://ustr.gov/sites/default/files/Proclamation_9902.pdf (accessed 18 July 2019).

'Generalized System of Preferences (GSP): Overview and Issues for Congress', *EveryCRSReport.com*, 8 January 2019. Available at https://www.everycrsreport.com/reports/RL33663.html.

IMF, 'World Economic Outlook Database', April 2019. Available at https://www.imf.org/external/pubs/ft/weo/2019/01/weodata/index.aspx (accessed 1 July 2019).

Intelligence Unit, 'Graduating from LDC: Will the Benefits Outweigh the Losses?', *The Economist*, 18 March 2018. Available at http://country.eiu.com/article.aspx?articleid=276572011&Country=Bangladesh&topic=Economy_1 (accessed 20 February 2019).

Jha, Lalit K. 'US Seeks More Progress from Bangladesh to Restore GSP', *Dhaka Tribune*, 3 March 2018. Available at https://www.dhakatribune.com/business/2018/03/02/us-seeks-progress-bangladesh-restore-gsp (accessed 1 July 2019).

Miles, Tom, 'US Drafts WTO Reforms to Halt Handouts for Big and Rich States', *Reuters*, 16 February 2019. Available at https://www.reuters.com/article/us-usa-trade-wto/u-s-drafts-wto-reform-to-halt-handouts-for-big-and-rich-states-idUSKCN1Q426T (accessed 20 May 2019).

Milner, Chris, Oliver Morrisey, and Evios Zgovu. 2010. *Policy Response to Trade Preference Erosion Options: Options for Developing Countries.* London: Commonwealth Secretariat.

Palit, Amitendu. 2014. 'New Regional Trade Architectures: Implications for LD Cs and Small States', Commonwealth Trade Policy Discussion Papers, Commonwealth Secretariat, London. Available at https://www.thecommonwealth-ilibrary (accessed 17 March 2019).

Rahman, Mustafizur. 2014. 'Trade Benefits for Least Developed Countries: The Bangladesh Case (CDP Background Paper No. 18)'. New York, NY: United Nations Department of Economic and Social Affairs.

Regulation (EU) No. 978/2012, Articles 9, 14 and 15 and Annexe 17, European Parliament and of the Council, of 25 October 2012, Applying a Scheme of Generalised Tariff Preferences and Repealing Council Regulation (EC) No. 732/2008', *Official Journal of the European Union*, 31 October 2012. Available at https://eur-lex.europa.eu/legal-content/EN/TXT/PDF/?uri=CELEX:32012R0978&from=EN (accessed 1 July 2019).

Senior Correspondent, 'GSP is an 'Image Issue' for Bangladesh: Tipu Munshi', *bdnews24.com*, 14 March 2019; https://bdnews24.com/bangladesh/2019/03/14/gsp-is-an-image-issue-for-bangladesh-tipu-munshi (accessed 19 May 2019).

Start Business Report, 'Bangladesh on the Path to GSP plus with EU', *The Daily Star*, 19 May 2019. Available at https://www.thedailystar.net/business/bangladesh-the-path-gsp-plus-eu-1315237 (accessed on 19 May 2019).

UN LDC Portal, 'South Asian Free Trade Area', Committee for Development Policy, UN. Available at https://www.un.org/ldcportal/south-asian-free-trade-area/ (accessed 1 July 2019).

US GSP Guidebook, Office of the United States Trade Representative, Executive Office of the President, Washington, D.C., November 2018. Available at file:///C:/Users/isasap/Dropbox/India%20US%20trade/GSP%20Guidebook%20November%202018.pdf (accessed 1 July 2019).

WTO. Bangladesh Member Profile. Available at https://www.wto.org/english/res_e/statis_e/daily_update_e/trade_profiles/BD_e.pdf (accessed on 17 May 2019).

WTO. Development: Trade and Development Committee. 'Special and Differential Treatment Provisions'. Available at https://www.wto.org/english/tratop_e/devel_e/dev_special_differential_provisions_e.htm (accessed 1 July 2019).

———. 'Generalized System of Preferences—European Union, Preferential Trade Arrangements'. Available at http://ptadb.wto.org/ptaTradeInfo.aspx (accessed 19 May 2019).

———. Preferential Trade Arrangements. Available at http://ptadb.wto.org/ptaTradeInfo.aspx (accessed 17 May 2019).

3

The Challenges of the Readymade Garment (RMG) Industry in Bangladesh

SELIM RAIHAN

Over the past 45 years since independence, Bangladesh has increased its per capita income four-fold, cut poverty by more than half, and is well set to achieve most of the millennium development goals (MDGs). Notwithstanding many external and internal shocks, the per capita income of the country has risen continuously, and steady progress has been made in lowering poverty. Bangladesh witnessed decades of slow economic growth until 1990. The growth rate started to rise since early-1990s. During the first decade of the twenty-first century, the average economic growth rate exceeded 6.5 per cent per annum. Bangladesh's economic growth rates in recent years have been higher than most of the South Asian countries and many of the sub-Saharan African countries. Bangladesh has also made significant, recent progress in reducing poverty. The decline in poverty in Bangladesh stems in large part from a strong, decade-long economic growth.

One of the major drivers of economic growth in Bangladesh has been the exports of readymade garments (RMGs). Over the past three-and-a-half decades, RMG has become the flagship export product of Bangladesh. Starting from a very small base of only around $31 million in 1984, RMG exports have grown to around $31 billion by 2017, accounting for more than 80 per cent of export earnings. The growth of RMG exports makes a major contribution to the national economy in four areas. First, the rapid expansion of the RMG exports contributed to important structural transformations of the economy. The manufacturing share in Gross Domestic Product (GDP) and employment increased gradually as RMG exports accelerated. Second, the positive impact on the macroeconomy is seen through the substantial increase in foreign exchange earnings, which converted the once aid-dependent economy to a trade-oriented economy. Third, the RMG sector has been an important contributor to growth and employment generation in Bangladesh. It provides direct employment to around 3.5 million people. More than 50 per cent of the manufacturing labour force is now employed in this sector. Fourth, female participation in the formal labour market underwent a major shift with the rise of the RMG industry in Bangladesh as 60 per cent of the labour force that are employed in this sector are female.

The growth of the RMG industry in Bangladesh is accompanied by the major structural shift in industrial and trade policies that took place during the 1980s and 1990s, from an import-substitution strategy to an export-oriented one. After independence in 1971, Bangladesh followed an import-substitution industrialisation and trade strategy, characterised by high tariffs and non-tariff barriers to trade, and an overvalued exchange rate system. This inward-looking approach to development was pursued with the aim of improving the balance of payments position of the country and creating a protected internal market for the domestic manufacturing industries. Like in many other developing countries, the import-substituting trade and industrial policies pursued by Bangladesh failed to deliver the desired outcomes. It was against the backdrop of the serious macroeconomic imbalances of the early 1980s and stagnating export performance that the policy of reforms for stabilisation and structural adjustment was undertaken along the guidelines specified by the World Bank and the International Monetary Fund (IMF) (Mahmud 1995). This adjustment programme put forward a wide range of policy reforms in Bangladesh, which included reforms in trade policy, industrial policy, monetary and fiscal policy, exchange rate policy, privatisation of the state-owned enterprises, and promotion of foreign direct investment (FDI). The policy reversal that took place in Bangladesh favouring the export-oriented development strategy was in line with the various structural adjustment programmes.

The growth of the manufacturing sector in Bangladesh over the past two decades has been the story of the success of the RMG sector (Raihan 2015). However, despite its success, the RMG industry in Bangladesh faces numerous challenges. These challenges are related to retaining competitiveness in the context of the domestic environment of high cost of doing business, diversification within the RMG industry, workplace safety and compliance, employment loss due to increased automation in the RMG sector, changing global trade regime, and challenges related to the country's graduation from the LDC status,. This chapter provides an analysis of these challenges and suggests ways to address them.

Overview of the RMG Industry in Bangladesh

The RMG exports from Bangladesh saw a remarkable rise over the past three-and-a-half decades. Figure 3.1 shows that during 1983–84, RMG exports were very insignificant, which by 2017–18 increased to $30.6 billion. Riding on the growth of the RMG exports, the country's total export of goods and services also saw a significant rise over the same period, from $0.8 billion to $36.7 billion. Figure 3.1 also shows that the share of RMG in total exports increased from only 3.9 per cent in 1983–84 to as high as 83.5 per cent in 2017–18. Also, in recent years, the export basket has become more and more concentrated around RMG exports. It then follows that despite the impressive growth record, the export base and the export markets have remained rather narrow for Bangladesh, which is a matter of concern. Undiversified exports, both in terms of product range and markets, are likely to be much more vulnerable to various shocks than well-diversified exports. Despite the policy reforms and various incentives offered, it seems that Bangladesh has failed to develop a diversified export structure.

Figure 3.2 shows that in recent years, Bangladesh's share of RMG exports in global RMG exports increased steadily. In 2012, the share was 4.66 per cent, which increased to 6.19 per cent in 2017. This increased share in the global export of RMG shows that despite numerous challenges, the RMG industry of Bangladesh has been able to strengthen its market share at the global level. With the increased share in the world market, in recent years, Bangladesh has become the second-largest exporter of RMG in the world (Figure 3.3). It also appears that after China, the closest competitors of Bangladesh are Vietnam and India.

It is also important to note that RMG export markets for Bangladesh have been highly concentrated, with the European

Figure 3.1 Total Exports and RMG Exports in Billion US$, and Per Cent Share of RMG Exports in Total Exports of Bangladesh

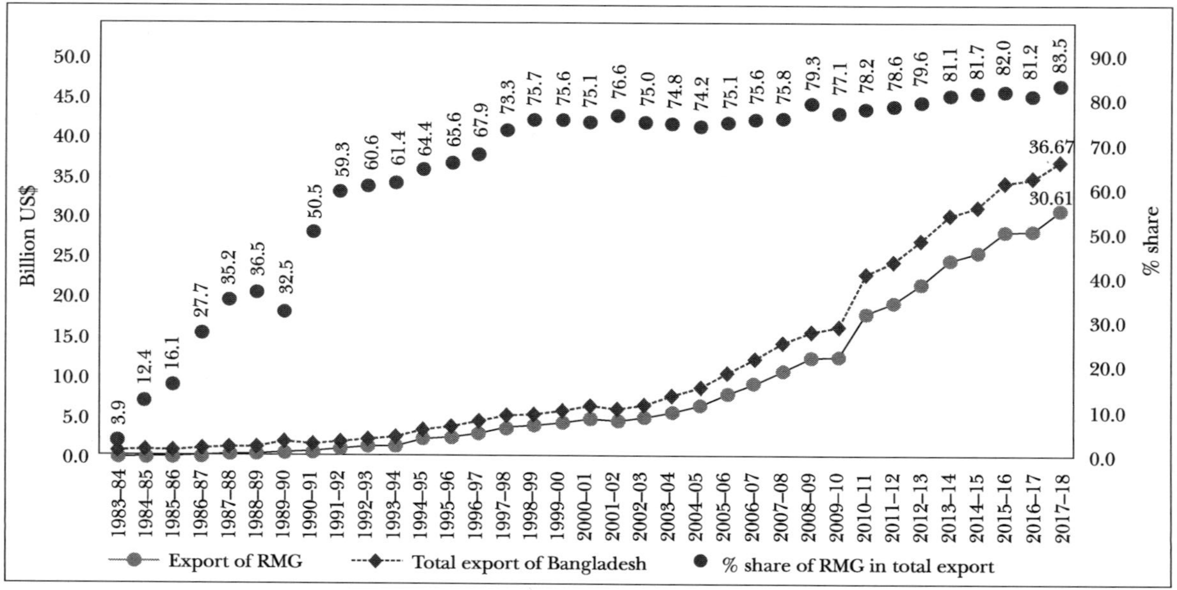

Source: Raihan (2019a).

Figure 3.2 Bangladesh's RMG Export Share in World Export of RMG

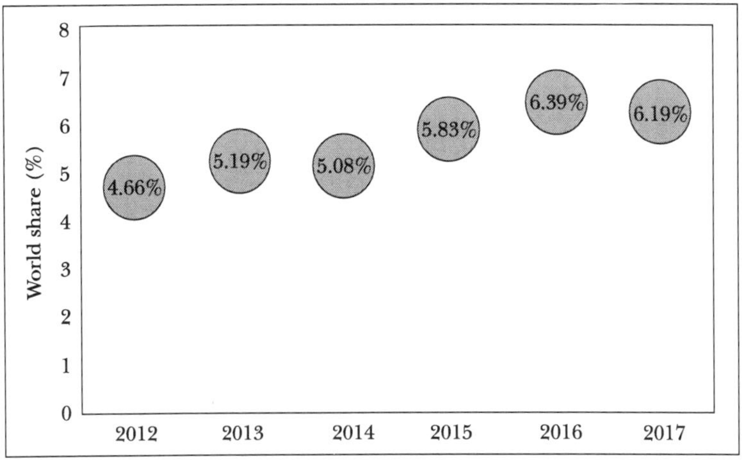

Source: Raihan (2019a).

Figure 3.3 Top 10 Exporters of Clothing in 2017 (Exports in Billion US$ and Growth Rate in Per Cent)

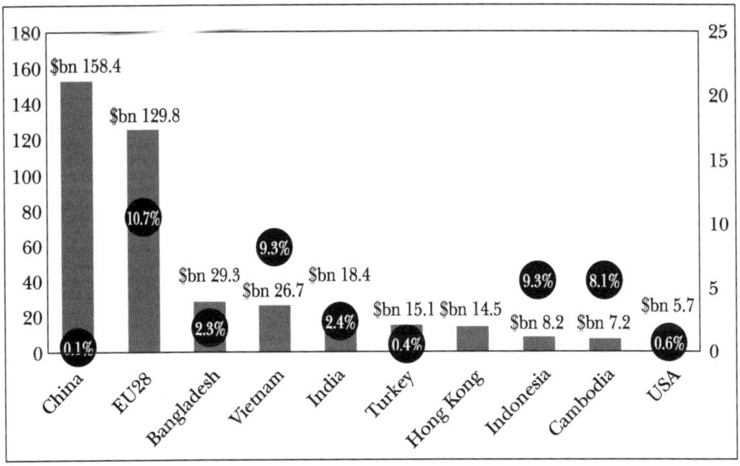

Source: World Trade Statistical Review 2018, Chapter VIII: Statistical tables, Table A23.

Union (EU) and North America being the major destinations. In 2018, around 62.5 per cent of the country's RMG exports went to the EU, while another 21 per cent was destined for North America (Figure 3.4).

Figure 3.4 Major Destinations of RMG Export of Bangladesh in 2018

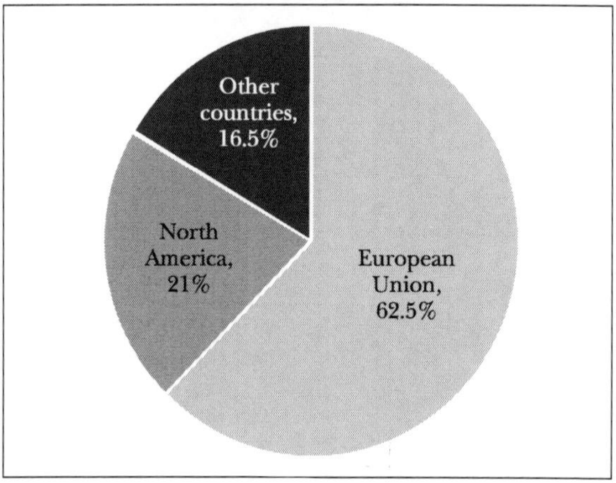

Source: Raihan (2019a).

Factors Affecting the Success of the RMG Industry in Bangladesh

The growth of Bangladesh's RMG exports was largely attributed to the international trade regime in textiles and clothing, which, until 2004, was governed by the Multi-fibre Arrangement (MFA) quotas. The quota system restricted competition in the global market by providing reserved markets for a number of developing countries, including Bangladesh, where textiles and clothing items have not been traditional exports. The duty-free access for Bangladesh's RMG products in the EU has also greatly supported the growth of the sector.

Abdur Razzaque and I (2007) highlighted that an important element of trade policy reform in Bangladesh has been the use of a set of generous support and promotional measures for exports. While import liberalisation was meant to correct the domestic incentive structure by reducing protection for import-substituting sectors, export promotion schemes were undertaken to provide exporters with an environment where the previous bias against export-oriented investment could be reduced significantly. Important export incentive schemes available in Bangladesh include, among others, subsidised rates of interest on bank loans, duty-free import of machinery and intermediate inputs, cash subsidy, and exemption from value-added and excise taxes. Table 3.1 summarises some of the most important incentive schemes that have been put in place in the country. A few sectors, especially the RMG sector, have been major beneficiaries of these reforms.

Table 3.1 Important Export-incentive Schemes in Bangladesh

Scheme	*Nature of operation*
Export Performance Benefit (XPB)	This scheme was in operation from the mid-1970s up to 1992. It allowed the exporters of non-traditional items to cash a certain proportion of their earnings (known as entitlements) at a higher exchange rate of WES. In 1992, with the unification of the exchange rate system, the XPB scheme ceased.
Bonded Warehouse	Exporters of manufactured goods are able to import raw materials and inputs without payment of duties and taxes. The raw materials and inputs are kept in the bonded warehouse. On the submission of evidence of production for exports, the required amount of inputs is released from the warehouse. This facility is extended to exporters of RMGs, of specialised textiles such as towels and socks, leather, ceramic, printed matter and packaging materials, who are required to export at least 70 per cent of their produce.
Duty Drawback	Exporters of manufactured products are given a refund of customs duties and sales taxes paid on the imported raw materials that are used in the production of goods exported. Exporters can also obtain drawbacks on the Value Added Tax on local inputs going into production.
Duty-free Import of Machinery	Import of machineries without payment of any duties for production in the export sectors.

Table 3.1 Contd.

Table 3.1 Contd.

Scheme	*Nature of operation*
Back to Back Letter of Credits (L/Cs)	It allowed the exporters to open L/Cs for the required import of raw materials against their export L/Cs in such sectors as the RMG and leather goods. This system is considered one of the most important incentive schemes for RMG export.
Cash Subsidy	This scheme was introduced in 1986. This facility is available mainly to exporters of textiles and clothing, who choose not to use bonded warehouse or duty drawback facilities. Currently, the cash subsidy is 25 per cent of the free onboard export value. In recent times, cash subsidies have been offered to agro-products exporters.
Interest Rate Subsidy	It allows the exporters to borrow from the banks at lower bands of interest rates of 8–10 per cent against 14–16 per cent of normal charge.
Tax Holiday	First introduced under the Industrial Policy of 1991–93, this incentive allows a tax holiday to an exporter for five to 12 years, depending on various conditions.
Income Tax Rebate	Exporters are given rebates on income tax. Recently, this benefit has been increased. The advance income tax for the exporters has been reduced from 0.50 per cent of export receipts to 0.25 per cent.
Retention of Earnings in Foreign Currency	Exporters are now allowed to retain a portion of their export earnings in foreign currency. The entitlement varies in accordance with the local value addition in exportable. The maximum limit is 40 per cent of the total earnings, although for low value-added products such as RMGs, the current ceiling is only at 7.5 per cent.
Export Credit Guarantee Scheme	Introduced in 1978 to insure loans in respect of export finance, it provides pre-shipment and post-shipment (and both) guarantee schemes.
Special Facilities for Export Processing Zones (EPZs)	To promote exports, currently a number of EPZs are in operation. The export units located in EPZs enjoy various other incentives such as tax holiday for 10 years, duty-free imports of spare parts, exemption from Value Added Taxes and other duties.

Source: Raihan and Razzaque (2007: 24–62).

M. Khan (2012) highlighted that the success that the RMG industry enjoyed was not replicated in any other major sectors. The critical element in the institutional arrangement, which allowed the take-off of this industry, was the global institutional mechanism with the MFA. The MFA facilitated fortuitous rents on terms that assisted the learning-by-doing that was critical for the sector. Khan further pointed out that the authoritarian clientelism during the early phases of the sector's take-off allowed for the rapid solution to a number of additional institutional constraints facing the sector. According to him, there was a 'political settlement'[1] among the elites in Bangladesh on the RMG industry.

However, while Khan (2012) rightly mentioned the institutional perspectives behind the growth of the RMG sector, his narrative of the 'political settlement' is somehow narrow and elite-centric. I have argued (Raihan 2017) that Khan's 'political settlement' is primarily an 'elite agreement' and it overlooks the critical nexus between elites and non-elites within the society. I have further argued that as the RMG sector is one of the growth drivers in Bangladesh, there must be some substances by which these growth drivers are fuelled; and I call these substances 'political capital'. The usual meaning of 'political capital' is a feeling of trust that politicians build among the common people, through which they exert their influence in the society. But, in my opinion, 'political capital' is an outcome of agreements among the political elites, and support from the non-elites on such agreements over certain growth drivers in the economy. In order to source such support, the elites ensure some critical benefits for non-elites. Over the past three decades, Bangladesh has been able to generate crucial stock and flow of 'political capital' in favour of its growth drivers. Bangladesh is not rich in natural resources, which prevented the generation of substantial rents for the political elites. Thus, the elites found the RMG sector to be a source of rent generation, and they were able to draw support from the non-elite through the creation of large-scale employment opportunities in the RMG sector, which helped increase female participation in the labour force and the alleviation of poverty.

Mirza Hassan and I (2017) offer another explanation for the growth of the RMG sector in Bangladesh through the lens of the 'deals space' of Pritchett, Sen and Werker (2017).[2] We argue that the sector as a whole enjoys closed deals. Parts of these closed deals actually have legal and quasi-legal bases (bonded warehouse schemes, cash incentives, statutory regulatory ordinances, etc.), but they tend to be highly exclusive in nature.

I have argued (Raihan 2019b) that the growth in the RMG sector in Bangladesh has also been, to a large extent, driven by some sizeable 'rents' generated in this sector, and there are possibilities of the sizes of such 'rents' shrinking in future due to both domestic and international factors. There have been five major sources of such 'rents': MFA quota (which no longer exists) and GSPs, different forms of subsidies, tax exemption, maintenance of the labour regime, and weak compliance. However, there are threats with regard to the continuation of GSP facilities in future on the grounds of lack of compliance, weak labour standards and conflicting political situations in Bangladesh. There are also budgetary constraints on the continuation or enlargement of subsidies or the exemption of taxes. Also, the recent labour unrest over the hike of the minimum wage in this sector, and pressure from the international community has exerted serious challenge over the 'sustainability' of the labour regime, which has been maintained with a kind of political settlement over the years. Similarly, from a lack of compliance, especially with regard to working environment and factory standards, in the context of weak regulatory institutions, 'rent' has become highly unsustainable. This is further due to the serious international pressure to enforce compliance in the wake of recent incidents of fire and building collapses, which resulted in the deaths of a large number of RMG workers.

The Challenges of the RMG Industry in Bangladesh

Competitiveness in an Environment of High Cost of Doing Business

There is no denying that apart from challenges on the external front, there are crucial supply-side constraints associated with production and exporting activities. Overcoming these constraints will be important for the future of RMG exports. An unusually long time required for supplies to reach importing countries from the date of receiving export orders, known as the lead time, is a major concern. Compared to many other competitors, Bangladesh is geographically located at a disadvantageous position, requiring a relatively long time to ship its products to major markets of North America and the EU. Also, as most of the raw materials for the finished products have to be imported from abroad, and are generally procured under back-to-back L/C arrangements, the delivery chain involves a two-way shipping. Unfavourable geographical location then serves to aggravate the situation further.

Apart from contributing to a longer lead time, inefficient ports also raise the cost of doing business in Bangladesh. Ports are plagued by labour problems, poor management and lack of equipment. All these factors make the Chittagong port one of the most expensive routes to international trade. Inefficiencies and excessive costs at ports are further exacerbated by poor customs services.

The state of physical infrastructure is weak in Bangladesh. Poor infrastructure requires firms to devote more resources to such tasks as procuring inputs and getting their products to market. This can undermine the competitiveness of exporting enterprises. There are two dimensions of poor infrastructure; one is the unavailability of a certain service or utility (such as telephone, water, electricity, roads and highways, etc.), and the other is the unreliability of the services provided. In Bangladesh, there are problems on both fronts. Most RMG firms have to rely on generators for uninterrupted power supply. But since the electricity produced from generators is much more expensive than the supplies from the national grid, excessive costs undermine the competitiveness of exporters.

Although Bangladesh is a labour-abundant country, shortage of skilled workforce is perceived to be a major constraint for manufacturing production. Backward integration of the RMG sector, as well as many other production activities in the sector such as fashion and design will require skilled manpower. Therefore, supply capacity is preconditioned by the availability of skilled workers.

Business enterprises in Bangladesh are subject to invisible costs arising from widespread corruption and malpractices. These activities impose direct costs, thus undermining the competitiveness of trading enterprises. Corruption and a hostile political situation together make the domestic environment business-unfriendly, discouraging new investment in exporting activities, both from local and foreign sources. Figure 3.5 suggests that in terms of the components of the Ease of Doing Business Index of the World Bank, Bangladesh is seriously lagging behind its major competitors like India, China and Vietnam.

Diversification within the RMG Sector and the Quality Issue

While the export basket in Bangladesh remained highly concentrated around the RMG exports, diversification within the RMG sector also persisted as a big challenge. Table 3.2 shows that at the six-digit HS code level, only 10 RMG products occupied 70 per cent of the total RMG exports from Bangladesh in 2017–18. Only two products (t-shirt and men's trousers) accounted for 36 per cent of the RMG exports in this period. Looking at these products, it

Table 3.2 Top 10 RMG Exports of Bangladesh in 2017–18

HS Code of Top 10 RMG Exports of Bangladesh in 2017–18	*Percentage Share in 2017–18*
610910: T-shirts, singlets and other vests, of cotton, knitted or crocheted	19.16
620342: Men's or boys' trousers, breeches, etc., of cotton	17.01
620462: Women's or girls' trousers, breeches, etc., of cotton	9.40
611020: Jerseys, pullovers, etc., of cotton, knitted or crocheted	6.29
620520: Men's or boys' shirts of cotton	5.45
611030: Jerseys, pullovers, etc., of man-made fibres, knitted or crocheted	3.50
610462: Women's or girls' trousers, etc., of cotton, knitted or crocheted	2.68
610510: Men's or boys' shirts of cotton, knitted or crocheted	2.57
620343: Men's or boys' trousers, breeches of synthetic fibres	2.11
611090: Jerseys, pullovers, etc., of other textiles, net, knitted or crocheted	1.80
Top 10 Share in Total RMG Export in 2017–18 (in Per cent)	69.97

Source: Raihan (2019a).

is obvious that these are low-value added and low-priced products. Therefore, moving up the ladder of high-value added and high-quality products within the RMG industry has also not been very successful. Figure 3.6 suggests that at the four-digit level, Bangladesh had higher quality in only three RMG products, as compared to its major competitors like China, India and Vietnam.

Workplace Safety and Compliance

There have been concerns regarding compliance issues and workplace safety in the RMG industry in Bangladesh; and in the last few years, especially after the infamous Rana Plaza accident in 2013, these issues have become extremely critical for the future of this industry. There is strong international pressure, in the form of the threat of cancelling large preferences in the markets of Western countries, if labour conditions are not improved. Quality competitiveness is receiving increased priority over price competitiveness, and of course, the quality of a product embodies the standard of living of labour being used in the production process. These concerns should be addressed in a positive way as an opportunity to build the industry's reputation in the global market. This calls for, among many other things, the need to deal with labour issues in the RMG industry carefully. In this context, issues like wage, workplace security, fringe benefits, workplace environment, etc., need to be resolved on a priority basis. Current labour practices prevalent in the RMG industry need to be improved in order to make the sector sustainable. Improvement of the labour condition is closely linked to the enhancement of the productivity of labour. There is equally a need to invest in training workers to move up to the higher-value added garment products.

A recent study by the International Labour Organization-South Asian Network of Economic Modelling (ILO-SANEM) (2018) suggests that despite some improvements after the Rana Plaza accident in 2013, there still remain unresolved issues related to occupational safety, hours of work and leave, fixation and execution of minimum wage provision, workplace training, workplace harassment and gender equality. The RMG manufacturers and exporters associations and the government should collaborate with each other, with help

Figure 3.5 Quality Index of RMG Products (Four-digit Level)

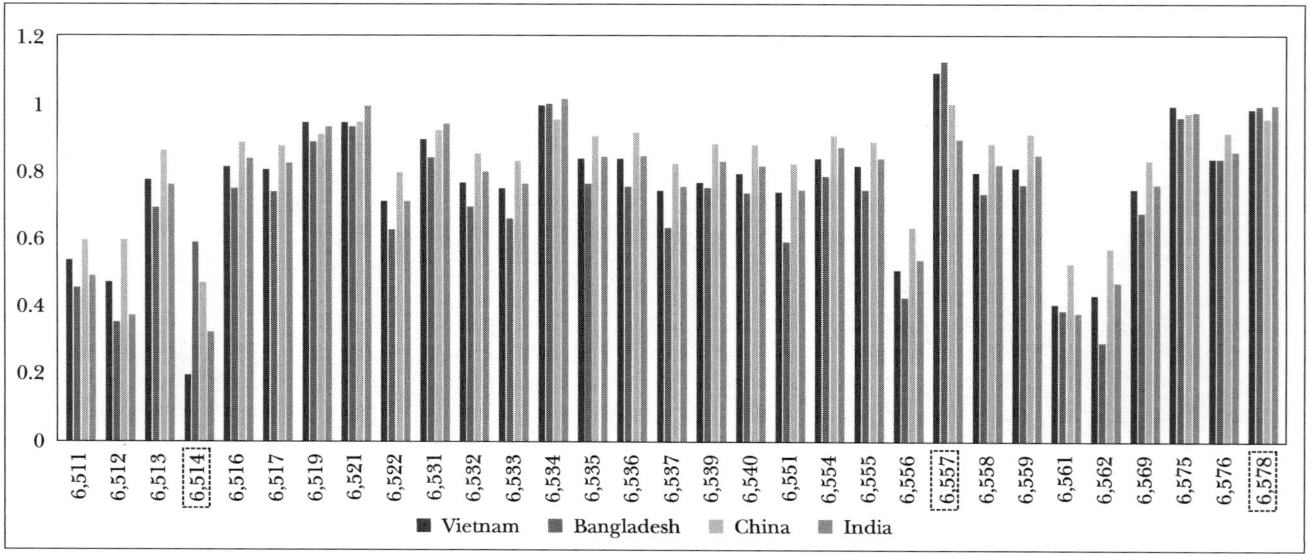

Source: Raihan (2019a).

from relevant international agencies, to be able to work effectively in this area.

Automation in the RMG Sector and Implications for Job Creation

Technological advances associated with the automation raises the concern that new technologies will lead to widespread job losses in manufacturing industries in countries like Bangladesh. What is perhaps different now is that the new, interconnected digital technologies will likely have a broader and more far-reaching array of abilities. Thus, the prospect of new kinds of jobs may well be diminished or be limited to increasingly sophisticated domains, such as machine-learning. In addition, new technologies are now not just replacing jobs, but they are also enabling the disruption and restructuring of entire industries (Hamann 2018).

Between 2013 and 2016–17, manufacturing jobs in Bangladesh declined by 0.8 million, and a major part of it happened in the RMG industry (Bangladesh Bureau of Statistics [BBS] 2017). Increased use of automation also changed the composition of labour in the RMG sector. Bidisha and I (2018) showed that the RMG factories that were closed down after the Rana Plaza event in 2013 were mostly ones that were comparatively female labour-intensive. Furthermore, the introduction of labour-saving machinery was speeded up after the Rana Plaza event to replace the kinds of jobs that were previously done mostly by low-skilled female workers, which caused employment loss of the female labour. Also, the perceived threat to employment by automation affects women disproportionately.

Changing Global Trade Regime

The idea of globalisation and free trade has gained prominence in the world since the 1980s. Despite a few limitations, globalisation and a free trade regime are seen as beneficial for economic development, poverty reduction and enhanced integration among countries. Recently, with the emergence of a trade war between the US and its leading trade partners, especially China, the question appears to be whether globalisation has started walking in the opposite direction. It is true that until very recently, nobody had anticipated such an unprecedented event. After the formation of the General Agreement on Tariffs and Trade (GATT) in 1948, and eventually, with the emergence of the World Trade Organization (WTO) in 1995, trade agreements and rules have prevented such a trade war. It is also important to mention that WTO rules have compelled even powerful countries to honour international agreements on trade rules.

The effect of the war between the US and its leading trade partners in the global market depends on how long this war will last and how intense it will get. Its effect can be both short- and medium-term, and even long-term. In the short term, the imposition of substantial additional tariffs by the US on imports from its leading trade partners, especially from China, and vice versa, will significantly affect the volume of bilateral trade between them. This may lead to a rise in exports from some countries, like from Bangladesh to the US, as the US would then seek cheaper imports from these countries. If the trade war continues in the medium- to long-term and intensifies, with the involvement of more countries, there is a high risk of a global economic recession as the trade war would affect consumer demand in the major economies of the world, especially in North America and the EU.

It is, however, important to note that the length and depth of the trade war are yet to be clear, which is creating a lot of uncertainties around the global trade regime. An uncertain trade regime is not conducive to developing countries like Bangladesh that have become trade-dependent over the years. When the global trade regime is guided by a set of rules and principles, which have been achieved over the past six decades through the GATT and WTO processes, all countries, in general, and the developing countries, in particular, are benefitted from these rules and principles. However, with the escalation of the ongoing trade war, the effectiveness of the rules and principles is at stake. In particular, the role of the WTO is greatly undermined, which can lead us to an uncertain global trade regime. If the US pulls out of the WTO, the global trade regime will probably face the biggest challenge after the Second World War. As RMG is the major export item of Bangladesh in the markets of North America and the EU, such an uncertain trade regime runs the risk of hurting Bangladesh's future growth prospect of the RMG exports.

Challenges of LDC-Graduation

Bangladesh has successfully met all three criteria for LDC-graduation in the first review in March 2018. It is expected that Bangladesh will be able to meet the graduation criteria in the second review in 2021, and will finally graduate from LDC status in 2024. There is a risk of erosion of preference for Bangladesh, which is associated with its graduation from the LDC status. I have suggested (Raihan 2019c), using the global dynamic general equilibrium model, that due to the loss of preferences of Bangladesh, after the graduation from the LDC status, in the markets of the EU, Canada, Australia, Japan, India and China, there might be a sizeable drop in exports of RMGs from Bangladesh compared to the business-as-usual scenario. As Figure 3.6 shows, according to the model simulation, the drop in RMG exports would be $5.4 billion in 2024 (13.5 per cent of RMG exports); this could increase to $5.8 billion by 2030 (10.8 per cent of RMG exports).

Figure 3.6 LDC Graduation: Impact on RMG Export (Percentage Change from the Business-as-usual Scenario)

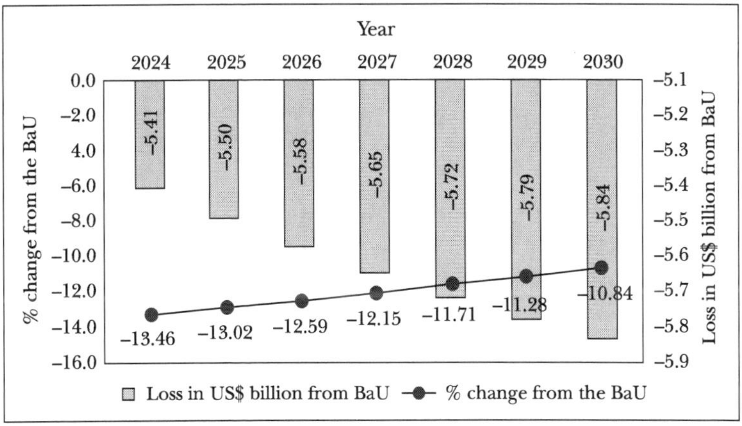

Source: Raihan (2019c).

Table 3.3 presents the impact on RMG exports by destination. In 2024, RMG exports in the EU, the largest export destination of Bangladesh, would fall by 33.6 per cent, which would be 30.3 per cent in 2030. The largest fall, in terms of percentage change, would be in Canada, as 50 per cent of the RMG exports would fall in 2024, which would be 45 per cent in 2030. In all other major export destinations, too, where Bangladesh enjoys preferences, there will be a loss in RMG exports. However, in other markets (shown in the category of rest of the world), there would be a rise in exports of RMGs, which would be 36 per cent in 2024 and 32.5 per cent in 2030.

Table 3.3 Impact on RMG Export by Destination (Percentage Change from the Business-as-usual Scenario)

	2024	*2025*	*2026*	*2027*	*2028*	*2029*	*2030*
EU	–33.6	–33.09	–32.53	–31.96	–31.40	–30.84	–30.3
Australia	–24.9	–24.45	–24.04	–23.62	–23.21	–22.80	–22.4
Canada	–50.0	–49.96	–49.96	–49.96	–49.96	–49.96	–45.0
Japan	–22.9	–22.94	–22.94	–22.94	–22.94	–22.94	–20.6
China	–17.9	–17.86	–17.86	–17.86	–17.86	–17.86	–16.1
India	–26.1	–26.12	–26.12	–26.12	–26.12	–26.12	–23.5
Rest of the World	36.1	36.11	36.11	36.11	36.11	36.11	32.5

Source: Raihan (2019c).

Concluding Remarks

The future of the RMG industry will be critical for Bangladesh's socio-economic development. The growth of RMG exports in Bangladesh has been associated with the overall economic growth of the country, accompanied by a remarkable progress in poverty alleviation and large-scale employment creation. The sustainability of this industry also depends on how carefully and properly the issues related to the welfare of the workers are addressed.

The RMG industry of Bangladesh is now at a crossroads. It is now time to focus on how Bangladesh could retain its comparative advantage and continue its success story. Reliance on only the mass pool of unskilled labour doing things in the old way would not be sufficient. Careful examination of Bangladesh's comparative advantage in the RMG industry reveals the fact that the nature of this advantage is primarily static. This suggests that retaining the static comparative advantage will be highly challenging in future, given the increased competition from other countries, growing stringent compliance issues, and the question of the extent to which the country will be able to enhance its competitiveness in doing business. Therefore, the sector should aim for generating dynamic comparative advantage, which would ensure its sustainability in future. There is a critical need for enhancing labour productivity, moving up to the higher-value added products by introducing new technology along the production line, thus spurring innovation, and enhancing Bangladesh's competitiveness by reducing the cost of doing business.

It is also essential to keep in mind that comparative advantage does not necessarily translate into a competitive advantage. Given the environment of the high cost of doing business, in order to maintain a competitive advantage, there is a tendency of putting downward pressure on workers' wages and benefits. In this context, for the workers' welfare, there is a critical need for reducing the cost of doing business in Bangladesh. The RMG industry is constrained by a host of such costs. These factors will eventually determine the competitive advantage of Bangladesh's RMG industry and exports. Addressing these issues requires strategic planning and its adroit implementation.

Notes

1. According to Khan (2018), the political settlements framework shows how the distribution of organisational power determines the institutions and policies that are likely to persist as well as the ones most likely to be developmental in this context, and how the relative power and capabilities of relevant organisations may be changing over time.
2. Deals, in contrast to rules, among the political and economic elites, can be open (access is open to all) or closed (access is restricted); and also, they can be ordered (deals are respected) or disordered (deals are not respected). The countries are likely to exhibit high

growth when deals are open and ordered. However, such deals-space framework is also elite-centric.

References

BBS. 2017. Dhaka, Bangladesh.

Hamann, Ralph. 'Developing Countries Need to Wake up to the Risks of New Technologies', University of Cape Town, 5 January 2018. Available at https://www.news.uct.ac.za/article/-2018-01-05-developing-countries-need-to-wake-up-to-the-risks-of-new-technologies (accessed 3 June 2019).

Hassan, Mirza, and Selim Raihan. 'Navigating the Deals World: The Politics of Economic Growth in Bangladesh'. In Lant Pritchett, Kunal Sen, and Eric Werker (eds), *Deals and Development*, pp. 96–128. Oxford: Oxford University Press, 2017.

ILO-SANEM. *Baseline Study of the Improving Working Conditions in the Bangladesh Ready-Made Garment Sector Programme*. Dhaka: ILO, 2018.

Khan, M. 2012. 'Technological Upgrading in Bangladeshi Manufacturing: Governance Constraints and Policy Responses in the Ready-Made Garments Industry', School of Oriental and African Studies (SOAS), University of London

———. 2018. 'Political Settlements and the Analysis of Institutions', *African Affairs* 117(469): 636–55.

Mahmud, W. 1995. 'Recent Macroeconomics Developments in Centre for Policy Dialogue'. In Rehman Sobhan (ed.), *Experiences with Economic Reform: A Review of Bangladesh's Development*, Dhaka: Dhaka University Press Limited.

Pritchett, Lant, Kunal Sen, and Eric Werker. *The Political Dynamics of Growth Episodes.* Oxford: Oxford University Press. 2017.

Raihan, Selim, 'Our Garment Industry at a Crossroad', *The Daily Star*, 27 June 2015. Available at https://www.thedailystar.net/op-ed/business-analysis/our-garment-industry-crossroad-103471 (accessed 3 June 2019).

———, 'Can Bangladesh Continue to Grow without "Good Governance"?', *The Daily Star*, 14 June 2017. Available at https://www.thedailystar.net/op-ed/economics/can-bangladesh-continue-grow-without-good-governance-1419685 (accessed 3 June 2019).

———. 2019a. 'Institutional Challenges of Export Diversification in Bangladesh in the Context of the Dominant RMG Sector', Paper

Prepared for the 'Bangladesh Institutional Diagnostic Tool' Research Project of Economic Development and Institutions Research Programme, Oxford Policy and Management and UkAid, London. Available at https://www.imf.org/external/datamapper/datasets/SPRLU.

———, 'Hiccups of Development Surprise', *The Daily Star*, 8 April 2019b. Available at https://www.thedailystar.net/opinion/governance/news/hiccups-development-surprise-1726366 (accessed 3 June 2019).

———. 2019c. 'Economy-wide Implications of Bangladesh's Graduation from the LDC Status', Background Paper for the Planning Commission of Bangladesh, Dhaka, Bangladesh.

Raihan, Selim, and Abdur Razzaque. 2007. 'A Review of the Evolution of Trade and Industrial Policies in Bangladesh'. In Abdur Razzaque and Selim Raihan (eds), *Trade and Industrial Policy Environment in Bangladesh with Special Emphasis on Some Non-Traditional Export Sectors*, pp. 24–62. Dhaka: Pathak Samabesh.

Raihan, Selim, and Sayema Haque Bidisha. 2018. 'Female Employment Stagnation in Bangladesh', EDIG Research Paper, ODI, The Asia Foundation and UKaid, London.

World Trade Statistical Review 2018, Chapter VIII. Available at https://www.wto.org/english/res_e/statis_e/wts2018_e/wts18_toc_e.pdf (accessed 17 December 2019).

4

Role of Multilateral Agencies and NGOs in the Development of Bangladesh

S. NARAYAN

Bangladesh's Gross Domestic Product (GDP) growth rate has been steady since the early-1980s, and there has been a significant rise in GDP per capita since 1985. In 2017, the GDP per capita exceeded \$1,400, rising from just under \$600 in 2004. This has been possible due to a steady GDP growth rate of over 6 per cent after 2004. Social indicators have improved after 1980. Infant mortality, female literacy and life expectancy levels have grown significantly since the same year. Life expectancy at 72 years is higher than in India, where it is 68 years. Population growth rates have fallen from a high of 3.2 per cent in 1967 to 1.05 per cent in 2017, which is considerably below the Net Reproduction Rate (NRR). These are clear indicators of the progress in human development, which Bangladesh has made in the last three decades.

This chapter examines the role of multilateral agencies and non-governmental organisations (NGOs) in this journey, and argues that certain special circumstances in the country's policies enabled this success. The chapter specifically looks at four programmes: a) the population programme, b) the Grameen bank, c) Bangladesh Rural Advancement Committee (BRAC) models, and d) Proshikha. It provides a brief narrative on each programme, and gives the reasons for the success of these programmes.

In the initial years after independence, Bangladesh remained heavily dependent on foreign aid for its development programmes. Multilateral aid agencies considered Bangladesh a willing recipient, ready to accede to programme content and delivery mandated by the donors. During this period, most of the development needs of the country were financed by grants rather than by loan receipts, which were repayable with interests. Both components of these foreign aids came either as food aid, project aid, or as commodity aid from the major development partners, including the World Bank, Asian Development Bank (ADB), United States Agency for International Development (USAID), United Nations Population Fund (UNFPA), United Nations Development Programme (UNDP), Japan International Co-operation Agency (JICA), Department for International Development (DFID), Australian Aid (AUSAID), Canadian International Development Agency (CIDA), Deutsche Gesellschaft für Internationale Zusammenarbeit (GIZ), etc. (Wahab 2015).

The flow of foreign aid in the initial years of the country's formation enabled development initiatives, especially in the health, population and education sectors, to be taken. After the 1980s, there was also focus on industry and foreign investment. Around the same time, there was also stability in political governance despite changes of regimes. There was substantial improvement in economic indicators like education, health, poverty, population, family planning, women's empowerment, micro-finance and all the broad sectors of the economy (agriculture, manufacturing and services), which contributed to growth acceleration in the country. Table 4.1 shows some of the economic indicators and their growth over the

Table 4.1 Economic Indicators Showing Socio-economic Development in the Post-war Period in Bangladesh

Economic Indicators	*1980*	*1990*	*2000*	*2010*	*2016*
Growth rate of GDP (annual percentage)	0.819	5.62	5.29	5.57	7.11
Gini Index	25.9 (1983)	27.6 (1991)	33.4	32.1	32.4
Primary school enrolment (in Billion)	18.13	39.60	53.37	115.28	221.42
Life expectancy at birth	53.48	58.4	65.32	70.20	72.49
Maternal mortality ratio (per 1,00,000 live births)	–	569	399	242	188 (2014)
Employment-to-population ratio (age 15+)	54.11 (1984)	83.86 (1991)	69.71	56.60	56.10
Employment-to-population ratio (female age 15+)	9.58 (1984)	63.8 (1991)	54.02	33.94	33.19

Source: World Bank Open Data.

years that can be attributed to Bangladesh's development from the 1980s till date.

The 1990s witnessed a policy shift among donors—away from programme assistance—towards providing support for liberalisation and good governance reforms. At about the same time, institutional shortcomings in the Bangladesh government resulted in the emergence of NGOs promoted by the donors as they superseded the public programmes in terms of efficiency and delivery. Foreign aid created a multiplier effect on the evolution of social stability and economic dynamism in Bangladesh (OECD 2018). The aid to the government was replaced by greater assistance to select NGOs during later years (Figures 4.1 and 4.2).

The Population Programme

Among all the programmes, the population control programme, initiated by the UNFPA, and soon supported by the World Bank and other multilateral agencies, was a highly significant one in terms of the results that it achieved (UNFPA 2000, 2015). When the UNFPA started operating in Bangladesh during the early-1970s, the country was listed as a Less Developed Country (LDC), with

Figure 4.1 Net Receipts of Official Development Assistance (ODA) by Bangladesh from 1970–2016

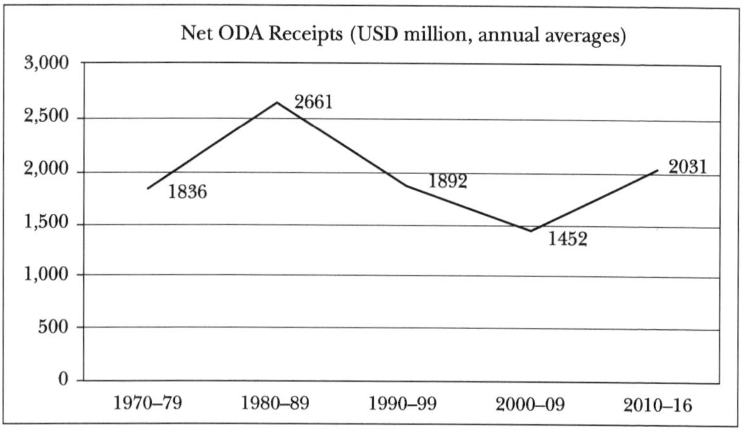

Source: OECD (2018).

Figure 4.2 Change in Composition of Loans and Grants in Total Foreign Aid

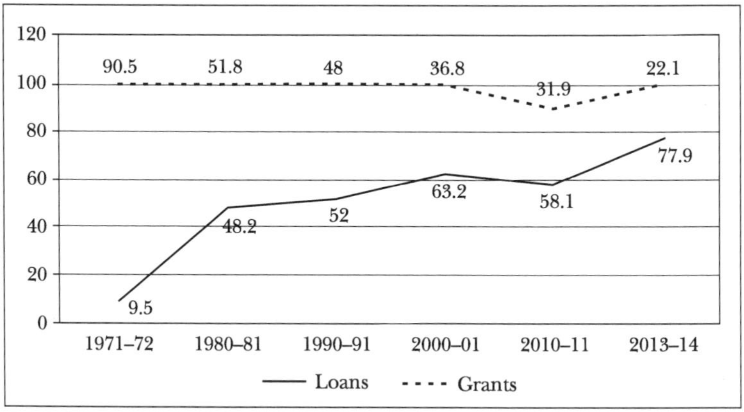

Source: Hasan (2011).

more than 60 million population, and a total fertility rate as high as 6.3 children per women in 1975 (World Bank Website). Some of the major challenges for the UNFPA were adolescent pregnancy, low proportion of institutional delivery of child births, the unmet need for family planning, high drop-out rate among family planning acceptors, and the high level of gender-based violence.

During 1974, the UNFPA committed $10 million in a contract with the government of Bangladesh over three years for the training of family-planning workers, census development, introducing population curriculum in medical schools, etc. In the 1990s, there were 13 UN organisations which provided operational assistance to the Ministry of Health and Family Welfare (MoHFW), accounting for 45 per cent of foreign aid receipt (Buse 2002). These multilateral organisations formed an important feature in the aid regime supporting the health sector of the country. In the period after the 1990s, the proportion of aid in the health programmes declined. From 1993–2000, the proportion of external aid in the health budget was between 31 per cent and 40 per cent, while the government contribution to health expenditure was between 60 per cent and 69 per cent. The magnitude of external aid in the health sector started declining after 2000. Under the Health, Nutrition and Population Sector Programme (HNPSP), an initiative of the government of Bangladesh in the mid-2000s, the development partners supported 27 per cent of the budget, while the remaining was provided by the government.

There were three distinct phases in Bangladesh's population policy. The first phase started in early-1973 and continued up to 1996. This phase was marked by the implementation of a target-driven Family Planning (FP) programme focusing on the reduction of population growth. In the first five-year planning period, the FP programme was targetted towards developing maternal and child health-based service delivery systems, deploying field workers to provide services at clients' homes, expanding the availability of contraceptives and their usage, promoting multi-sectoral collaboration, and motivating people to use family planning services (Barkat-e-Khuda and Barkat 2010). The second phase in the country's population control policy started in 1997. There was a transition in the population control mechanism, from a target-driven to a client-centred approach during the second phase. During 1997–2002 (fifth five-year plan period), emphasis was given to a broader range of reproductive health issues covering larger population groups, in contrast to the need for targetting family planning alone. During 1998–2003, the health and family planning facilities and personnel were integrated to provide an Essential Services Package (ESP), in which reproductive health was one of the core components. Finally, the third phase population policy was developed and approved formally in 2004. The main objective of the Bangladesh Population Policy 2004 was to achieve the Net Rate of Reproduction (NRR) of one by 2010, and to have a stable population by 2060. Table 4.2 provides the progressive impact of these policies.

Interestingly, even though there were several changes in governments and different regimes, the focus on population control remained important for every government. Soon after independence, in 1973, the government of Sheikh Mujibur Rahman targetted reduction of population growth. In 1975, two administrative bodies, the Directorate of Family Planning and the National Population Council, were formed, and the Ministry of Health and the maternal and child health programme were transferred to the Directorate of Family Planning. At a meeting of the National Population Council in June 1976, under a different government, population was declared

Table 4.2 Population Growth

Indicators	*Phase I* *1973–96*	*Phase II* *1997–2003*	*Phase III* *2004–11*
Population growth rate (average)	2.43	1.95	1.22
Population density (average people per sq. km of land)	714.51	1,010.37	1,128.91
Infant mortality rate (average out of 1,000)	116.84	64.28	44.65
Adolescent fertility rate (average out of 1,000)	173.00	112.61	94.46
Contraceptives prevalence method (average percentage)	24.95	52.05	55.65
Adults (15 years and above) newly infected with HIV (average in 1,000)	114.28	654.28	1,542.85

Source: Data extracted from World Bank, World Development Indicators.

as the number one problem for the country. The government emphasised the urgent need to make the FP programme an integral part of the development process. The second five-year plan of the government (1980–85) aimed to reduce population growth from 2.8 per cent to 1.5 per cent, which was further revised to 1.8 per cent (from 2.4 per cent) in the third five-year plan (1985–90).[1]

The government population control programme lost pace in the mid-1990s for several reasons. There was inadequate funding by the government of Bangladesh; inadequate staffing; lack of a regular, reliable and uninterrupted supply of contraceptives; lack of strong technical and managerial leadership; and a limited role of the NGOs and the private sector in the health sector. The services emphasised particular contraceptive methods, omitting health service needs. While evaluating the programme, it was found that the family health assistants focused more on the better-educated women rather than the poor, uneducated female population. Also, the exclusion of men while reaching out to couples as a part of the outreach programme reduced the efforts of the programme (Barkat-e-Khuda and Barkat 2010).

Notwithstanding these criticisms, it is clear that Bangladesh has been able to effectively manage the system in order to control high fertility rates, high infant mortality, and also to reduce the growth rate of the population to near-replenishment levels. Given that

Bangladesh was a very poor country at the time of its independence, with very low literacy and a very conservative rural population, this story appears to be remarkable. The population growth rates of the country appear to be currently lower than those in India and Pakistan, and this achievement must be recognised as a success in its development story.

The success of the population programme in Bangladesh could perhaps be attributed to three causes. First, a willingness on the part of the government to accept external aid not only in financial terms, but also in the form of programme formulation and implementation by aid agencies. This was perhaps necessitated by the weakness in institutional capabilities in the government immediately after independence, when aid as well as advice was welcome by the Bangladesh government. Second, there was a sustained focus on population control over changing political regimes, coups and elections. It could be argued that fears stemming from earlier famines and the pressure that the population created on food supply enabled the government to focus on this aspect as a vital aspect of the development process. Third, the administrative hierarchy and existing institutional machinery was suited to use the aid funds and programmes to strengthen their own position within the administrative structure of government. People working on the programme, within the government, earned power and prestige through its implementation, apart from gaining recognition from international agencies.

This requires further analysis. When Bangladesh gained independence, governmental institutions were weak, and the administrative hierarchy and attendant processes had to be rebuilt. There were inadequate resources for addressing any of the pressing problems. It was therefore somewhat natural that the country turned to external assistance, both in terms of programme funding, and for conceptualisation and implementation. Its priorities were set by the donors. Once the programmes got underway, it was natural that benefit-seekers developed, both within the government and outside, to leverage these programmes for their individual benefits.

As in other developing countries, in Bangladesh, during the post-independence era, there existed a strong relation of power, conflict and cooperation among various social forces like the state, the market, the dominant class, the working class, and the NGOs supported by foreign donors. For Bangladesh, the NGOs gained importance and started influencing the political and economic domains of the country, and especially, the power and legitimacy of the government. Immediately after the post-liberalisation period, since the 1980s, both international and local NGOs, namely Terre des Hommes, BRAC, Proshika, Gano Shahajjo Sangstha (GSS), and Association for Social Development (ASA) prioritised their operation of relief and rehabilitation activities, and distributed food, medicine, blankets, etc., among war-affected people. During the mid-1970s and 1980s, the role of the NGOs started changing. With the impact of globalisation and the transfer of state power, there was more emphasis on integrated community development programmes. To support this, the NGOs started receiving foreign funds, and they played an important role in bringing self-reliance among local development sectors. Thus, in alliance with the foreign donors, the NGOs started competing with the government and posed a threat for sharing political power at the local level. One of the crucial indicators for expanding power was their takeover of the basic facilities of the nation, such as healthcare services, education, micro-finance, small industries, sanitation, etc.

Therefore, in the health sector, the trend suggested the diminishing role of the government ministries and agencies, and the increasing prominence of foreign organisations. The majority of the NGO members were women who played a role in politics and in influencing election outcomes. In local government institutions, these female members played a significant role in mobilising voters in favour of their candidates and getting elected to the local bodies. The government became relatively dependent on these NGOs for public support, stability and legitimacy, and thus, there was a growing public indifference towards the role played by the government in the health sector. In 2000, an election result showed that more than 40 per cent of the elected female members in local governments were involved in NGO activities. In contrast to the state agencies, the NGOs had a more popular image, a large number of rural memberships, and extensive informal training programmes for generating socio-political awareness. All of this, coupled with better service and publicity, strengthened their social position and influence in relation to the government (Haque 2002).

Grameen Bank

In the post-independence era, under the socio-economic setup, the financial sector of Bangladesh was underdeveloped and was dominated by state-owned commercial banks and specialised banks (Nguyen, Islam, and Ali 2011). The Bangladesh government maintained strong control over the whole financial sector, where a majority of all the major industries were under government control, following the nationalisation policy in 1972.

There were broadly three categories of financial institutions in the initial phase: a) the formal sector, including banks, non-bank financial institutions (FIs), insurance companies, capital market intermediaries like brokerage houses, merchant banks and micro-finance institutions (MFIs); b) the semi-formal sector, including Specialised Financial Institutions, which do not fall under the jurisdiction of the Central Bank or other enacted financial regulators, and; c) the informal sector, which included unregulated private intermediaries. As Barai and Adhikary (2013) stated in their work, the formal financial institutions were based on a collateral and codified system of risk assessing, which failed to finance the credit needs of poor people. Moreover, the monitoring mechanism was also not adequate to cover large numbers of small borrowers, and to cope with uncertainties in micro-finance. On the other hand, the unregulated and unorganised informal sector was characterised by high interest rates, for example, 10 per cent per month. Additionally, there was a supply constraint to the financing of small and micro-finance sectors. The micro-credit industry was born in Bangladesh prior to the 1970s, as cooperative societies failed to become self-sustaining due to their inability to both accumulate deposits and reduce loan defaults (Suzuki, Barai, Kumar and Wanniarachchige 2011). Although almost all of the financial institutions were nationalised, the public-sector enterprises failed to run efficiently and profitably due to several financial difficulties. According to Nguyen, Islam and Ali (2011), there was excessive government intervention, political connections, economic and political corruptions, lack of market discipline and competitiveness, and operational and managerial inefficiency in the banking sector, which affected economic development, industrialisation and poverty elimination in the country. This marked the beginning of economic liberalisation and reform in the financial sector (Lee and Islam 2011).

Against this backdrop, Muhammad Yunus initiated the Grameen Bank project in August 1976, which gained immense popularity as a self-sustaining micro-credit initiative. The Grameen Bank emerged as a micro-finance institution mainly due to the inefficiency of both the formal and informal credit market, which failed to cater to the credit needs of the rural poor of the country. According to the traditional banking system, the corollary of collateral-based lending practices was that the poor was not bankable (Zohir 2004).

The Grameen Bank realised that granting credit to the poor is costly and relies on foreign aid in the initial phase for fund-raising. At the initial stage of its inception, the Bank collected funding from different international donor agencies at low rates. The Grameen Bank secured concessionary loans from international agencies such as the International Fund for Agricultural Development (IFAD), Royal Norwegian Development Cooperation (RNDC), Swedish International Development Agency (SIDA), Japan Bank for International Cooperation (JBIC) and the Ford Foundation. In addition to such foreign agencies, the Grameen Bank also received loans from the Central Bank of Bangladesh and from other commercial banks within the country.

The pattern started changing during the mid-1990s, when the bank reduced dependency on external funds in relative terms, from 98 per cent of total resources in 1988 to 4 per cent in 1994. By the mid-1990s, the bank started to get most of its funding from the Central Bank of Bangladesh. Figure 4.3 shows the change in the share of foreign funds and the Grameen Bank's path towards self-sustainability.

The Grameen Bank initiated a credit-based poverty alleviation programme for the rural poor, particularly for women who had less than half-an-acre of land in possession, or whose asset value was less than 1 acre of land (Neer, Ohashi and Nagahata 2002). The Bank provided credit for small-scale non-farm activities, housing loans,

Figure 4.3 Share of Foreign Funds in the Total Fund of the Grameen Bank from 1986–94

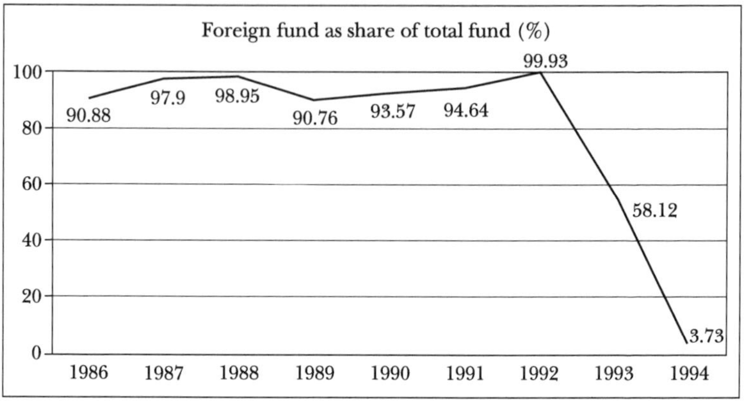

Source: Khandker, Khalily and Khan (1995).

as well as loans for irrigation, drinking water or sanitation facilities. It also provided small amounts of loans, which are as low as $60–$100 to the poorest of poor in the rural areas of Bangladesh. The basic objective of the Bank was to provide necessary capital to these poor to channelise their skills into viable productive enterprises (Hossain 2000). The success of the Grameen Bank, starting from its inception till today, is shown in Table 4.3, which reveals that there has been an enormous increase in terms of loans disbursed, total deposits and profit gains of the Bank in the past few decades, that is, from the 1970s till 2016.

The bank targetted women, and participation of women reached 97 per cent in over 80,000 villages by 2016. The model ensured that recovery rates remained high, at close to 98 per cent. As the burden of loan repayment and any lapses in repayment went to the group taking the loan and not on any individual, this helped in the screening of good borrowers from bad borrowers. The group members also contributed to the defaulted amount, with the intention of collecting the money from the default member at a later period. The Grameen Bank's policy did not encourage further credit-lending to the group in which any member had defaulted, and thus, due to peer pressure from within the group, repayment became more likely. The bank supervisors are involved in vigorous

Table 4.3 Loans Disbursed by the Grameen Bank

Year	*Total Loans Disbursed (in Million $)*	*Total Deposits (in Million $)*	*Number of Members*	*Number of Villages Covered*	*Percentage of Female Members*	*Profit/Loss for the Year (in Million $)*
1976	0.001	—	10	8	20	—
1980	1.310	0.10	14,830	363	31	—
1986	56.510	4.10	2,34,343	5,170	74	0.0003
1990	248.080	25.86	8,69,538	19,536	91	0.0027
1996	1,691.740	90.83	20,59,510	36,420	94	0.4600
2000	3,060.440	100.54	23,78,356	40,225	95	0.2100
2006	5,954.020	390.48	69,08,704	74,462	97	20.0000
2010	10,124.640	800.48	83,40,623	81,376	97	10.7600
2016	20,674.260	1,640.37	89,01,610	81,395	97	17.7400

Source: Grameen Bank (2017a).

monitoring, which also helped to reduce the moral hazard of the members, led to an increase in productivity, and created incentives to receive additional credits (Suzuki, Barai, Kumar and Wanniarachchige 2011).

There were criticisms of this approach. An important criticism was that the amount of micro-credit received by the borrowers failed to have any significant impact on their household income (Debnath and Mahmud 2014). Micro-credit provided by the Grameen Bank is often termed as a 'death trap' by many economists, who felt that poor people may take up loans even without thinking of the consequences, and may enter into the system of irresponsible borrowing and debt trap for their entire lifetime (Levin 2012).

The failure of micro-finance ventures also led to the depletion of family savings and diversion of remittance flows to repayment. Families sell off their land and other household assets under cash constraint to repay loans in order to avoid being in the default list with the bank (Bateman 2014).

Importantly, risk appraisal for credit, especially for micro-enterprises, is weak, based on the assumption that group guarantees provide adequate security cover. There are several cases where projects that are not viable have been funded (Wahid 1994). Wahid commented that in terms of cost-efficiency, the Bank was performing well and was maintaining moderate economic profit as long as it was relatively small in size and operation until 1986; but it started to lose persistently when it started expanding after 1986. The operating profit of the bank was 409 (thousand Taka) and 17 (thousand Taka), respectively, in 1985 and 1986, which fell to –3,000 (thousand Taka), and –75,000 (thousand Taka) in 1987 and 1990, respectively. It was found that the loan recovery rate for repeated borrowers was relatively low when compared to the recovery rate of first-time borrowers. The reason was that the amount of loan given for the second time seemed to be very small for the borrowers who have already lifted their economic conditions above the poverty line. With the horizontal expansion of the bank slowing down in later years, the bank workers' and field workers' prospects for promotion started diminishing. Thus, without a better incentive structure, dissatisfaction among the workers had a negative effect on the loan recovery process of the Bank.

Hanley (2003), in his article, mentioned that, there were several instances and incidents when the Grameen Bank faced challenges from the two major political parties in Bangladesh—the Bangladesh Nationalist Party (BNP) and the Awami League—during the 1990s. The first came from within the Bank when the BNP incited its members to form trade unions and targetted to unionise all the employees. As a consequence of this process, several centre buildings of the Grameen Bank where the borrowers met were destroyed. This affected the repayment process of the Bank. The second disruption in the Bank's process took place when a former borrower's dissatisfaction with the savings policy turned into a political issue throughout the country. Borrowers started withdrawing their savings, including 'group tax'[2] from the Bank, and this dissatisfaction grew into a political debate. The political parties in opposition to the Bank encouraged the borrowers to leave the Bank and stop the repayment of loans. According to the Bank, repayment suffered immensely during this period. Finally, during the 1991 general election, in order to boost their chances of a win, both the parties targetted the Grameen Bank and promised to write off all agricultural loans under $1,000 if they were elected. The news created a sensation, and repayment stopped in some parts of the country. Many Grameen

Bank branches were hit hard by this announcement. Although repayment had mixed effects, there was an increased percentage of borrowers who were late in their repayment.

Despite these criticisms and challenges, the Bank continued its expansion in Bangladesh. The number of villages covered under the Bank grew from one in 1976 to 37,937 in 2017, and the number of branches also increased from one in 1976 to 1,105 in 2017. The Bank's net profit for 2017 was 2,275.30 million (Taka), which enabled the bank to declare 30 per cent cash dividend to the shareholders, including the government of Bangladesh (Grameen Bank 2017b).

The political and military rule soon after independence in 1971 was not characterised by the development or strengthening of institutions. Rather, it was characterised by political mobilisation. Even in the 1980s, the phase of elected, democratic governments was only marginally more stable than that of the military regimes (Haque 2002). NGOs gained greater leverage due to the intensive competition between the two main parties, the BNP and the Awami League, which needed to expand their grassroots support through these NGOs. Against such a political backdrop, donors and development researchers felt that NGOs could effectively deliver development services to the poor and landless in comparison to the government agencies, and thus, they started supporting the rapid expansion of NGOs to foster development. The leading NGOs worked to provide micro-finance, and services on sanitation, healthcare and education to the rural poor population. The proliferation of NGOs in Bangladesh and the broadcasting of their success stories created pressure on the government, fostered by aid agencies, to utilise them for development activities, which widened their funding sources both from the government and foreign donors. As mentioned by Chen (2013), in the post-independence era, the Bangladesh government encouraged all kinds of philanthropic institutions, and there were no rules regarding establishing NGOs. Hence, the role of NGOs, their contribution to development, and their accountability have been publicly debated and questioned by the government and other sectors of the society (Ahmed, Hopper and Wickramsinghe 2012).

The success of the Grameen Bank could be attributed to the government of Bangladesh ceding space to micro-finance institutions to fill the gap between scheduled bank-lending and the needs of small borrowers. The management structure of the Bank, built around close supervision and mutual collateral, could not be replicated within the formal banking systems.

It is interesting to compare policies in India targetted towards enterprise loans for the poor. The nationalisation of banks in the 1970s, and a large programme of subsidy-supported rural entrepreneur loans attempted to bring small borrowers into the fold of formal banking systems. Over the past four decades, while programmes have changed, the policy approach has been to support lending to the poor through the banking sector, subsidising interest rates as well as inputs, and controlling output markets. Multilateral agencies were able to access the poor only through governmental structures and institutions. The pattern also focused on keeping interest rates low, thus causing stress to the banks as well as to government budgets. On the other hand, in Bangladesh, with little budgetary funds, the Grameen Bank became an example of privatising loans to the poor, with the help of multilateral agencies. Most importantly, there was no cap on interest rates, which enabled the Bank to expand.

BRAC

Following the war of independence in 1971, millions of refugees returned to Bangladesh from India, and the government of Bangladesh lacked funds for reconstruction. It was during this time that Fazle Hasan Abed, a devotee of the Bangladesh independence war, returned to Bangladesh from London in 1972, with a grant of £96,000 from the Oxford Committee for Famine Relief (OXFAM) and started the Bangladesh Rehabilitation Assistance Committee (BRAC) to establish a temporary relief organisation for supporting refugees. Towards the end of 1972, after the first phase of relief work was over, BRAC concentrated on the long-term development needs of the country (Talapatro 2012). The name of the organisation was changed to Bangladesh Rural Advancement Committee in 1974. It highlighted multiple social problems and development strategies to support the poor, especially in areas where government agencies failed to deliver services (Seelos and Mair 2006). BRAC focused on credit-based income and employment-generation programmes for vulnerable groups, human rights and legal support, essential healthcare, livestock and poultry, fisheries, sericulture, and lending assistance to micro-enterprises. The relationship between BRAC and the government had several phases; during the early 1970s, the new government tried to establish its own credibility, and thus, considered BRAC to be its 'rival'.

During the 1980s, the government was unable to address the large number of social problems that exceeded both their capability and capacity. During this phase, the government tolerated the initiatives of BRAC, and finally in the phase of the 1990s, the government started outsourcing projects to BRAC. The lack of manpower and of access to poor and vulnerable groups were some of the other reasons why the government started their phase of cooperation and collaboration with BRAC as an important channel to reach the poor. BRAC never identified itself with any political parties, but maintained a close relation with elites and had a good public image (Hulme and Moore 2006), which led it to become the government's biggest partner in Bangladesh. According to Haque (2004), collaboration between the government and BRAC resulted in a mutually beneficial relationship. BRAC received benefits for the support of their programmes, and the government could also ensure its accountability for programme performance. In its initial days, BRAC was funded by many bilateral and multilateral donors like the OXFAM, SIDA, Overseas Development Agency (ODA), UK, Kreditanstalt für Wiederaufbau (KWF), Germany, European Economic Committee, etc.

Although BRAC is present in all areas of rural development, its largest contribution has been through its education programme (Lovell and Fatema 1989). BRAC initiated the primary education programme for the rural poor in Bangladesh and opened 22 experimental schools in 1985. By 2001, the number nearly reached 2,000. BRAC's objective was to develop a replicable primary education model in a three-year period, where basic literacy and numeracy skills can be provided to the poorest rural children failing to attend formal school. BRAC started two types of schools for two different age groups. The first was a three-year programme for children in the age group of 8–10 years, who had never enrolled in a school or had dropped out during the first year. This was called the Non-Formal Primary Education (NFPE). The second one started in 1988; it was a two-year programme for children in the age group of 11–14 years, who had never attended school. This programme was called the Primary Education for Older Children (PEOC). In this programme, girl children formed 75 per cent of the students.

During this phase, it was observed that nearly half of the primary school-age students were not enrolled in government primary schools, and more than half of them dropped out of schools before completing the fifth grade. Government schools suffered from non-availability or absence of teachers, high teacher–student ratio, irrelevant curriculum, lack of books and study materials, unequal treatment of poor children, and unauthorised fees. In contrast, since the inception of BRAC schools during 1985–88, the percentage of drop-out students has reduced significantly. As para-professional teachers, young men and women of the villages were selected and given basic as well as refresher training courses and structured guidance on teaching children. The teachers were given a nominal monthly stipend, and were selected based on the criteria of having completed nine to 10 years of schooling, and of being married. In BRAC schools, 75 per cent of the teachers are female, in contrast to 86 per cent of male primary teachers in government schools. With almost no paid work for women in the villages, BRAC employment for teachers gave the women a small but steady income round the year, as well as social respect. Some other initiatives under BRAC included Early Childhood Development Schools, School Meal Programme, *Shishu Niketon* Programme, BRAC libraries and creating platforms with interactive multimedia content for English language learning for adolescents (United Nations Educational, Scientific and Cultural Organization [UNESCO] Institute for Lifelong Learning, BRAC Education Programme 2016).

Despite these positive features, BRAC has been criticised by many researchers, scholars, governments, and other communities or groups for operating as a commercial enterprise (Muneer 2017). It generates around 70 per cent of its own income through numerous BRAC-branded enterprises. There are many instances where BRAC runs successful businesses, like cold storage, press, real estate companies and restaurants, which are highly profitable. By not being dependent on the government, and by funding its own programmes, it has developed a great degree of independence from governmental policies and is able to pursue its own agenda for development. It is said that the donors of BRAC are mostly influential foreign Western governments who are criticised for entering into countries' affairs by means of NGOs.

PROSHIKSHA

Proshiksha is an NGO in Bangladesh aiming at contributing to the socio-economic development of the country. Started in 1975 in few villages of Dhaka and Comilla district (Chowdhury 2014), the organisation was established with a view to creating a self-reliant process among the rural poor by providing support to collective or group efforts to improve their socio-economic condition (Alam 1993). The main objectives of Proshiksha are:

- Structural poverty alleviation;
- Environmental protection and regeneration;
- Improvement in women's status;
- Increasing people's participation in public institutions; and
- Enhancing people's capacity to exercise democratic and human rights.

To attain these objectives, Proshiksha extended credit assistance for income and employment-generation projects in different fields like agriculture, irrigation, pond fishery and open-water fishing, sericulture, bee keeping, cattle- and poultry-rearing, homestead gardening, social forestry, handicrafts and cottage industry, etc. (Alam 1993). Through organisation-building, education and training, Proshiksha initiated health and nutrition education, literacy and women's programmes, and extended programmes for the development of the urban poor in 1990. In the field of agriculture, the organisation advised group members on the selection of their unused land with irrigation facilities and to produce homestead vegetables and other tree seedlings. The saplings produced were sold in the local market and other neighbouring villages. To create a strong social impact, the organisation used popular theatre with themes like women's rights against polygamy, spread of preventive healthcare, awareness on legal rights, the need to participate in elections, etc., for the dissemination of knowledge among its clients As a consequence, unlike BRAC, Proshiksha also received criticisms from Islamic communities and Madrasas for teachings regarding marriage, women's inheritance, and the like, which they considered un-Islamic (Moniruzzaman 2007). The coverage of the organisation is 21,272 villages and 2,380 urban slums in 55 districts, with nearly 5.5 million programme beneficiaries. Additionally, the programme has generated 12.33 million employment and self-employment, and 1.24 million households have been made poverty-free by the organisation.

Although the organisation reached certain milestones including socio-economic development of the country, it faced some major setbacks, which had a high impact on its operation and employment. Proshikha was banned from operation in 2003 and in 2007 on charges of misappropriation of funds, corruption within the organisation, and various internal conflicts (Sadia 2014). The NGO Affairs Bureau blocked huge amounts of donor funds and accused the organisation of being politically aligned with the opposition party. Internal conflicts in 2007 was another major incident when the National Board of Revenue, Bangladesh asked all the commercial banks to freeze the accounts of Proshikha chairpersons and their family members. Following this, the organisation received very little donor funds, and the micro-finance activities ran in a deficit in 2009 (Chowdhury 2009). Among some strong criticisms against the organisation, it was found that it had started an internet and software business, which were mostly market-oriented, with the objective to earn profits through long-term capital investments. The government criticised the organisation, stating that although it is registered under the 1961 Ordinance, Proshiksha developed a transport company, the garment industry, a press and video library with huge initial investments, which had no social motive but were targetted at profit-earning (Sadia 2014). Proshiksha was termed not just as an NGO, but also as an 'NGO conglomerate', and was criticised on the point that like other NGOs, it had diverted from the objective that it had during its initial phase, when the organisation first emerged as a meaningful player in the country (Karns, Shaffer and Ghere 2008).

Concluding Remarks

The discussion in this chapter clearly illustrates the role of non-state actors in Bangladesh's development initiatives. The population control programme owes its success to multilateral agencies, credit delivery to small enterprises to the Grameen Bank, and the inititaives in education, especially women's education, to BRAC. How was this possible? There could be several reasons.

Immediately after independence in 1971, state activities were largely focused around urban areas. Lack of administrative institutions and personnel, and financial constraints prevented the government of the day from extending its activities to remote and rural areas. Therefore, the government did not try to restrict the activities of the NGOs there (Kennedy 1999). The fact that these organisations were able to attract foreign capital, at a time when the state budget was extremely constrained, also contributed to the government's support to these institutions.

Second, the government of Bangladesh, especially after the Mujib period, was not constrained by an ideological adherence to a socialistic pattern of society, with the heights of governance and development in the hands of the state. Successive governments encouraged private enterprise, followed an export-led growth model rather than an import substitution model, thus encouraging foreign investment and technology, especially in the textile and garments sectors.

Third, the areas that the Grameen Bank and BRAC focused on, namely micro-enterprise, rural education and women's welfare, were not high on the state development agenda in the initial decades after independence. The state was focused on building infrastructure and energy as well as on stabilising institutions, and it was content to cede space to the NGOs in areas where it had little financial leverage. With regard to population control, the argument was different. This was such an important priority that the state was eager to access all external aid available, and it was willing to cede institutional space to aid agencies to implement programmes, as it had little funds or machinery of its own, especially in the early years.

Finally, the structure of democracy as it emerged in Bangladesh appears to be very different than that in India. In India, policies target the poorest, and all programmes, grants and subsidies are focused on the poor; and a considerable portion of state administration and finances are spent on targetted programmes for the poor. There is a total absence of this approach in Bangladesh. Bangladesh elections appear to be much more an urban phenomenon, with entrenched beneficiaries from governmental programmes appearing to direct electoral movements.

It is difficult to escape the argument that the absence of a socialist ideological pattern of policy led to the development of parallel institutions that were market-oriented and less regulated. Governance remained in urban hands rather than in the remote villages. This liberal ideological approach could well have been the reason why non-state actors were able to contribute so much to the development of Bangladesh, even in the social sectors.

Notes

1. The following is an excerpt from the section, Second Five-Year Plan, Population Control and Family Planning, Population Planning section, the Planning Commission of Bangladesh:

   > Bangladesh's population plan is aimed at achieving a replacement rate of 1 by 1990, a population size of 117 million by the year 2000, and a stationary population of about 175 million by the mid-2000s. On the basis of this long-term goal, the Second 5-year Plan (1980–85) calls for reducing the present total fertility rate of 5.85 to 4.1 by 1985 and the crude birth rate from 43.25 to 31.56/1000 (Bangladesh Planning Commission 1980: 28).

2. A levy that was akin to a membership fee, deposited with the Bank, liable to be refunded when the group got dissolved or became dysfunctional.

References

Ahmed, Z., T. Hopper, and D. Wickramsinghe. 2012. Hegemony, Counter Hegemony and NGO Accountability Change: BRAC in Bangladesh. Available at http://apira2010.econ.usyd.edu.au/conference_proceedings/APIRA-2010-239-Ahmed-Hegemony-counter-hegemony-and-NGO-accountability.pdf.

Alam, K. Q. 1993. 'Proshika Manobik Unnayan Kendra—Bangladesh', Food and Agriculture Organization of the United Nations, RAP PUBLICATION: 1996/44. Available at http://www.fao.org/3/ac772e/ac772e03.htm#TopOfPage.

Bangladesh Planning Commission, Population Planning Section. 1980. 'Second Five Year Plan: Population Control and Family Planning', Unpublished, p. 28.

Barai, M., and B. Adhikary. 2013. 'The Success of Microcredit in Bangladesh: Supplementing "Group Lending" Explanation with Institutional Understanding', *Review of Integrated Business and Economic Research* 2: 471–90.

Barkat-e-Khuda and S. Barkat. 2010. *The Bangladesh Family Planning Programme*, UNFPA-ICOMP Regional Consultation.

Bateman, M. 2014. 'The Rise and Fall of Muhammad Yunus and the Microcredit Model', IDS Working Paper 001.

BRAC Education Programme, Bangladesh, 31 August 2016, UNESCO Institute for Lifelong Learning. Available at https://uil.unesco.org/case-study/effective-practices-database-litbase-0/brac-education-programme-bangladesh.

Buse, K. 2002. 'The Coordination of United Nations Health Sector Support in Bangladesh: Necessary, Insufficient, and Misguided?', *Global Governance* 8(2): 221–46.

Chen, Y. 2013. 'Microfinance Program in BRAC—the Largest NGO in the World', International Organizations and Economic Development (IEPM 3110).

Chowdhury, A. 2009. 'Microfinance as a Poverty Reduction Tool—A Critical Assessment', DESA Working Paper No. 89.

Chowdhury, M. 2014. 'An Analysis on Proshika'. Available at https://www.slideshare.net/Mahamuda/an-analysis-on-proshika.

Debnath, S., and K. Mahmud. 2014. 'The Myth of Microcredit in Poverty Alleviation: Perspective from the Grameen Bank in Bangladesh', *World Applied Sciences Journal* 31(6): 1025–32.

Grameen Bank. 2017a. *Grameen Bank Historical Data Series 1976–2017 (Amount in Million USD)*. Available at http://www.grameen.com/data-and-report/historical-data-series-in-usd/.

———. 2017b. *Grameen Bank Annual Report 2017: Dedicated to Create A Poverty Free Bangladesh.* Available at http://www.grameen.com/wp-content/uploads/bsk-pdf-manager/GB-2017.pdf.

Hanley, D. 2003. 'Grameen Bank', The Board of Trustees of the Leland Stanford Junior University, SM-116.

Haque, M. 2002. 'The Changing Balance of Power between the Government and NGOs in Bangladesh', *International Political Science Review* 23(4) 411–35.

———. 2004. 'Governance-based on Partnership with NGOs: Implications for Development and Empowerment in Rural Bangladesh', *International Review of Administrative Sciences* 70(2): 271–90.

Hasan, M. 2011. 'Foreign Aid Dependency of Bangladesh: An Evaluation', *The Chittagong University Journal of Business Administration* 26: 281–94.

Hossain, I. 2000. 'Micro-credit and Good Governance: Models of Poverty Alleviation', *Southeast Asian Journal of Social Science* 28(1): 185–208.

Hulme, D., and K. Moore. 2006. 'Why Has Microfinance Been a Policy Success in Bangladesh (And Beyond)?', Global Poverty Research Group, WPS 041.

Karns, M. P., J. T. Shaffer, and K. R. Ghere. 2008. 'The Challenges of Accountability for International Nongovernmental and Civil Society'. Available at https://www.academia.edu/398233/The_Challenges_of_Accountability_for_International_Nongovernmental_and_Civil-Society_Organizations.

Kennedy, H. C. 1999. 'Reconsidering the Relationship between the State, Donors, and NGOs in Bangladesh', *Pakistan Development Review* 38(4): 489–510.

Khandker, S., B. Khalily, and Z. Khan. 1995. 'Grameen Bank: Performance and Sustainability'. World Bank Discussion Papers, no. 306.

Lee, K. K., and M. Islam. 2011. 'Financial Development and Financing Constraints in a Developing Country: The Case of Bangladesh', *Indian Economic Review* 46(1): 41–67.

Levin, G. 2012. 'Critique of Microcredit as a Development Model Pursuit', *The Journal of Undergraduate Research at the University of Tennessee* 4(1): Article 9.

Lovell, H., and K. Fatema. 1989. *The BRAC Non-formal Primary Education Programme in Bangladesh.* UNICEF, UNE/ICEF(02)/L6. Available at https://digitallibrary.un.org/record/150210?ln=en.

Moniruzzaman, M. 2007. 'Group Formation and Empowerment: The Case of Brac and Proshika in Bangladesh', *Intellectual Discourse* 15(1): 37–58.

Muneer, I. K., 'Ngo-isation of Bangladesh', *Geonorntnka.ru/Carthago delenda est*, 1 July 2017. Available at https://www.geopolitica.ru/en/article/ngo-isation-bangladesh.

Neer, S., M. Ohashi, and M. Nagahata. 2002. Rural Development Credit Project, Grameen Bank, Bangladesh.

Nguyen, C., A. Islam, and M. Ali. 2011. 'The Current State of the Financial Sector of Bangladesh: An Analysis', AIUB Business and Economics Working Paper Series, Office of Research and Publications (ORP), American International University-Bangladesh (AIUB).

OECD. 2018. Development Aid at a Glance: Statistics by Region. Available at the Global Picture of Official Development Assistance (ODA). Available at http://www.oecd.org/dac/financing-sustainable-development/development-finance-data/Asia-Development-Aid-at-a-Glance-2018.pdf.

Sadia, S., 'Criticism of NGOs in Bangladesh', *Wordpress.com*, 16 September 2014. Available at https://salmajune.wordpress.com/2014/09/16/121/.

Seelos, C., and J. Mair. 2006. 'BRAC—An Enabling Structure for Social and Economic Development', Study 34, IESE Business School, University of Navarra, Barcelona, Spain.

Suzuki, Y., M. Barai, B. Kumar, and M. Wanniarachchige. 2011. 'The Grameen Bank "Empowering the Poor" Model of Microcredit: An Institutional Comparison with the Traditional Mode of the Japanese Banking System', *Journal of Comparative Asian Development* 10(1): 129–56.

Talapatro, D., 'What is BRAC? All about BRAC NGO and its Activity in Bangladesh', ReportBD.Com: Website for Students and Educators, 22 December 2012. Available at https://www.reportbd.com/articles/3048/1/What-is-BRAC-All-about-BRAC-NGO-and-its-activity-in-Bangladesh/Page1.html.

UNFPA. 2000. Annual Report, United Nations.

———. 2015. 'The Impact of the Demographic Transition on Socioeconomic Development in Bangladesh: Future Prospects and Implications for Public Policy', United Nations.

Wahab, F. 2015. 'Foreign Aid 101: The Story of a Bottomless Basket'. Available at https://ces.ulab.edu.bd/wp-content/uploads/sites/18/2015/07/Wahab_presentation.pdf.

Wahid, A. 1994. 'The Grameen Bank and Poverty Alleviation in Bangladesh: Theory, Evidence and Limitation', *The American Journal of Economics and Sociology* 53(1): 1–15.

World Bank Open Data. 2018. Available at https://data.worldbank.org/.

World Bank Website. Available at https://data.worldbank.org/indicator/SP.DYN.TFRT.IN?locations=BD (accessed 18 August 2019).

World Development Indicators, World Bank. Available at https://databank.worldbank.org.aspx?source=2&country=BGD#advancedDownloadOptions (accessed 21 November 2019).

Zohir, S. 2004. 'NGO Sector in Bangladesh: An Overview', *Economic and Political Weekly* 39(36): 4109–13.

5

Policy Stances and Financial-Sector Developments in Bangladesh

SALEHUDDIN AHMED

After the independence of Bangladesh in 1972, continued policy efforts have successfully resulted in the development of the country. Bangladesh has reached two milestones: a) it has become a lower-middle-income country, and b) it has graduated to the status of a developing country. This growth has been achieved over time, with moderate inflation rates. Table 5.1 below shows the picture of the growth rates of Bangladesh in various years at financial year (FY) 2006 constant price.[1]

Table 5.1 Growth Rates in Bangladesh FY 2006 (Constant Prices)

Period	*Growth rates (in Per Cent)*
FY 2009–18 (Average)	6.4
FY 2017 (2016–17)	7.3
FY 2018 (2017–18)	7.9

Source: Bangladesh Bank (2019a).

As observed from Table 5.2, the inflation rate movements also give a satisfactory picture.

Table 5.2 Annual Average Consumer Price Index (CPI)-based Inflation (FY 2006 = 100)

Period	*Inflation rate (in Per Cent)*
FY 2015	6.40
FY 2016	5.92
FY 2017	5.44
FY 2018	5.78

Source: Ibid.

The financial sector and reforms in its policies play a vital part in this growth story. This chapter discusses the contribution and the role of monetary policy and the financial sector in Bangladesh's growth story.

Bangladesh's financial sector consists of the Bangladesh Bank (the Central Bank), six state-owned commercial banks (SCBs), three specialised banks (SBs), five non-scheduled banks, nine foreign commercial banks (FCBs), 34 non-bank financial institutions (NBFIs), 41 private commercial banks (PCBs), 62 insurance companies, micro-finance institutions (MFIs) and the capital market (Bangladesh Bank 2019b).

Bank is the most important institution in the financial sector of Bangladesh. In the 1970s, all banks were nationalised. The management and financial norms were decided by government directives. The lending rate, amounts of loan and types of borrowers were decided by the government. Lending was focused on state-owned enterprises. These practices resulted in large Non-Performing Loans (NPL). Bangladesh Bank—the central Bank of the country—did not have many tools of monetary policy because of the administered prices and interest policy of the government. The focus of the nationalised banks was to extend bank branches to cover large geographical areas without considering financial viability. Therefore, the contribution of the financial sector to the efforts of economic growth was not very significant in the beginning (Ahmed 2007).

A major policy shift occurred in the early-1980s with the emergence of 10 new private commercial banks. From the mid-1990s till the early-2000s, more private commercial banks were licensed by Bangladesh Bank. The impetus of this policy shift came, first, from the politicians, and then it was taken up by the Central Bank to give it a practical shape and implement it. The then President of Bangladesh, Abdur Rahman Biswas (1991–96), set up a committee headed by a Minister to explore the feasibility of operating private banks. The recommendation of the committee was to allow privately owned banks to come in. This was given the green signal by the succeeding President of Bangladesh, Shahabuddin Ahmed (1996–2001). Therefore, the policy shift was a result of the combined efforts of politicians and professionals. With the initiatives of the

World Bank and the International Monetary Fund (IMF), a major reform programme, namely the Financial Sector Reform Program (FSRP), was taken up in the 1990s. This programme was designed to increase the efficiency of the monetary policy instruments and strengthen Bangladesh Bank. The administered interest rate practice was abandoned, open market operation of treasury bills by the Central Bank was introduced, and governance of the financial sector improved (Ahmed 2007).

In the early-2000s, a multi-dimensional second phase of policy reforms began. The rationale and background work of these reforms were prepared by the professionals of the Central Bank, with a view to matching them to the needs of the financial sector. A major step towards operationalising the reforms came from the policymakers in the form of legal reforms. A brief of some major aspects of the reforms are as follows:

- Legal aspects: Bangladesh Bank Order, 1972 was reformed to extend autonomy to Bangladesh Bank. The Money Loan Courts Act was passed to recover default loan and laws to combat money laundering offences. In the late-2000s, this law was extended to include measures to prevent finance for terrorism, following the resolutions of the United Nations Convention against Corruption (UNCAC). The Non-Bank Financial Institutions Act (NBFI Act) was promulgated to create institutions for leasing, housing finance, and long-term lending.
- Prudential norms: With the advent of private commercial banks, there was a need to introduce strict prudential norms. These included raising the Minimum Capital Requirements (MCR) of banks from the initial 400 million Taka to 1,000 million Taka, and finally, in 2007, to 4,000 million Taka or 10 per cent of Risk Weighted Asset (RWA) (whichever is higher). Loans rescheduling conditions were introduced to stop even greening of Non-Performing Loan (NPL). Strict conditions for writing off bad loans were introduced and conditions for bank's exposure to a single borrower were also introduced.
- Risk management guidelines: Risk management is a core function of banking. There was an emphasis on managing six core risks, namely credit risk, foreign exchange risk,

asset liability risk, internal control compliance risk, anti-money laundering risk, and information and communication technology (ICT) risk.

- Management and governance norms: In approving the appointment of Bank Directors, Chief Executive Officers (CEOs) and Advisors, the Central Bank introduced a fit and proper test, and their roles were defined in the Terms of Reference (ToRs). Mandatory Audit Committees were set up in each bank, the Capital adequacy, Assets, Management capability, Earnings, Liquidity, Sensitivity (CAMELS) rating and the Early Warning System (EWS), and disclosure standards were introduced (Bangladesh Bank 2009).

Despite these reforms, there were some other issues in the sector. These include governance and regulatory issues of commercial banks, concentration of bank loans to a small number of big borrowers and corruption. The alarming issue of Non-Performing Loans (NPL) in banks is depicted in Table 5.3.

Table 5.3 Net NPL Ratios to Total Loans (in Per Cent)

Types of Banks	*2010*	*2011*	*2012*	*2013*	*2014*	*2015*	*2016*	*2017*	*End-June 2018*
State-owned Commercial Banks (SCBs)	1.9	–0.3	12.8	1.7	6.1	9.2	11.1	11.2	11.7
Development Finance Institutions (DFIs)	16	17	20.4	19.7	25.5	6.9	10.5	9.7	7.4
Private Commercial Banks (PCBs)	0	0.2	0.9	0.6	0.8	0.6	0.1	0.2	0.8
(Foreign Commercial Banks) FCBs	–1.7	–1.8	–0.9	–0.4	–0.9	–0.2	1.9	0.7	0.8
Total	1.3	0.7	4.4	2	2.7	2.3	2.3	2.2	2.7

Source: Bangladesh Bank (2019a).

Non-Bank Financial Institutions (NBFIs)

The third and current phase of policy reforms which started in the mid-2000s (especially from 2005) focused attention on the foreign exchange market, capital market and insurance market. Owing to the fast-changing structure and functions of various components of the financial sector, policymakers and banking professionals initiated this phase of reforms to cope with their ever-changing needs.

In the foreign exchange market, Bangladesh moved from a fixed exchange rate system to a market-based flexible exchange rate system in June 2003. The foreign exchange operations and payment system were simplified and adapted to the needs of the economy (Bangladesh Bank 2006).

As elsewhere, with regard to capital markets, NBFIs like leasing companies and mortgage banks are considered important institutions in capital markets. In order for the NBFIs to contribute significantly to the development of capital markets, suitable policy measures are required. In Bangladesh, 57 companies are now listed as merchant banks, out of which 54 are full-fledged, two are issue managers, and one is an issue manager with underwriter authorisation. Only nine NBFIs have registered with the Bangladesh Security Exchange Commission (BSEC) for performing merchant banking activities (Bangladesh Bank, Financial System 2019). However, the contribution of NBFIs in the capital market is limited. The success of NBFIs, especially merchant banking operations, is largely linked to the development of the security market in Bangladesh. Table 5.4 provides the data on assets and liabilities of NBFIs in Bangladesh.

Table 5.4 NBFIs: Assets, Liabilities and Deposits (in Billion Bangladeshi Taka [BBT])

Particulars	*2012*	*2013*	*2014*	*2015*	*2016*	*2017*	*2018**
Total assets	333.9	436.3	520.1	611	713.9	841.07	870.3
Total liabilities	274.3	350.4	424.2	509	606.46	725.95	762.04
Liabilities–assets ratio	82.2	80.3	81.5	83.3	84.95	86.36	87.56
Total deposit	145.4	198.3	238.5	318.1	382.43	467.98	480.1
Deposit as per cent of total liabilities	53	56.6	56.2	62.5	63.1	64.41	63

* As of 30 June 2018.

Source: Bangladesh Bank (2019a).

The NBFIs offer some essential financial products with a comparatively narrow profit margin. Therefore, consideration should be given to whether the tax treatment for NBFIs can be more congenial for their development. Compared to banks, the role of NBFIs in providing loans and advances is not significant. To give a picture of the same, in FYs 2017 and 2018, industrial-term loans of the banking sector were 528 and 587 billion Taka, respectively, whereas during the same period, the NBFIs provided 93 and 121 billion Taka, respectively (Bangladesh Bank, Financial System 2019).

MFIs

Empirical evidence suggests that the non-governmental organisations (NGOs) as well as MFIs, or the NGO-MFIs in Bangladesh can undertake most of the work for which the specialised banks (SBs) were established. Statistics provided by the Microcredit Regulatory Authority (MRA) show that till June 2017, NGO-MFIs rendered their services to 24.8 million beneficiaries, with an outstanding loan of 581.6 billion Taka. Meanwhile, their outstanding savings were recorded at 216.1 billion Taka (Bangladesh Bank 2017). Besides, more than 80 per cent of the economy's outstanding micro-credit belongs to the top 10 NGO-MFIs. The high recovery rate (more than 90 per cent) is an achievement of the Bangladeshi NGO-MFIs. The Bangladesh Rural Advancement Committee (BRAC)[2] has also gone for micro-credit securitisation to opening a new horizon for funding micro-credit operations.

In July 2006, the parliament of Bangladesh passed the Microcredit Regulatory Authority Act. Under this Act, the government established a separate MRA and constituted its Board of Directors with the Governor of Bangladesh Bank as the chairperson. This authority is now responsible for giving registration license to NGO-MFIs and to provide the financial and operational norms to be followed by the operators of micro-credit.

Capital Market

The capital market, comprising debt and equity instruments, plays a key role in economic development by channelling surplus resources to the most productive uses. The stock market in Bangladesh started its operation around 50 years ago. However, its contribution to the capital market is still not significant. Owing to the absence of proper regulatory measures and slow institutional development, the capital market remains weak. The result of this is reflected in the state of financing long-term investment, as compared to the banks and non-bank financial institutions.

The stock market is not effective in raising capital for the real sector. Funds raised from the Initial Public Offering (IPO) in the capital market is insignificant compared to the funds raised through loans and advances (Chowdhury 2014).

A typical characteristic of the capital market in Bangladesh is its low level of capitalisation, that is, the lack of liquidity and depth. It lacks active trading in fixed income securities, such as bonds and debentures. Several steps, including the de-mutualisation of the Dhaka Stock Exchange (DSE) and Chittagong Stock Exchange (CSE), have already been adopted to develop the capital market of Bangladesh.

Bond Market Developments

With economic development, debt financing of businesses and industries as a proportion of all financing increases. The debt market as well as the capital markets provide a significant proportion of investible resources. However, this is not the case in Bangladesh, where debt markets are dormant and equity markets do not yield sufficient capital for entrepreneurs.

The debt market in Bangladesh is not yet developed. Only 30 per cent of total domestic savings are invested in bond market instruments, and the remaining 70 per cent goes in the banks and financial institutions. The Bangladesh bond market is overwhelmingly dominated by short- and long-term government securities. There are hardly any corporate bonds (only 1 per cent of the total debt market) from which business corporates can mobilise funds. Some companies issue debentures (unsecured bonds), but its impact on the bond market is negligible.

At present, there is hardly a vibrant secondary bond market in Bangladesh. There are other problems like the absence of fixed income securities, lack of access to contractual savings instruments (like pension and gratuity funds), absence of municipal bonds, and lack of adequate incentives for the corporate sector to issue bonds. Depth and size for the bond market require a proper regulatory framework with transparent rules and regulations, an enabling tax regime, market rules, good settlement and custody systems, a reliable rating system, and awareness among corporate directors and private investors. Presently, the government, with the help of Bangladesh Bank and the Bangladesh Security Exchange Commission (BSEC), is trying to develop the bond market.

Developments in the Insurance Sector

Insurance is an important component of the financial sector of a country. The insurance industry in Bangladesh is fairly big, with 62 insurance companies covering both life and non-life insurances. Of these, two are state-owned companies, one each for life and non-life insurances. Historically, the regulatory system of this sector was relatively weak and under-developed. The Controller of Insurance used to be appointed by the government, and the office was under the direct control of the Ministry of Commerce (Ahmed 2007). There was a lack of transparency and governance in the insurance companies, and the rules could not be properly enforced by the regulatory authority. To improve the situation, and to improve the role of the sector in the overall financial market of the country, the government established an independent regulatory body called the Insurance Development and Regulatory Authority (IDRA) in 2010. This body has, since then, been working to ensure good governance and management of the insurance companies. However, it is necessary that the IDRA connects with other regulators like Bangladesh Bank and BSEC in order to ensure satisfactory compliance of the regulatory norms by the insurance companies.

Financial Inclusion

The Central Bank of Bangladesh, Bangladesh Bank, has pursued many strategies of financial inclusion to reach out to unserved and underserved sections of services and economic industries. Some of these strategies are discussed below (Ahmed 2016a).

Provision and Advancement of Agriculture Lending

Apart from the farm loans of two state-run farm credit institutions (Bangladesh Krishi Bank and Rajshahi Krishi Unnayan Bank), all Bangladesh-based commercial banks (owned by the public or the private sector) now provide farm credits directly, either via MFIs or through value-chain intermediaries. Total agricultural loan disbursements are on a steadily increasing trend; between FY 2014 and FY 2018, agricultural loan disbursements increased from 160.37 billion Taka to 213.93 billion Taka, respectively.

Credit for Sharecroppers

In the case of the smallholders' agricultural farming, namely sharecropping, where a sizeable number consists of women, the Central Bank, in 2008, formulated a guideline for all banks to provide credit to the sharecroppers. Agriculture credit, totalling 10.86 billion Taka, was disbursed by these banks in FY 2012 to around 500,000 sharecroppers. BRAC, the largest NGO in Bangladesh, has taken a pioneering role in this field.

Bank Accounts for Farmers and Other Disadvantaged Groups

Within the inclusion initiative, banks opened more than 10 million fresh bank accounts, with nominal original deposits as low as 10 Taka (around 12 US cents), on behalf of small farmers and other small-scale, rural and urban populations, without charge. These accounts are used as a means of savings and payments by account holders for the receipt of input subsidies to agriculture, net social security payments, etc.

Finance for Women Entrepreneurs

Under Bangladesh Bank's refinancing system, Small and Medium-sized Entrepreneurs (SMEs) took numerous steps to guarantee that female entrepreneurs have access, on easy terms and conditions, to economic services. A decreased interest rate of 10 per cent (Bangladesh Bank of 2018) was assigned at least 15 per cent of the refinancing funds for the SME industry. Up to 2.5 million Taka, women and businessmen may receive collateral-free loans from banks and economic institutions, but only against their personal guarantee. An initiative to include micro-enterprises included a group lending policy, according to which up to 50,000 Taka or higher could be lent out (Bangladesh Bank 2018).

E-BANKING

The cornerstone of a modern banking system is e-commerce or online banking. The use of ICT in banking, so that the debit or credit card, Automated Teller Machine (ATM) and Society for Worldwide Inter-bank Financial Telecommunication (SWIFT) system can be used, are all parts of a massive digitisation process in Bangladesh.

The introduction of online banking (e-banking) by the scheduled banks in Bangladesh has aided customers in urban areas to transfer money between locations easily, as it ensures a safer and time-saving way of making payments and carrying out transactions. As of December 2018, out of 59 scheduled banks in Bangladesh, 50 banks (41 PCBs and 9 FCBs) have adopted online banking services.

The use of the debit card, credit card and ATM as smart payments and transaction products and services has been increasing rapidly. In October 2018, ATM facility was available in 51 banks, and the number of debit and credit cardholders were 1,35,39,087 and 10, 61,407, respectively.

Although the objective of the government is to move to a digital environment across all the sectors of the economy, the process has become slightly slow because of the lack of adequate attention of the managers of different companies and financial institutions. Adequate funds are also not allocated for this purpose. There have been cases of ICT security lapses in some companies and financial institutions (including the Central Bank) in Bangladesh. These have given rise to apprehension among people. Proper attention should be given to ICT security, and to develop an efficient, safe and user-friendly digital financial system in Bangladesh.

Modernisation of the Financial Sector of Bangladesh

Automation in the banking sector in the last several years has been achieved with significant progress (Bangladesh Bank, Financial System 2019). The Bangladesh Bank has taken several initiatives in this regard. These include the creation of a data bank for potential and current borrowers in order to improve risk management. Improvement in digital services, integration with best international practices, and the introduction of mobile-based banking services are some of the innovations introduced. Bangladesh ranks very high in the use of mobile phones for financial transactions.

Regulatory Development

Banks and financial institutions in Bangladesh have been working under a diversified regulatory development over the last few years. These developments were a result of felt needs on the part of the regulators, mainly the Central Bank, to bring about efficiency and discipline in the financial sector. A few of the main regulatory developments are discussed below:

- Reform of monetary policy tools: The first step was to make the monetary policy more effective and relevant to the economy. Instruments like 'repo', 'reverse repo', 'open market operations' to auction government securities and foreign exchange management tools were built in the Monetary Policy Statement (MPS) of Bangladesh Bank. The first MPS was formally announced to the public by Bangladesh Bank in January 2006. The policy statement was independently prepared by the Central Bank, without any intervention of the government. After that, a six monthly MPS is issued in January and July of every year, which is an example of the autonomy of the central bank.
- In January 2015, Basel-III was phased in and complete capital ratios were implemented from the beginning of 2019.
- Risk management guidelines on environmental and climate change, for banks, were distributed. Green banking policy guidelines were released as well.

- Stress-testing guidelines were published for banks and financial institutions to evaluate banks' and financial institutions' resilience under various negative conditions.
- Banks had to construct a distinct risk management unit to manage risk thoroughly and intensively.
- Banks were ordered to build a distinct capital market subsidiary, and they are now being carefully controlled in terms of capital market activities.
- To increase bank involvement in Corporate Social Responsibility (CSR), the guidelines of Bangladesh Bank have been issued.
- Guidelines for money-changers, insurance companies, and postal transfers have already been circulated to meet the international standard on Anti-Money Laundering (AML) and Combating Terrorist Finance (CFT).

To ensure proper financial disclosures and true audit reports of companies and institutions, the government established an independent regulatory body called the Financial Reporting Council (FRC) in 2007. This body examines the audit reports that will lead to ensuring good governance. This will help capital market development by ensuring proper audit reports of those companies that would like to issue IPOs to raise funds from the share market.

Reforms Following International Norms

The global financial scenario has been fast-changing. Bangladesh must keep pace with the global movements and adopt measures in tandem with global practices. The Asian Financial Crisis of 1997 and the Global Financial Crisis of 2007 taught the world that once the financial sector is infected, the financial contagion spreads to the real sector of a country and beyond its borders (Ahmed 2016b).

After the Asian Financial Crisis of 1997, like many countries, Bangladesh also took measures to strengthen corporate governance. To this end, the Companies Act, 2013 (for all companies of Bangladesh) and the Bank Company Act (Amendment) 2013 reiterated relevant issues and measures to ensure corporate governance. Under the corporate governance of the banks, the board needs to chalk out strategies and work plans on an annual basis for banks, and set the Key Performance Indicators (KPIs) for the CEO and other senior executives of a bank. The Audit Committee of banks is a part of good governance.

As mentioned earlier, on the recommendations of the UNCAC, the government of Bangladesh enacted the Money Laundering Prevention Act, 2012 and the Anti-terrorism Act, 2009 (to control terrorist financing risks). To implement these laws, the Bangladesh Financial Intelligence Unit (BFIU) was set up in Bangladesh Bank in 2002. In 2018, BFIU became autonomous under the Ministry of Finance, Bangladesh.

Basel norms (Basel I, Basel II and Basel III) provide the best international practices in the banking sector. The Basel Accords have been introduced in the Bangladesh Bank regulations and norms to regulate and monitor operations of all banks in accordance with Basel norms.

The Role of an Independent Regulator

Central bank autonomy is a debatable but crucial issue. However, for the central bank to achieve its objectives, such as inflation control, economic stability, better financial management, etc., it is necessary for the bank to be free from all external influences. Thus, the bank should be fully autonomous in all its functional and decisional activities.

Some attributes of interdependence are whether the central bank can refuse credit to the government; whether it can meet its expenses without depending on the government; whether its Governor or Board of Directors can function independently; whether its governor is independent in following the monetary policy; whether it is free to choose its monetary instruments; and finally, whether it is free to regulate the banking policy and the banks.

The main responsibilities of Bangladesh Bank are monetary policy functions, to be a bankers' bank, a banker of the government and regulators, as well as the supervisor of the commercial banks. The Bank of England (BoE), which deals with monetary policy functions, among others, is regulated by the Prudential Regulation Authority (PRA) and Financial Conduct Authority (FCA), two independent bodies under the overall guidance of BoE. Most of the Central Banks have dual functions, like those of Bangladesh Bank. Therefore, its tasks are enormous. The performance of the economy and that of the different sectors are closely linked with the performance of Bangladesh Bank. The vision and mission given below state the functions of Bangladesh Bank.

- Currency and payment management policy;
- Management of the foreign exchange scheme and controlling the foreign exchange market;
- Managing foreign exchange reserves and foreign exchange regulation;
- Regulating and overseeing banks as well as financial institutions, and advising the government on the interaction and effects of fiscal, monetary and other economic policies (Bangladesh Bank, Financial System 2019).

Implementing the vision and mission of Bangladesh Bank has faced serious challenges and limitations. In the context of Bangladesh Bank, the debates on macro-economic issues centred around how Bangladesh Bank can set up monetary targets without political pressure, and how far monetary policy can be implemented without any political and structural limitations. The authority of the Bangladesh Bank over the constituent banks and financial institutions recently shows some limitations in terms of controlling corruption, increasing non-performing loans, lack of good governance, weak management, and finally, erosion of public faith in the bank. It seems that Bangladesh Bank, due to both 'internal' (within the bank itself) and 'external' (outside the preview of the bank) hurdles, finds it difficult to exert effective control over the banking sector. The pressure groups of the stakeholders, namely the Bangladesh Association of Bankers (BAB)—an association of bank owners—and the Association of Bankers, Bangladesh (ABB)—an association of CEOs/Managing Directors (MDs) of banks—play vital roles in the regulatory aspects of the banking sector.

In order for Bangladesh Bank to be independent and effective, the necessary aspects are:

(a) More focus on core banking issues by the central bank;

(b) Appropriate and strong prudential and management norms of the Central Bank, which are not subject to frequent changes due to external political/administrative pressure; and
(c) A system of prompt corrective actions for management of crises, and for legal/administrative actions against persons responsible for crises in a particular bank or in the banking 'system' as a whole (Ahmed 2019).

In real-world situations, extraordinary independence and full autonomy of the Central Bank may not be easily achieved. Therefore, a Central Bank like Bangladesh Bank can minimise political and other external pressures by constantly engaging with them and gaining public support for actions, which in turn may make Bangladesh Bank autonomous and effective. Whether in good or bad times, supervisors always face pressure from lobbyists and from politicians that can undermine the stability of the financial system.

For Bangladesh Bank to be successful in regulating the financial sector, it must have very relevant and pragmatic 'policies', prudential management rules, and must ensure that these are fully followed by all banks and financial institutions. 'Discretionary' powers or 'ad-hoc measures' must be avoided to safeguard the independence and autonomy of Bangladesh Bank. The typical case of 'policy' versus 'discretion' must be resolved by the strong stance of Bangladesh Bank, where policies and rules, and not the discretionary powers of any individual and agency, will be supreme. The time has come for Bangladesh Bank to strike a balance, showing an appropriate professional stance, while avoiding the danger of politically motivated reforms in a highly technical domain.

Concluding Remarks

The notable resilience of the Bangladesh economy, as exhibited by key macroeconomic indicators so far, lends strong support to the outlook that Bangladesh may be able to achieve the target of GDP growth rate of 7 per cent and above, given that its present performance is sustained, and development is accelerated. However, the resilience of the economy, with stability and development along with equity, will have adverse consequences if the major challenges mentioned in this chapter are not met properly (Ahmed 2016c).

To meet the challenges, one of the most important tasks is to make the financial sector (banks, non-banks, insurance, and the capital market and micro-finance market) more competitive and service-oriented, which can cater to the needs of all types of clients across all the areas of Bangladesh. Along with this, the challenges of the external sectors (exports, imports of goods and financial services) are also to be met by the financial sector.

The country needs to enforce strict adherence to regulatory and prudential guidelines that are effectively integrated among all institutions in the monetary and financial sectors. The global financial crises of 2007, and the present state of somewhat low global growth outlook, points to the fact that fiscal and monetary policies cannot be substituted with prudent government interventions and careful regulations, even when market-based, liberalised structures operate. Therefore, a symbiotic relationship should prevail between fiscal and monetary policies.

The policy stances towards the financial sector of Bangladesh resulted from action on two fronts: on the one side, the stakeholders, mainly the business people, clients of banks and other users (internal and external) articulated the need for and the kind of changes required in the sector; on the other hand, the policymakers (which includes politicians and advisors to the government), on their own, and as a response to the stakeholders' demands, initiated the process of reforms and changes (Muqtada 2018). Therefore, changes took place in different phases to take the country forward. However, the challenge of backing the tasks to be undertaken by 'political will' remains, and the actions to be taken should be based on facts or data, and the knowledge of the decision-makers and implementers.

The policies and activities of the financial sector directly impact productive activities, covering both income and employment, and income and asset distribution. The indirect impacts of the financial sector operate through its effects on the fiscal and monetary policy stances. In this context, the macro policy stances and the financial sector are critical to the accelerated and sustainable development of Bangladesh.

Notes

1. FY for Bangladesh covers 12 months from July–June. For example, FY 2006 means July 2005–June 2006.
2. BRAC is a big NGO, which has programmes on credit, health, education, environment and other related fields of development.

References

Ahmed, S. 2007. 'The Road Map to Financial System Standards for Middle Income Bangladesh', *Journal of The Asiatic Society of Bangladesh (Humanities)*, 52(2): 342–43.

———. 2016a. *South–South and Triangular Cooperation in Asia* (DP/15). Incheon: Economic and Social Commission for Asia and the Pacific (UNESCAP).

———. 2016b. *Impact of the Global Financial Crisis on the Bangladesh Economy. In Collected Papers on Economic Issues.* First ed. Dhaka: Aloghar Prokashona.

———. 2016c. *Bangladesh Economy: Development Trends and Challenges. In Collected Papers on Economic Issues.* First ed. Dhaka: Aloghar Prokashona.

———, 'Bangladesh Bank's Role as an Independent Regulatory Body', *The Daily Star*, 15 February 2019, Available at https://www.thedailystar.net/supplements/strong-institution-good-governance/news/bangladesh-banks-role-independent-regulatory-body-1701913.

Bangladesh Bank. 2006. *Monetary Policy Review* 2(1), DCP, Bangladesh Bank, Dhaka.

———. 2009. 'Financial Sector Review', DCP, Bangladesh Bank, Dhaka.

———. 2017. 'Financial Stability Report (8)', DCP, Bangladesh Bank, Dhaka.

———. 2018. 'Survey on MSME Financial Inclusion Indicators (2016)', Research Department, Bangladesh Bank, Dhaka.

———. 2019a. 'Annual Report: 2017–18', Department of Communications and Publications (DCP), Bangladesh Bank, Dhaka.

———. 2019b. 'Financial System'. Available at https://www.bb.org.bd/fnansys/recent_dev.php.

Chowdhury, M. N., 'Capital Market for Industrial Development', *The Daily Star*, 2 February 2014. Available at https://www.thedailystar.net/capital-market-for-industrial-development-9512.

Muqtada, M. 2018. 'Macroeconomic Policy, Price Stability and Inclusive Growth in Bangladesh', CPD Working Paper Series, Macroeconomic Performance Analysis, 115.

6

Bangladesh

Examining the Contemporary Politico-social *Fabric*

Sreeradha Datta

Standing close to five decades of independence, Bangladesh has taken enviable strides in positioning itself as a strong South Asian entity, recording remarkable all-round progress. As one of the fastest-growing economies in recent times, Bangladesh is uniquely poised today as a critical regional player. As per the trend, Bangladesh is likely to record an 8 per cent growth rate in the present financial year. Its present nominal Gross Domestic Product (GDP) per capita is at $1,888—up from $273 per capita in 1975 (Asian Development Bank [ADB], Bangladesh and ADB). It has improved upon its Human Development Index (HDI), while deftly controlling its population growth and poverty levels.

The country has had to overcome its inherent socio-political and economic constraints, including changing identities, varying political systems, dynastic politics, improving growth, and dealing and tasking with the anti-Liberation War elements to achieve sustained progress since independence. Over the years, Bangladesh's journey has been perceived differently—from being a 'bottomless basket',[1] to a 'model Muslim nation' (Jahan 2003: 228), to the 'next Afghanistan' (Karlekar 2005), to being a 'developing giant in the world stage'. It has manoeuvred through all of these phases successfully, overtaking many of its neighbours in socio-economic indicators. More importantly, the country has moved ahead despite many constraints, and has managed to deliver to an ever-burgeoning middle-income population, attracting substantial foreign direct investment (FDI) and foreign remittance.

Notwithstanding its growth story, Bangladesh polity still has a long way to go, and its democratic norms remain debatable. A cursory survey of the political developments in Bangladesh raises some concerns regarding its political stability. The country could very well be said to be a study in contrasts, and depending on the direction it takes, the perspectives on this will dramatically differ.

The political trajectory of Bangladesh has taken it through forms of parliamentary democracy, interspersed with direct and indirect military rule. Nearly five decades after its birth, Bangladesh is now standing at the crossroads of a political transition. In 1971, when it broke away from Pakistan, Bangladesh held out a promise of an independent democratic state based on cultural values, and freedom of thought and life. At the present juncture, following the latest parliamentary elections—the eleventh Jatiya Sangsad (JS) held in December 2018—the underlying authoritarian tendencies that were witnessed not only during the 15 years of military rule, but were also glimpsed during the early years under Sheikh Mujibur Rahman, seem to be returning.

The country is currently headed by the Sheikh Hasina-led Awami league government, which is in its third consecutive term, with a rather weakened opposition. The last electoral win of 2018, which brought in the Awami League coalition with brute majority, has led to a distinct consolidation of power in a single (coalition) party. This has led many to suggest that the parliamentary election of 2018 could be the tipping point in Bangladesh between a multi-party political system and a cemented one-party rule. The lines are blurring rapidly, and the survival of a multi-party democracy is presently being questioned.

In the South Asian context, it has often been argued that the holding of periodic elections and the completion of an elected term through the due processes of law largely constitutes being a successful democracy. Arguably, that may be so. However, the present political developments in Bangladesh, while broadly adhering to the above factors, appear to be signalling a move away from a multi-party democracy towards a single coalition-party system. Political manoeuvring is not unknown to Bangladesh or South Asia, but the long-term implications of these developments can be lasting, and can prove to be destabilising at both the domestic and regional levels.

This chapter examines some of the broad issues surrounding Bangladesh's political journey and its impact on its society. The chapter is divided into three broad sections. The first section examines the political developments and issues of governance, including the holding of free and fair elections, the manipulation of the JS, and issues of decentralisation of power. The second section considers the issues that impact the society, including the level of political violence, corruption and increasing Islamisation. The third and final section examines the present civil–military relations. This chapter, while summarising the past developments of Bangladesh, focuses more on the contemporary events, given the changing scenario.

Political Systems and Developments

The polity of Bangladesh continues to be dominated by dynastic politics, weak institutions, absence of political accountability, lack of a responsible opposition, and a pronouncedly weak law-and-order situation. Individually, these factors are neither unique to Bangladesh, nor a serious challenge. However, their prolongation would not only weaken the democratic norms, but might also undermine its stability (Datta 2004: 57). In 1971, Sheikh Mujibur Rahman, the first Prime Minister of Bangladesh, and the leader of the Awami League, introduced Bangladesh to parliamentary democracy, imbibing tenets of socialism and secularism. Meandering through the demands of nation-building, he even briefly experimented with a one-party rule, of the Bangladesh Krishak Sramik Awami League (popularly referred to as the BAKSAL), moving towards a presidential system. The instability worsened with the assassination of Mujibur Rahman, triggering coups and counter-coups ultimately leading to military takeover (Rashiduzzaman 1977). The next 15 years saw the rule of General Ziaur Rahman, who took over as the President (1977–80) and formed the Bangladesh Nationalist Party (BNP), followed by General Hussain Mohammad Ershad and his Jatiya Party (1981–91).

In 1991, prolonged political movements and protests from a cross-section of people led to the re-introduction of multi-party parliamentary democracy in Bangladesh. This period, ironically, strengthened, consolidated and institutionalised the personal animosity between the two leading families in Bangladesh politics—

the Awami League and the BNP. Sheikh Hasina took over the reins of the Awami League from Mujibur Rahman, and Khaleeda Zia headed the BNP post-Ziaur Rahman. Since then, Bangladesh's polity has been shaped by these two leaders. The other two main political parties, that is, the Jatiya Party and the Jamaat-e-Islami (there is an appeal against its ban waiting to be heard) have played a critical role by extending support to the party that formed the government. Interestingly, both these *netris* (women leaders), who catapulted into politics following the assassination of their close relatives, blatantly sought to capitalise on their personal tragedies, and in their bid to consolidate their dynastic rule, have institutionalised feudalism in Bangladesh's polity. The political discourse, thus, reflected their mutual acrimony spilling over into personal animosity and vendetta. Until 2006, the anti-incumbency factor was seen at play with either a BNP-led or an Awami League-led coalition government in Dhaka. Polling behaviour suggested that both the*netris* were able to receive support from one-third of the electorate, and the final verdict usually lay with the other one-third swing factor, which seemed to follow the anti-incumbency trend.[2]

Having been under military rule for over a decade-and-a-half, Bangladesh's transition to a parliamentary democracy was no mean achievement. The stabilisation of democracy, building of institutions, growth of free and fair media, and the creation of an enabling space for political freedom and individual liberty differentiated it from other experiences in the regional neighbourhood. However, recent political developments have cast a shadow over the role of the JS in the independence of other branches of the government, that is, the Judiciary, the Election Commission and even the Media.

Weakened Jatiya Sangsad

The parliament plays a crucial role in a democracy. Its strength lies in its ability to work with the opposition. This, however, is not the case in Bangladesh, where the opposition prefers to protest about the electoral mandate, and the ruling party is neither keen to initiate any serious discussions, nor accommodate some of the opposition's demands. Howard Schaffer, a diplomat having served in Bangladesh, notes, '[t]he unfair treatment of the opposition in Parliament, government and ruling-party maltreatment of opposition supporters, manipulation by the government of by-election results, and unacceptable partisanship in the administration of the country have all figured almost routinely' (Schaffer 2002). For such reasons and more, the opposition has usually preferred to stay outside the parliament, indulging in street protests, parliament boycotts and prolonged *hartals*,[3] causing a complete cessation of public activities during a political strike. For the greater part of most parliamentary working sessions, the opposition usually stays out, only entering the parliament when it is on the verge of disqualification.

Usually, the Bangladeshi parliament would largely reflect the broad political divide represented by the two political viewpoints, manifested through the two main political parties—the Awami League and the BNP. However, due to some piquant developments, the last two JS elections have been one-sided affairs, with a negligible opposition. The present 300-member (with an additional 50 reserved seats) parliament consists of a 16-member coalition led by Sheikh Hasina, which managed to garner 288 seats (258 seats for the Awami League, with its partner JP winning 20 seats).[4] In this one-sided election, with the numbers hugely stacked in favour of the ruling coalition, the BNP, which could win only six seats, initially refused to be a part of an 'illegitimate parliament', although its other coalition partner (Gono Forum, which had two seats) joined the JS. It was only on the last day of April 2019, and on the ninetieth day of the first session of the fourteenth JS parliament, that four elected members of the BNP were sworn in to avoid the cancellation of their membership. The BNP had initially held out, hoping that the turn of events during the first parliamentary session would annul the electoral results, which did not happen. In the previous election of 2014, although the Awami League had a comfortable win with 234 seats, a peculiar situation evolved with the JP—an Awami League alliance member—filling in for the opposition, while its leader General Ershad became a special envoy of the Prime Minister, enjoying the position of a minister, along with three JP members of the parliament being inducted into the Council of Ministers.

This brute majority in the parliament enabled the government to implement measures with far-reaching consequences. In fact, the present imbroglio has its genesis in the fifteenth constitutional amendment of June 2011, which abolished the Caretaker Government (CG) system; coincidentally, this was brought in through the thirteenth Amendment. The core mandate for the CG, consisting of a Chief Advisor, along with 10 other advisors, was to assist the Election Commission to hold free and fair elections. The neutrality of the CG was a critical criterion for its functioning.[5]

The demand for the holding of elections under the CG goes back to 1991 when the then president, General Ershad, gave in to the opposition demand, stepped down, and constituted a CG to successfully oversee Bangladesh's parliamentary elections that year. This marked the country's return to multi-party democracy. Interestingly, the CG system was legally introduced only in 1996, and was not without its share of controversy even then. However, once introduced, the CG system proved to be a stabilising factor, and elections thereafter in Bangladesh were held without much controversy, until the 2006 October imbroglio. This time round, the blatant manoeuvring of the then CG, the Election Commission, and the voters' list by the BNP government prior to the elections scheduled for October 2006, led the nation into another period of political instability and uncertainty.

The neutrality of the CG was questioned by the opposition, leading to an interregnum period starting October 2006, when a CG governed the country covertly, backed by the military and Army Chief, Mooen U. Ahmed, until the next multi-party election in December 2008 (Datta 2008: 39). While the CG introduced major reforms, it also revealed the pitfalls of a CG exceeding its brief and assuming a role larger than what was intended. Hence, Sheikh Hasina, who suffered indignity at the hands of the CG, revoked the system she had strongly advocated for in the past. Hasina decided to go ahead with the 2014 elections without the CG system, although, during the constitutional ruling, the Supreme Court provided for the system to remain in practice for the next two JS elections, for the sake of 'safety of the state and its people'. The Awami League's decision was unpopular, and the opposition led by the BNP decided to boycott the elections on the ground that a free and fair multi-party election was not possible without the CG. The opposition complained about the absence of an enabling atmosphere, and preferred to give a walkover of 153 seats. This made the ruling Awami League secure an overwhelming majority of over 234 seats. The political tension was palpable, leading to barely 25 per cent voter turnout, in contrast to the 87 per cent recorded during the previous elections. The BNP's protests against the government could not be sustained, and Hasina was able to complete the full term (2014–18).

In the face of the deep political divide, and in continuation of past trends, the Awami League government also used its machinery to supress the opposition; by the latest count, it had 37,000 complaints filed against the BNP members (*The Economist* 2016). As alleged by the opposition, the government did not ensure a level playing field, disallowing the opposition leaders to hold public meetings; it also went to the extent of imposing a transport blockade to stifle the movement of opposition leaders and activists. It randomly issued warrants against most of the BNP central leaders, and came down on prominent journalists and private TV channel owners because of their support for the BNP.

The Awami League government was able to send Khaleda Zia (BNP Chief, opposition leader) to prison on 22 charges of corruption. Her son, Tarique Rahman, who is the deputy Chairman of the BNP, and who is facing similar corruption charges, has not been able to return to Bangladesh. This has made the BNP weak and increasingly irrelevant. Inevitably, the leaderless and rudderless BNP's manifesto was all about scrapping 'black laws' and improving law enforcement measures. Its election promises were more fury than substance, lacking a serious roadmap for better governance. Its insistence on co-habiting with the Jamaat clearly boomeranged; and its earlier decision to not participate in the 2014 parliamentary elections made a number of its cadres and alliance partners unhappy.[6] In contrast, the war criminal trial, initiated by Hasina, had a mass appeal, and the young voters appreciated the perceptible economic growth (Lorch 2014).[7] Khaleda Zia playing the victim card was ineffective, and the BNP's last-minute coalition was unable to move the electorate.

BNP's coalition with the Unity Front Party led by Kamal Hossain was seen as a last-minute effort without much popular appeal. The opposition's chances dimmed further when Bikalpa Dhara, a political party formed by former President Badruddoza Chowdhury, disassociated itself from the coalition. The opposition political parties missed the opportunity to portray themselves as a consolidated and reliable front, and did not hold much appeal for the electorate. Thus, the Awami League seemed comfortably poised to make the required numbers. Not willing to leave anything to chance, the Awami League party machinery ensured outlandish electoral numbers, bettering its 2014 win. The electoral farce was loud and clear, chipping away at the credibility of the seats the Awami League would have won fair and square. The verdict also underscored Khaleda and BNP's alienation from the public.

Thus, despite regular and periodic elections, the question of political legitimacy continues to haunt Bangladesh. As we have seen, allegations of rigging, intimidation, and other forms of electoral malpractice by the opposition, especially, followed the last two JS elections. The rivalry between the two leaders has often been the root cause of dysfunctional democracy in Bangladesh (Transformation Index BTI, BTI 2018, Bangladesh Country Report). This has been a cause of deep concern, and a comment about the state of politics, although dated, still holds good in the present context. Both the parties failed to cooperate, 'not only because they underestimate each other's political strength, but also because each has an urge to establish a monopolistic rule by knocking out the other, believing that the losing party would simply fade away' (Hossain 2000: 521). Undeniably, as a recent report notes, 'democracy has been gradually undermined for years, suggesting that Bangladesh is now under autocratic rule' (Transformation Index BTI, BTI 2018, Bangladesh Country Report). The absence of a strong, credible opposition in the JS gives the ruling government unbridled power. As it appears, there is a discernible erosion in the institution of the parliament. Media and civil society groups have long identified these problems plaguing Bangladesh's fragile democratic political system. Political parties, however, have ignored their criticisms.

Separation of Powers

In any discussion about socio-political developments in Bangladesh, the question of governance predominates. While Bangladesh has made remarkable economic progress, the ability of the government to implement its policies, deliver public utilities to its citizens, and maintain law and order has been significantly difficult. Importantly, the organs of democracy—the legislature, judiciary and media—all seem to be closely linked to the political premier. This lack of separation of power has not allowed the organs to grow or function independently. Thus, not surprisingly, there have been several controversies surrounding the judiciary and the other organs. There is enough evidence to suggest that the judiciary in Bangladesh does not function independent of the executive, and is subservient to the latter.

In his recently published memoir, the former Chief Justice S. K. Sinha refers to specific cases of governmental interference in judicial decisions. Ironically, it was the CG of the 2006–08 period that was able to legally enable the separation of the judiciary from the executive on 16 January 2007. Interestingly, the separation of these two organs of the government was a delayed implementation of a Supreme Court ruling of December 1999, and one which was actually enshrined in the Constitution. The intentions have always been to keep the political stranglehold over the judiciary. Both the BNP and the Awami League, when in opposition, have argued for the independence of the judiciary, but once in power, both strived to retain control over it (Datta 2008). Indeed, when in 1999, the Supreme Court issued a directive for the separation of the judiciary from the executive, the decision was postponed as many as 20 times. The political parties supported the position while in opposition, but did a volte-face once in power. The shadows of political patronage are so overwhelming that the independence of the judiciary in real terms look unlikely under the prevailing conditions.

The Awami government had introduced the Sixteenth Amendment, allowing the parliament to remove a judge, the power of which was earlier vested with the judiciary itself. This Amendment snowballed into a controversy when the Supreme Court (the executive and judiciary) overturned the Amendment, leading to the resignation of the serving Chief Justice. Apart from the lack of independence and the technicalities of separation of power, there is a lack of an enabling atmosphere for these organs to work without the fear of interference and the fear of being watched over. In the words of Masder Hossain, a retired district judge, '[i]ndependence doesn't only mean separation. It implies the ability to adjudicate disputes without any interference or fear, it implies certainty of tenure and economic independence' (*The Daily Star* 2017). As another sign of unbound impunity, the Bangladeshi transport owners and workers are challenging the High Court as it continues to issue orders for compensation in road accident cases (*New Age*, Staff Correspondent 2019). While the judiciary continues to be under the shadow of political powers, the other critical organ of democracy, the Election Commission, faces similar issues.

The Election Commission plays a critical role in upholding democratic norms in a country. Unfortunately, many of the controversies surrounding the parliamentary elections, especially in the last few years, have emanated from the lack of independence of the Commission. For a variety of reasons, the Election Commission was not seen as non-partisan and neutral. The controversy surrounding the 2006 elections over the grossly incorrect voters list (at the behest of the BNP leaders) led to major protests, and ultimately, the prolongation of the CG. The Election Commission never acquired an independent status. Thus, the opposition parties have always questioned the ability of the Commission to hold free and fair elections without the CG.

Electoral reforms were first made in 1996, with the introduction of the election Code of Conduct, drafted in consultation with the political parties. Unfortunately, the subsequent delinking of the appointment of the Chief of the Election Commission as well as other members from the executive did not bring any semblance of independent behaviour (Hena 2013). This time around, too, as the situation unfolded, the Election Commission seemed largely under the influence of the ruling political party. Moreover, it was widely reported that the latest elections were not fairly conducted. Voters were coerced to vote for a particular alliance, opposition parties were disallowed to campaign in their constituencies, and electoral posters were displayed in public places, which violated the norms of a free and fair election. Also, in the 2018 elections, there was lack of consensus within the EC over the announcement of electoral dates. Mahbub Talukdar, one of the Election Commissioners, disagreed with the other members, which further magnified people's distrust in the Commission.

These evidences from 2018 as well as many instances from the 2014 elections buttress the allegations that the Election Commission lacks autonomy in the electoral process. It failed to muster people's faith in terms of overall organisational strength. The lack of neutrality in the Election Commission's behaviour led a former commissioner to opine, '[n]either the turnout at this election nor the winner surprised me in the least. It was inevitable. It was a manifestation of the people's loss of confidence in the election commission' (Hossain 2019). As a consequence of this loss of confidence perpetuated by the weak role played by these vital organisations, the ruling party is robbed of even the credible seats that it may have actually won, furthering the prejudice regarding the political machinery.

The lack of segregation of power in media, too, is very visible in Bangladesh. The governments have been known to monitor the media. With the introduction of the Digital Security Act, 2018, functioning of free and independent media has been greatly jeopardised. This Act allows greater government control over online publishing and social media, but it was not without its share of controversy and protests. The Sheikh Hasina government, however, has stood its ground. This was not unexpected, and with the consolidation of power, this government has made clear its displeasure towards any alternative view from the media. Internationally recognised journalists and editors, including Magsaysay Award recipients, have been charged repeatedly with sedition and defamation. Not only were they legally harassed, but their papers and channels have also been deprived of government revenue. The more recent incident of the well-known photographer, Shahidul Alam, who was arrested in August 2018, for 'spreading false information' about students protesting against unsafe traffic in Dhaka, is a case in point, of the government exerting its stronghold over media (Alam 2018). New social media, including Facebook, was also drawn into a similar controversy (*The Economist* 2018). Summing up the core problem, economist Rehman Sobhan observes:

> Bangladesh's parliamentary democracy has been transformed into electoral autocracy, raises grave concerns .... we have .... also become more unequal, more intolerant and hence more prone to violence in our social and political relations, I have written elsewhere

> that Bangladesh has graduated from two economies to two societies. This is dangerous to social and political stability and could even endanger our economic gains (Hassan and Bardhan 2017).

This is an unfortunate development, given the fact that Sheikh Hasina sought to bring about greater decentralisation in governance by increasing the number of regional administrative divisions in the country when she returned to power in 2008 (Sáez 2016). That environment, however, now seems to have changed drastically.

Bangladesh's recurring political instability is compounded by a lack of political accountability and the absence of a system of checks and balances. The lack of institutional mechanisms to restrict and curb authoritarian tendencies as well as the inability to establish the independence of various institutions has led to problems of governance. Nearing 50 years of independence, Bangladesh is yet to conceive, evolve and build strong institutions that would safeguard and guarantee the essence of democracy—a gap that needs to be addressed without any delay.

II

Political and Social Violence

Violence—political and social—constitutes a significant problem in Bangladesh. At every level of society, Bangladesh deals with and confronts acts of violence. Weak governance impedes the polity from effectively controlling violence—organised and unorganised—against different sections of the society. A society deeply polarised between haves and have-nots, with political schisms, and the growth of religious extremism have contributed to this trend. Political violence includes the violent tactics employed by political parties and groups opposed to the government, with an explicit desire to secure a political concession. It also includes protest actions that often transforms into violence or have proven to turn violent, such as *hartals*, *bandhs* (the complete cessation of public activities during a political strike), and other non-parliamentary methods adopted by various political parties. It is this vitiating atmosphere which enables political groups to resort to violence for expressing and achieving their political/social goals that contribute to this vicious cycle. It has been pointed out that the 'government has also indulged in acts of suppression and harassment of political opposition. Both parties have nurtured thugs and criminal elements to intimidate the opposition. Both have attempted to control government and non-government institutions by appointing partisan supporters to head key institutions' (Jahan 2003: 223).

As is well known, political parties employ extra-parliamentary protest actions as an effective means of unseating the elected government, and thereby plunge Bangladesh into perpetual political instability. They rely on street power, *hartals,* and other mass protests to achieve their objectives. Nowadays, religious violence against secular targets is being carried out with an explicit political agenda by Islamic militants. Bangladesh is witnessing signs of social fragmentation due to violence against minorities like the Chakmas, the Hindus and also against women in the form of acid attacks, which is the most lethal and frequently used method. For a country that has been ruled by women since 1991, Bangladesh has the dubious distinction of having a significant number of battered women in the world; as per a survey conducted in 2015, there 41.7 per cent woman affected by violence (Report on Violence against Women Survey 2015).

As evidenced through decades, the cause and growth of violence in Bangladesh is manifold (Datta 2005). Some of them are:

- Presence of an atmosphere of political intolerance and irresponsibility;
- Successive low levels of governance that have impeded effective control over violence, both organised and unorganised, unleashed against different sections of society;
- Complicity of political parties in not allowing the growth of democratic norms and institution-building, while encouraging religious conservatism, leading to extremism that has made the polity more susceptible to violence;
- The dividends of being in power are very high. Consequences of this for electoral gains are the potential for a high level of violence and malpractices.

The rampant political violence unleashed by the opposition has been met through many governmental mechanisms. Some have been controlled through the local police force. At times, the government has had to resort to other security apparatuses. One of the first instances of the government using the army to assist civil administration in fighting growing acts of terror and violence was in October 2002, in a nationwide operation called 'Operation Clean Heart' that lasted for a few months. The government's decision to rely on the army to tackle internal violence underscores a major problem facing Bangladesh. While the action was welcomed initially, it soon came to be perceived as another mechanism for political witch-hunting. Fears about the security forces being entangled 'in partisan conflict and corruption' is not a new trend (Jahan 2003: 225).

Moreover, the Joint Forces Indemnity Act (February 2003), passed by the JS amidst stiff opposition, granted immunity to the army for all its actions during the operation, adding to civilian fears and apprehensions. Subsequently, the BNP government launched a similar operation, 'Spider Web', in July 2003, involving 14,000 personnel from the police, the paramilitary Bangladesh Rifles, the Ansar Militia auxiliary force, and the Coast Guard. The present government has also resorted to dedicated forces to deal with domestic acts of terror. In the aftermath of a one-sided election, when the opposition took to the streets once again, 'rather than resolving the crisis through compromise, the government cracked down and reportedly detained hundreds of opposition activists' (Shah 2016: 132). While violence remains a problem, the concerns arise out of the government's practice to use it to accomplish other political goals. When Sheikh Hasina raised 'special units' within the police structure to deal with acts of terror, analysts cautioned against the government resisting the temptation to use the police for political, partisan ends, noting that the police are a source of instability and fear rather than a key component of a democratic society (International Crisis Group 2009). The spate of attacks against secular bloggers and the Holey Artisan Café attack reiterated the grave problem, that extremism had found its way in to the educated and wealthy social strata, giving the government more reasons to impose further strident security measures. While attacks against minorities have been a recurring problem—although they seemed to peak during the non-Awami rule—the human rights record of the Awami League government is not exemplary (*The Hindu* 2016).

The security apparatus has often been used for political witch-hunting in the face of the increasing number of terror attacks, law and order issues, drug problems; and the government has effectively used the state machinery to clamp them down (US Department of State 2018). In the process, a number of those in the opposition and those critical about the government have had to face severe consequences. As per one report, there are over 300 victims of enforced disappearances who have not been traced (Anam 2018). According to another report, there were 437 extrajudicial killings between January and October 2018, citing crossfire, encounters, etc. (US Department of State 2017). There are a number of similar reports, but the state remains unfazed. Shehryar Fazil summarises the issue succinctly in his report:

> If mainstream avenues of legitimate dissent remain closed and the protections of the law continue to be denied, a rising number of the government's opponents may feel compelled to view violence and violent groups as the most effective alternative force for change. Islamist extremists would then be the ultimate winners (Fazil 2016).

Electoral violence is rampant in Bangladesh. The last Union Parishad (Council) elections held in 2016 (from March through June) 'were carried out with a full panoply of electoral irregularities, including attacks on election officials, and candidate and voter intimidation' (Sáez 2016: 43–49). The last general elections of 2018 were particularly bloody, and it witnessed more than 40 opposition candidates pulling out of the race due to violence over vote-rigging and ballot manipulation. Interestingly, both the major parties dismiss political violence as being natural and do not see any alarming tendencies. In the words of an Awami League senior leader, '... Awami League is a huge political party. There are people with different perspectives which lead to conflicts' (Raju 2018). Similarly, for the BNP, which has fought most of its politics in a bloody battle on the streets, a senior leader explains its behaviour as 'some disputes among the leadership and activists which leads to the clashes. It is completely normal' (ibid.). While violence continues to dominate the polity, the other entrenched issue, that of corruption, continues to vitiate the atmosphere.

Corruption

One of the persistent maladies that plagues Bangladesh is that of corruption; Khaleda Zia continues to serve a prison term on corruption charges. Whether highlighted by multilateral organisations, to recall the fracas over the Padma Bridge project that the World Bank walked out of, or by civil society movements, this toxic issue raises its head periodically. As per a latest report, Bangladesh has scored 26 out of 100 points, and is reasonably well-positioned in South Asia (Transparency International Report 2019). Its ranking at the position of 149 from the top among 180 countries, is marginally better than the previous record of the position of 143 in 2017. While this record is a progress from Bangladesh being the most corrupt country between 2001 and 2005, the present ranking is barely encouraging. The report identifies the systemic issues and points to the 'lack of strong and independent democratic institutions that can deliver checks and balances, and a strong-handed central government that limits or suppresses free and open media and citizen participation' (ibid.). The problem is age-old. As pointed out by Rounaq Jahan, a political scientist, 'Even Sheikh Mujibur Rahman stated repeatedly that he could not get the country moving to rebuild *Sonar Bangla* (golden Bengal) because of widespread corruption around him' (Jahan 2003: 228). This affects every citizen every day in myriad ways, and the international indictment is clear and unambiguous:

> Corruption is a serious problem, and anticorruption efforts have been weakened by politicized enforcement. Due process guarantees are poorly upheld and security forces carry out a range of human right abuses with near impunity. The threat posed by Islamist extremists has receded since 2016, when the government enacted a harsh crackdown that saw the arrest of some 15,000 people (Freedom House 2019).

The pervasive nature of corruption in Bangladesh is also reflective of a general degeneration of societal values and violation of human rights, and a breach of the rule of law. It has been suggested that 'corruption of public morals is at the roots of all corruption in Bangladesh' (Hasmi 2017). While the political leadership has laid the genesis of the problem squarely with the previous military leaders and their practices, after the return of multi-party democracy, successive governments in Dhaka have introduced commissions and other mechanisms for redressal (*The Daily Star* 2019).[8]

This endemic issue has affected a wide variety of sectors—from large infrastructure projects like the Padma Bridge, to the present crises in the state-owned Biman Bangladesh Airlines that has incurred huge losses in recent times. The Anti-Corruption Commission (ACC) has identified a total of 74 sectors—a pervasive problem within Bangladesh. Even local governance is not spared from this malaise, as the distribution of public resources has provisions that appear to be reinforcing a similar culture. The ACC identified 'excessive arbitrary power' by tax officials as one of the biggest sources of corruption (*The Daily Star*, Star Business Report 2018). In an attempt to showcase governmental resolve to address this issue, some 634 government officials were punished for their involvement in irregularities and corruption (*Dhaka Tribune*, Tribune Desk 2019). Not quite unexpectedly, given the schism in the polity, ACC has not been spared the label of being corrupt (*The Daily Star*, Start Business Report 2018).

The stereotypical blame game continues in all aspects of life, including education. Ranging from false certificates, through obtaining certificates on payment, to the pre-planned leakage of question papers, schooling has taken on an entirely different face. Often short-term measures like the recent banning of coaching centres during the ensuing secondary and higher secondary examination period have been undertaken, but these may lead to further complexities (Rahman 2019). This is likely to give rise to other illegal practices and create further layers of graft. Corruption can be traced to the administration of key institutes. While addressing corruption is often shown as the core of political agenda of any government, the commitment needs to move beyond paper and involve the creation of independent functional and accountable institutes. This remains, as yet, unrealised.

Despite the pronounced anti-corruption resolve of the Awami League's leadership, corruption in Bangladesh spans a wide spectrum—from political parties, to businesses to social sectors. Senior politicians on both sides have common business interests and know that corruption charges can never be prosecuted to the full extent because of systemic inefficiency. Significantly, corruption has also been used as a convenient whipping tool in the hands of the government to pursue the opposition. Typically, both political parties, when in power, have used corruption as a political tool against the opposition. In the past, the BNP government had filed a series of corruption cases against the members of the former Sheikh Hasina government, banning a number of Awami personalities from leaving the country, and imprisoning many. In a move reminiscent of personal vendetta, the Awami League government, having faced the brunt of this tool, has now ensured the marginalisation of the opposition on the grounds of corruption. Paradoxically, instances of Awami League leaders continuing to be similarly tainted are not unknown, and the media has been heckled for raising this issue now and again. One of the better-known cases pertains to that of the Railways Minister who retained his position despite being involved in a bribery scandal in 2012. Despite attempts to reform the 'toothless tiger', ACC, which still needs government approval to investigate officials, the institution has not been able to play a bipartisan role (*bdnews24.com* 2011). Although the Bangladesh economy is progressing significantly, it would do better without the debilitating effect of the all-pervasive corruption. Society in Bangladesh has changed through the years, and the introduction of political Islam changed the political discourse for good.

Cohabitation with the Islamists

One of the underlying reasons for East Pakistan, that is, Bangladesh, breaking away from Pakistan was rooted in its seeking cultural autonomy. However, the military leaders engineered constitutional changes, replacing Bengali nationalism with Bangladeshi nationalism, which emphasised the Muslim identity of its citizens and removed secularism from the Constitution. While Mujibur Rahman's idea of *Sonar Bangla* was one that included the tenets of secularism, socialism, democracy and Bengali nationalism, his invitation to join the Organisation of Islamic Cooperation (OIC) in Pakistan in 1974 was a reflection of the growing Bangladeshi need to reinforce its Muslim identity (Rashiduzzaman 1977: 797). The BNP, given its different lineage of belonging to the barracks, positioned itself differently and did not hesitate to reach out to religion to seek sanctity and differentiate itself from the Awami League. As it unfolded, for the post-Mujibur leaders, Islam emerged as the identity and the mobilising force, and the Islamic identity of the State began to be the focus and agenda of the leaders. Gradually, Islamisation of the society started taking place at the political, cultural, and constitutional levels. However, after General Ziaur Rahman's military coup, the Constitution was amended, and 'Bangladeshi' nationalism, with an emphasis on Islamic identity, was introduced. The new Constitution, introduced in 1977, eliminated secularism, replacing it with 'absolute trust and faith in the almighty Allah'. In the post-1979 elections, Bangladesh began its move towards Islamic 'legalism' (Pipes 1983: 208), and the Preamble was amended to begin with a salutation to Allah. Unlike in the Mujibur Rahman era, Islamic groups were allowed to form political parties. Islam was declared a State religion in 1988, excluding more than 12 per cent of Hindu minorities from the concept of a nation-state.

In the post-Mujibur Rahman era, the 'concept of Bangladeshi nationalism evolved into the principal ideology for a large section of Bangladesh's political and military establishment', and was soon adopted by the Centre-Right and Rightist political parties (Absar 2014). This contestation over differing conceptions of national identity—a cultural/ethnic 'Bengali' nationalism associated with the Awami League, and the more religious 'Bangladeshi' nationalism—is rooted in its liberation history (Shah 2016). As Islamisation was gaining ground, the Awami League, which was popularly viewed through the lens of secularism, was unable to alienate the mass appeal of religion, and yet was wary of embracing extremist positions. The BNP, in contrast, has been receptive towards, and even encouraged, the Islamisation process, and some have argued that the BNP is no different from the Jamaat-e-Islami or the JP—

the harbinger of Islamisation of Bangladesh (Murshid 1995). The expansion of the Gulf-backed Wahabi Islamist agenda in Bangladesh happened subsequently. In the past, military leaders sought legitimacy through the Islamic religious leaders. Now every shade of political leader, including those from the Awami League, has chosen to stay on the right side of the Islamists, not taking into account the long-term consequences of their narrower agenda.

Since 1991, the Awami League has courted Islamic groups, and prior to the 2014 elections, struck an alliance with the hardliner Hefazat-i-Islam—a move carried out to protect its political ground in the country. This forcible realignment of the polity to the right of Islam was done within the framework and dynamics of a pluralist democracy. After its 1991 defeat, the once firmly secularist Awami League began using Islamic language in a rhetorical shift that added legitimacy to political Islam (Alamgir 2009). In this context, the 2001 elections assumed critical importance. For the first time, the Jamaat-e-Islami (coalition partner with the BNP) was given two vital ministerial berths. Various government measures provided tacit support to the Islamists, attributed to the presence of the Jamaat-e-Islami in the ruling coalition (Riaz 2005). Since then, there has been no looking back. Arguably, Sheikh Hasina attempted to restore the 1972 secular Constitution through the fifteenth Amendment, but Islam remains the State religion, and interestingly, the Court took just two minutes to dismiss a petition that challenged Islam's role as the State religion in March 2016 (*The Economist* 2016).

Despite the Amendment, there is a distinct consolidation of the Islamist agenda, or a reversal to the politics of the ideological centre. The growth of fundamentalism, the atmosphere of social and political intolerance, and the lack of secular space have all contributed to a growing 'religiousness' in the State. A report states, 'When, for political convenience, a majoritarian community starts aggressively projecting its self-righteousness above all and seeks to compel others to conform, it transgresses a red line and strays into very murky territory that is defined by intolerance and contemptuous rejection of "the other"' (Karim 2018). The political leaders courting the strident Islamists points towards a deeper issue that confronts the Bangladeshi polity presently. In contradictory moves, while the country protested against the light sentence delivered to a Jamaat leader and an impromptu movement in Shahbag Square that was started by students, secularists and activists, it was Hefazat-e-Islam that openly attacked the secular protesters, killing one and injuring several others, while murdering several prosecution witnesses from the country's Hindu minority, which has traditionally supported the Awami League (Shah 2016: 134). The dichotomy between the secular ethos and Islamic stridency was, in fact, put to rest when the Awami League government allowed the secular movement to be overtaken by the Islamists.

Some of the key factors that aid the extremists' growth in Bangladesh, which exploit people via political violence, include the presence of an increasingly polarised political situation and the politicisation of state institutions. This has indirectly created an atmosphere for the Islamic State and home-grown extremist groups to thrive in (Khan 2017). Singapore's deportation of 26 Bangladeshi labourers for supporting the armed *jihad* (a struggle guided by belief) ideology has pointed to domestic groups having established networks among expatriate Bangladeshis (BTI 2018 Country Report). In a bid to stop the alienation, the government moved to recognise Madrasa degrees as equivalent to university degrees in 2017, enabling 1.4 million students studying in 14,000 Qawami Madrasas (Ahmed 2015) to compete with students from the mainstream education system. The jury remains out on this decision. While it may bring about greater assimilation of the youth with the mainstream, it may also have several implications in terms of diluting the education standards and norms that Bangladeshi educationists are working to make internationally relevant.

III

Civil–Military Relation

As the political institutions in Bangladesh remain fragile, the role of the military and its influence over the political developments remain a concern. As was seen, given their role in the Liberation War and subsequent events, the military has always been highly politicised, and the coups and counter-coups during the early years revealed a deep ideological split within the military (Maniruzzaman 1992: 204).

The army, which went back to the barracks in 1990, continues to wield influence in numerous ways, and its role still remains open-ended. While it is popularly argued that the military is content to stay behind the scenes, much of it is owing to international pressure and not wanting to jeopardise its rather lucrative annual earnings (estimated to be more than five times its earnings in Bangladesh) from its United Nations (UN) peacekeeping role (Haque 2012). The military's ability to wield influence over the political system in Bangladesh, however, still remains intact. Not only was their actual strength increased during General Ershad's government, but the substantial increase in the defence budget and provisions for opening up corporate sectors as well as civilian posts for military personnel has also changed the course of history (Maniruzzaman 1992: 204).

Continuing with past practices, retired military personnel have an active public life, and this has been encouraged and has been evident under different governments. The willingness of the leaders of the Awami League and the BNP to engage with the military was obvious during many instances, even in the post-1991 period. Thus, when Khaleda Zia brought in the army to improve the law-and-order situation in Bangladesh in the period 2001–06, launching a countrywide 'Operation Clean Heart', the main opposition, the Awami League, neither opposed nor questioned the legality of this action (Jahan 2003: 222).

The military's role was certainly most distinct during the two years of the CG. The imposition of Emergency and the suspension of certain rights by the CG would not have been possible without the backing of the army (two of the 10 advisors to the Chief Advisor, Fakhruddin, were retired generals). Likewise, Choudhury, who revamped the ACC successfully, was also a retired army officer. Above all, the CG could expand its functions and mandate, primarily because of the backing of the armed forces. The military was actively involved in the revision and updating of electoral rolls. The political reforms undertaken during the 23-month period were possible only with the support of the military and its influence over political life. The military emerged as a real power behind the CG. Interfering in the unfolding political developments, the Chief of Staff, Lt. Gen. Moeen U. Ahmed, went to the extent of redefining democracy in

Bangladeshi terms (*The Daily Star* 2007). The military during this period was said to be behind the infamous 'minus two formula', which would not have endeared the CG to either of the *netris*, with both of them having to serve prison terms briefly during that CG period. While many have questioned the military's position to stay behind the scenes, it has been argued that the 'military's complete takeover would have raised serious questions about its credibility in imposing democratic and legitimate governments in other parts of the world under the UN auspices' (Uz Zaman and Biswas 2014: 325).

Historically, the BNP was closer to the military establishment, while the Awami League's appeal lay more with the civil society. One of the first challenges that Sheikh Hasina faced was the mutiny by the paramilitary Bangladesh Rifles. Although it was quelled quickly, the government soon took measures to work with them closely, and there was a clear twinning happening between the Awami League and the military.

Through various mechanisms, the military pay scales have risen, the arms budget has grown, with expansion in manpower, firepower, equipment, and additions to the army's business portfolio, including another luxury hotel as well as a cattle ranch. The government has used military agencies to carry out many of their demands.[9] As per a recent Global Fire Power Index, Bangladesh has been ranked the fifty-seventh most powerful military power in the world for a country that has limited security threat perception. This says much. As noted by a commentator, ' ... [AL] they have taken complete control of the military, not by using power but by sharing the money .... The risks are obvious .... the military is getting used to these augmented privileges. This is absolutely dangerous for the sustaining of democracy in this country' (Mallet 2015). In a growing trend, retired army officers are pledging support to the Awami League.

Although written in an earlier context, this assessment still holds well in the present situation:

> It has been widely recognized that the failure of Bangladeshi leaders to reform and democratize the polity would result in undemocratic tendencies in the long run. Absence of any far-reaching systemic changes within the polity is an invitation for military intervention

> and the next time round the army might be more ambitious than during the tenure of this CG (Datta 2008: 16).

In the long term, democracy rests on a stable civil–military relationship. The fear of the military not using restraint in an unstable political situation can never be fully allayed. Political instability would be an open invitation for military intervention. Without formally taking over the reins of power, the military might use an unelected interim administration to rule Bangladesh. Given the history of coups and counter-coups, internecine domestic confrontation always opens up the window for the military to intervene. In one of the last such actions, the challenge came in the form of a bloody mutiny by paramilitary border guards, who took army officers hostage, and slew 56 of them in late-February 2009 (Alamgir 2009: 52). Given the uncertainties in the evolving situation, the civil society keenly engaged with the implications of such eventualities on different occasions, by suggesting the introduction of greater checks and balances through the formation of institutions and structures for national security. The political leadership, however, has shown no interest (*Prothom Alo*, Staff Correspondent 2016).

The civil–military relations in Bangladesh have seen varying hues in the last few years. The military's political ambition and the possibility of the wild card element can never be ruled out. At the same time, the Awami League's growing close association with the military, in the hope of political dividends, may also counter their political ambition. An interesting argument about the role of the military is premised on the role played by them in the post-liberation phase, which has made it difficult to locate it in the traditional model of civil–military relations. Rashed Uz Zaman and Niloy Ranjan Biswas thus conclude that 'Bangladesh has been involved in an elusive quest for an appropriate framework to govern civil–military relations and delineate the armed forces' role vis-à-vis Bangladeshi society' (2014: 341). As has been pointed out, 'finding the right balance remains a challenge' (Alamgir 2009: 52). The role of the military in the political landscape of Bangladesh remains a matter of speculation. The complicity of the government is giving rise to most of the issues that afflict Bangladesh today, and this is where the problem lies.

Concluding Remarks

The slogan, 'It's the economy, stupid', was made immortal by the campaign managers of former US President, Bill Clinton. The present Bangladeshi leadership, too, seems to be internalising a similar narrative. There is much to celebrate, such as, overcoming the initial constraints, economic achievements, improvement in social indicators like mortality rate, life expectancy and immunisation, which have all been remarkable. The economic progress has led to an emerging middle class, but the nation's growth is not taking place in a vacuum; both internal and external factors will shape and influence the political discourse. Bangladesh is well-poised to use its locational advantage and leverage the regional and sub-regional momentum. Thus, how it manages some of its core governance issues will be critical for its journey ahead.

Much of Bangladesh's domestic volatility has been rooted in its inability to have a closure of its Liberation War. The war wounds remained open, and much of the political strife revolved around it. Bringing the collaborators to task was thus a highlight in the 2008 JS election campaign by Sheikh Hasina. Soon after taking charge, she set up the International Criminal Tribunals (ICT) in 2009 to examine and prosecute those who had acted against East Pakistan's struggle for liberation from West Pakistan. The exhaustive list, including those who had committed atrocities against innocent civilians during the nine-month war, seemed to be a sound ground to address the longstanding grievances. It was hoped that the ICT would help Bangladesh to put its history behind and build on its foundation rather than create dissonance. Unfortunately, both the composition of the panel of jurists and its judgements became rather controversial and led to further chaos.

Bangladeshis have demonstrated their impatience with authoritarian leaders in the past, and the last 50 years has been a struggle to ensure political freedom. People have taken to the streets when their political rights seemed to be slighted. Presently, the underlying concerns about democracy, rule of law, and fundamental human rights and freedom continue to arise. The concern is also that as Bangladeshis seems to be adjusting with the times, political tiredness seems palpable. After being subjected to political instability for years, people finally seem to be adapting to the stability and controlled environment that now exists. The priorities for the growing large section of the youth population revolves around the quality of life that the growing nation is able to offer and the services it provides. If Bangladesh's history is the window, suppression of political freedom, and stymying of liberal thoughts and choices will not be a way of life for long. The institutionalisation of democracy and allowing space for robust politics will lead to greater growth and progress. The onus lies on the political parties and the civil society to ensure a way forward.

NOTES

1. Attributed to Henry Kissinger in Dhaka during 1974.
2. In 1996, the Awami League won 50 seats, which the BNP had won five years earlier. In 2001, the BNP won 89 seats that the Awami League had won in 1996. And in 2008, the Awami League won 145 seats that the BNP had won in 2001.
3. *Hartal* essentially refers to closure of shops/offices/business establishments, and even transport systems as a protest or a mark of sorrow. This tool is often used by political leaders in the region.
4. The vote strength of the other political parties within the Awami League coalition include: Workers Party of Bangladesh, three seats, Jatiya Party, one seat, Bikalpadhara Bangladesh, two seats, and Jatiya Samajtantrik Dal, two seats.
5. The CG was to hold office for a maximum period of 90 days, within which the elections had to be held. The Chief Advisor was to be the last retired Chief Justice of the Supreme Court, who would form this interim government within 15 days of the dissolution of the parliament, with a group of specialists, chosen through the process of an all-party consensus.
6. The BNP, during its term, had a similar track record, and the arrest of Shariar Kabir, among many other intellectuals who protested against the attacks on Hindu minorities, is well-documented.
7. According to a survey conducted by the *Dhaka Tribune,* 74 per cent of the citizenry continued to support the war crime trials till the end of 2013, despite its serious legal flaws.
8. These mechanisms include the Anti-Corruption Commission, State Party to the UN Convention against Corruption, which we have the Right to Information (RTI) Act, and Whistle Blower Protection Act, National Integrity Strategy.

9. The government used military agencies to control the board of the Islami Bank, Bangladesh, through the physical removal of their board members in 2017.

References

'2018 Country Report', *Bertelsmann Stiftung's Transformation Index*, Bertelsmann Stiftung, 2018. Available at https://www.bti-project.org/fileadmin/files/BTI/Downloads/Reports/2018/pdf/BTI_2018_Bangladesh.pdf (accessed 7 May 2019).

Absar, A. B. M. Nviolurul. 2014. 'Muslim Identity, Bengali Nationalism: An Analysis on Nationalism in Bangladesh', *Academic Journal of Interdisciplinary Studies* 3(1): 444.

ADB, Bangladesh and ADB. Bangladesh, ADB Country Reports, Asian Development Outlook 2019. Available at https://www.adb.org/countries/bangladesh/economy (accessed 7 May 2019).

Ahmed, Mustak, '1.4 m Students Study in 14,000 Qawmi Madrasas', *Prothom Alo*, 24 May 2015. Available at https://en.prothomalo.com/bangladesh/14-lakh-students-study-in-14-000-Qawmi-madrasas (accessed 7 May 2019).

Alam, Shahidul, 'Jailed Journalist's Powerful Photos of Bangladesh', *BBC News*, 15 August 2018a. Available at https://www.bbc.com/news/world-asia-45173303 (accessed 7 May 2019).

———, 'Khan Denial is Not the End of Responsibility Between Policing and Serving', *The Daily Star*, 31 August 2018b. Available at https://www.thedailystar.net/news/opinion/strategically-speaking/between-policing-and-serving-1626691 (accessed 7 May 2019).

Alamgir, Jalal. 2009. 'Bangladesh's Fresh Start', *Journal of Democracy* 20(3): 44.

'Amendment to Strip ACC of Freedom', *bdnews24.com*, 29 January 2011. Available at https://bdnews24.com/business/2011/01/29/amendment-to-strip-acc-of-freedom-tib1 (accessed 7 November 2018).

'Bangladesh Should have Own Brand of Democracy', *The Daily Star*, 21 February 2008. Available at https://www.thedailystar.net/news-detail-24266 (accessed 7 May 2019).

'Bangladesh's Slide Towards Authoritarianism is Accelerating', *The Economist*, 4 October 2018. Available at https://www.economist.com/asia/2018/10/04/bangladeshs-slide-towards-authoritarianism-is-accelerating (accessed 7 May 2019).

'Campaign of Terror against Bangladesh's Liberal Voices', *The Economist*, 27 April 2016. Available at https://www.economist.com/asia/2016/04/27/campaign-of-terror-against-bangladeshs-liberal-voices (accessed 7 June 2019).

'Corruption Can be Found Even at ACC: NBR Chairman', *The Daily Star*, 12 November 2018. Available at https://www.thedailystar.net/business/news/corruption-can-be-found-even-acc-nbr-chairman-1659277 (accessed 7 May 2019).

Datta, Sreeradha. 2004. *Bangladesh: A Fragile Democracy*. New Delhi: Shipra Publications.

———. 2005. 'Political Violence in Bangladesh: Trends and Causes', *Strategic Analysis* 29(3): 441.

———. 2008. *Caretaking Democracy: Political Process in Bangladesh, 2006–08*. New Delhi: Magnum Books.

Fazil, Shehryar, 'Bangladesh Government Must Step Back from Chaos', *Crises Group Report*, 8 April 2016. Available at https://www.crisisgroup.org/asia/south-asia/bangladesh/bangladesh-government-must-step-back-chaos (accessed 7 May 2019).

'Freedom in the World Report 2019', *Freedom House*, 2019. Available at https://freedomhouse.org/report/freedom-world/2019/bangladesh (accessed 7 May 2019).

Haque, Nicolas, 'Bangladesh Troops Lead Global Peacekeeping', Al Jazeera, 30 May 2012. Available at https://www.aljazeera.com/indepth/features/2012/05/201252982553900996.html (accessed 7 May 2019).

Hasmi, Taj, 'Corruption in Bangladesh: Perception Vs Reality', *The Daily Star*, 4 February 2017.

Hassan, Sohrab, and Protik Bardhan, 'Interview: Polls Prospect Not Promising', *Prothom Alo*, 16 December 2017. Available at https://en.prothomalo.com/opinion/news/167979/Polls-prospect-not-promising-Rehman-Sobhan (accessed 12 June 2019).

Hena, Mohammad Abu, 'The Challenge Before the Election Commission', *The Daily Star*, 17 March 2013. Available at https://www.thedailystar.net/news/the-challenge-before-the-election-commission (accessed 7 May 2019).

Hossain, Akhtan. 2000. 'Anatomy of *Hartal* Politics in Bangladesh', *Asian Survey* 40(3): 521.

Hossain, M. Sakhawat, 'No Public Confidence in Election', *Prothom Alo*, 1 March 2019. Available at https://en.prothomalo.com/opinion/news/191876/No-public-confidence-in-election (accessed 7 May 2019).

International Crisis Group 2009. Report 182/Asia, 'Bangladesh Getting Police Reform on Track', *Crises Group,* 11 December 2009. Available at https://www.crisisgroup.org/asia/south-asia/bangladesh/bangladesh-getting-police-reform-track (accessed 7 May 2019).

Jahan, Rounaq. 2003. 'Bangladesh in 2002: Imperiled Democracy', *Asian Survey* 43(1): 222–29.

Jamal, Eresh Omar, 'Corruption is Anti-development', *The Daily Star,* 9 December 2017. Available at https://www.thedailystar.net/opinion/interviews/corruption-anti-development-1502296 (accessed 7 May 2019).

Karim, Tariq, 'Bangladesh's Travails: An Unendless Saga', *The Daily Star,* 12 June 2018. Available at https://www.thedailystar.net/opinion/bangladeshs-travails-relentless-saga-1589785 (accessed 7 May 2019).

Karlekar, Hiranmay. 2005. *Bangladesh: The Next Afghanistan.* New Delhi: Sage Publications.

Khan, Shahab Enam. 2017. 'Bangladesh: The Changing Dynamics of Violent, Extremism and the Response of the State', *Small Wars and Insurgencies* 28(1): 191–217.

Lorch, Jasmin, 'Elections in Bangladesh: Political Conflict and the Problem of Credibility', *International Security and Network,* 10 February 2014.

Mallet, Victor, 'Bangladesh Army Funded to Forget its Role as Neutral Referee', *Financial Times,* 26 April 2015. Available at https://www.ft.com/content/7baf6f5c-ea74-11e4-a701-00144feab7de (accessed 12 June 2019).

Maniruzzaman, Talukder. 1992. 'The Fall of the Military Dictator: 1991 Elections and the Prospect of Civilian Rule in Bangladesh', *Pacific Affairs* 65(2): 203–04.

Murshid, Tazeen M. 1995. 'Democracy in Bangladesh: Illusion or Reality', *Contemporary South Asia* 4(2): 203.

'No Hindus will be Left in Bangladesh after 30 Years: Professor', *The Hindu,* 2 November 2016. Available at https://www.thehindu.com/news/international/No-Hindus-will-be-left-in-Bangladesh-after-30-years-professor/article16675228.ece (accessed 7 May 2019).

Pipes, Daniel. 1983. *In the Path of God: Islam and Political Power.* New York: Basic Books.

Rahman, Mahmudur, 'When There is Corruption in Education', *Dhaka Tribune,* 24 January 2019. Available at https://www.dhakatribune.com/opinion/op-ed/2019/01/24/when-there-is-corruption-in-education (accessed 7 May 2019).

Raju, Fazlur Rahman, 'Five Years of Political Violence: 1,028 Deaths and 52,000 Injuries', *Dhaka Tribune*, 17 November 2018. Available at https://www.dhakatribune.com/bangladesh/2017/11/20/1028-deaths-53000-injuries (accessed 7 May 2019).

Rashiduzzaman, M. 1977. 'Changing Political Patterns in Bangladesh: Internal Constraints and External Fears', *Asian Survey* 17(9): 4.

Report, 'Violence against Women (VAW) Survey 2015', Statistics and Informatics Division, Ministry of Planning Government of the People's Republic of Bangladesh, August 2016. Available at http://evaw-global-database.unwomen.org/-/media/files/un%20women/vaw/vaw%20survey/bangladesh%20vaw%20survey%202015.pdf?vs=2125 (accessed 7 May 2019).

———, 'Bangladesh 2018 Human Right Report', US State Department, 2017. Available at https://www.state.gov/documents/organization/289486.pdf (accessed 7 May 2019).

Riaz, Ali. 2005. 'Bangladesh in 2004: The Politics of Vengeance and the Erosion of Democracy', *Asian Survey* 45(1): 113.

Schaffer, Howard B. 2002. 'Back and Forth in Bangladesh', *Journal of Democracy* 13(1): 79.

'Tiger in the Night', *The Economist*, 15 October 2016. Available at https://www.economist.com/asia/2016/10/15/tiger-in-the-night (accessed 7 May 2019).

Staff Correspondent, 'Civil Military Relation', *Prathom Alo*, 29 July 2016. Available at https://en.prothomalo.com/opinion/news/114111/Civil-military-relations (accessed 7 May 2019).

———, 'Owners, Workers May Quit Transport Business, Threatens Shajahan', *New Age*, 03 May 2019. Available at http://www.newagebd.net/article/71343/owners-workers-may-quit-transport-business-threatens-shajahan (accessed 12 June 2019).

Sáez, Lawrence. 2016. 'Bangladesh in 2016, Transition and Turmoil Intertwined', *Asian Survey* 57(1): 43–49.

Shah, Aqil, 'Democracy Deadlocked in Bangladesh', *Current History*, April 2016.

Star Business Report, 'Corruption can be Found Even at ACC: NBR Chairman', *The Daily Star*, 12 November 2018. Available at https://www.thedailystar.net/business/news/corruption-can-be-found-even-acc-nbr-chairman-1659277 (accessed 7 May 2019).

'Ten Years of Seperation of Judiciary and the State of Judicial Independence', *The Daily Star*, 21 November 2017. Available at https://www.thedailystar.net/law-our-rights/ten-years-separation-judiciary-and-the-state-judicial-independence-1494130 (accessed 7 May 2019).

Tribune Desk, '634 Govt Officials Punished for Irregularities, Corruption', *Dhaka Tribune,* 8 April 2019. Available at https://www.dhakatribune.com/bangladesh/government-affairs/2019/04/08/634-govt-officials-punished-for-irregularities-corruption (accessed 7 May 2019).

Transformation Index BTI. 2018, Bangladesh Country Report, 'BTI 2018: Bangladesh Country Report', *Bertelsmann Stiftung Transformation Index.* Available at https://www.bti-project.org/en/reports/country-reports/detail/itc/BGD/ (accessed 7 May 2019).

Transparency International Report, 'Asia Pacific: Little or No Progress on Anti-Progress', 29 January 2019. Available at https://www.transparency.org/news/feature/asia_pacific_makes_little_to_no_progress_on_anti_corruption (accessed 7 May 2019).

'Uproot Graft Drug Menance', *The Daily Star,* 21 January 2019. Available at https://www.thedailystar.net/country/free-bangladesh-from-corruption-drug-abuse-militancy-prime-minister-sheikh-hasina-1690213 (accessed 7 May 2019).

US Department of State. 2018. 'The Antinarcotics Drive during May–June 2017 Resulted in Approximately 230 Alleged Drug Dealers Killed and 17,000 Arrests: Bangladesh Human Rights Report 2017', State Department Report. Available at https://www.state.gov/documents/organization/289486.pdf (accessed 7 May 2019).

Uz Zaman, Rashed, and Niloy Ranjan Biswas. 2014. 'Bangladesh's Participation in UN Peacekeeping Missions and Challenges for Civil–Military Relations: A Case for Concordance Theory', *International Peacekeeping* 21(3): 324–44.

7

Women, Development and Empowerment

The Bangladesh Context

AMENA MOHSIN

Development and empowerment are problematic concepts from the perspective of women. This chapter argues that development and empowerment for women are as much linked to economics as they are to culture and societal factors. The idea of power and power relations between gender is integral to the processes of development and empowerment; for a woman, the personal is political, it is the arena where power relations, gender roles and spaces are defined. Taking this arithmetic into cognisance, this chapter traces, through the processes of development (this includes political, economic and societal factors) women's empowerment and their position within these processes. Indeed, the woman is not a homogenous category, and the location varies across class, religion, ethnicity and one's relationship to power. It may be noted that the factors are interlinked, and flow into each other. Empowerment is a process embedded in socio-political and economic factors. It also includes the participation of women in these processes, their voices, and the acquisition of their capability to take decisions that bring about positive changes in their lives, and through it, changes in the structures that regulate their lives. Change in power relations is the key factor in this empowerment process.

The internationalisation of the woman question by the United Nations (UN), and through it, the State taking cognisance of it at the policy levels, played a critical role in this process. This came through the activism of various rights and women's movements groups. Their demands led to the adoption of various conventions. In 1970, the General Assembly, for the first time, included in the International Development Strategy for the Second Development

Decade the importance of encouraging the full integration of women into the total development effort. The UN had declared 1975 as International Women's Year, and the first UN Conference on 'Women in Development' was held in 1975. The period from 1976–85 was declared as women's decade. The objectives of the Conference were peace, equality and development. Equality of women in all spheres of life was a major objective behind this movement, and thus, for women, development was not confined to economics; rather, it was a move towards empowerment, efficiency, equity and justice. The Conference emphasised that women's work needs to be recognised as work. This recognition was considered vital for the rightful and just place of women in society; and more critically, to visibilise them in the public sphere.

Over the years, States experimented with different approaches to integrate women into the development process. It was recognised that women had both practical and strategic needs. Practical needs addressed the day-to-day issues of women, and strategic needs questioned the fundamentals, that is, subordination of women. It was felt that it was necessary to make interventions in the socio-cultural practices that designated the woman into a stereotypical role and kept her within the private domain. Both religious and secular discourses are intertwined here (Mohsin 2016).

Women contribute to half of the world population and a considerable proportion of the labour force worldwide (globally, 47.862 per cent) (World Bank 2018). Many scholars in the development sector, especially Amartya Sen, as cited by Naila Kabeer (Kabeer 1999), see development from a humanitarian perspective where development focuses not only on economic growth, but also on the people who are the drivers of development. Skills and capabilities that enable a person to make critical life choices to advance in life on his/her terms, and their ability to exercise the same, are important to bring about development. Feminist scholars support the idea of a development process that can empower a woman economically and socially, that is, which can free women from gender roles and other diminishing social relations and norms. Kabeer sought to measure women's empowerment through their access to resources, not necessarily only the productive ones;

agency and achievements. Thus, women's access and control over the resources which they can actively decide and choose to act upon are similar to Amartya Sen's idea of capabilities, according to Kabeer (Kabeer 1999: 435–38).

The 'Human Development Report', prepared by the United Nations Development Programme (UNDP), has adopted the ideas of the capabilities approach and has introduced an analysis for measuring development by assessing three factors: life expectancy, knowledge or education, and standard of living (Gross National Income [GNI] per capita). The organisation also included a gender dimension in its report by segregating the male and female Human Development Index (HDI) and comparing their differences. Bangladesh is placed 136 in the HDI ranking and placed higher in Gross Domestic Income (GDI) (UNDP 2018). Women have higher life expectancy at the time of birth than men in Bangladesh, but in terms of other indicators, they lag behind men. In the Gender Inequality Index (GII), with education and life expectancy, the employment and political participation of women were considered. Bangladesh stood 134 out of 160 countries in this Index (ibid.). In the Global Gender Gap Report 2018 prepared by the World Economic Forum, Bangladesh ranked 47 among nearly 200 countries (World Economic Forum 2018).

The following is an attempt to trace the development and empowerment question in Bangladesh, through the paths taken and the interrogations made in addressing the woman question.

The Political Domain (Mohsin 2009)

The Constitution of Bangladesh, in its Articles 9, 10, 27, 28(1), 28(2), 28(3), 28(4) and 65(3), calls for equality of women in all spheres of life, and ensures women's participation in national and local politics. The Constitution also states that the government can make special laws for improving the status of women. The State is also a signatory to the Convention on Elimination of all Forms of Discrimination against Women (CEDAW).[1] Initially, it had imposed reservations on CEDAW Articles 2, 13(a), 16-1(c) and 16-1(f) on the ground that they conflict with the traditional law and the Sharia law based on the Holy Quran. In1997, the government withdrew its reservations from Articles 13(a) and 16-1(f). The reservations on Articles 2 and 16-1 (c), however, remain; the government position is that they are in conflict with the Sharia law.

It needs to be stressed that the State and the society have constructed gender roles and gender spaces. In this formulation, women are relegated to the private sphere, while men belong to the public sphere. The latter is in fact visible, while the private is the sacrosanct space, and needs to be protected by men and patriarchal ethos (Chatterjee 1989). Due to the private–public divide, women have remained under-represented in the formal arena of politics all over the world, and to redress their exclusion, quotas were considered as a global fast-track strategy (Mohsin 2010). It has been regarded as an effective tool for ensuring women's presence and visibility at various levels of political structure. This, however, raises the critical question of strategic gender needs, and if quotas could indeed pave the way for women's empowerment without addressing the core issue of power relations and the patriarchal structure of the society. Moreover, bringing in more women into the political arena without addressing the issue of patriarchal structure only reinforces the existing patriarchy, without addressing the power equation within the operating patriarchal paradigm.

Sincc 1991, Bangladesh has been in a unique position, where the leader in position and leader of the opposition are both women. The present parliament is an exception are both in the last two parliaments, Bangladesh has had a woman Speaker of the Parliament. Despite these, women's representation remains low in politics. Major factors behind this, as stated earlier, are patriarchy and the public–private divide. The divisions between public and private lives are, however, often blurred in the daily lives of women in Bangladesh, and their spaces and roles are defined repeatedly as private, resulting in exclusion from politics. The socio-cultural practices of sex-segregation and *purdah* (veil) are also responsible for restricting women's mobility to interact with the public. However, it needs to be emphasised that increasingly, *purdah* is being redefined by women as a mode of inclusion and of greater mobility in the public sphere; according to women, it provides them with greater social respectability and acceptability. Arguably, this is a male-centric argument, which allows a woman space in the public sphere, but within norms defined by men.

The Constitution of Bangladesh grants fundamental rights to its citizens, irrespective of sex, race and religion (Article 36–39), and it does not discriminate between women and men in respect of contesting and voting for public representative offices (Article 66, 122). In fact, through Article 65, the Constitution also provides for reserved seats for women in order to ensure their participation in the legislature and in local government institutions (Article 9). The Constitution articulates the necessary steps towards facilitating women's participation in all spheres of national life (Article 9), and grants permission to adopt special measures in favour of women and children (Article 28); this gives legitimacy for affirmative actions in order to attain gender equality and equity in the political arena.

The Constitution of Bangladesh also provides for a 300-member parliament known as the Jatiya Sangsad (National Parliament), with 50 seats reserved for women. Both men and women can contest directly for these 300 seats, while the 50 seats are reserved for women. The latter are nominated or elected indirectly by the elected members of parliament.

Despite the high visibility in politics of the two women leaders, Sheikh Hasina and Begum Khaleda Zia, an integrated presence of women in the top echelons of party leadership or in the ministerial cabinets could not be ensured. Ironically, as we will see later in this chapter, women are enthusiastic voters and their participation as voters is high. Political parties like the Awami League and the BNP have also incorporated gender concerns into their manifestos. They have mainly remained confined within the practical gender needs. Strategic needs are perhaps considered too volatile and sensitive as an electoral issue. Parties are regarded as the gatekeepers in the world of politics. Unless they categorically speak out for women, the dream of creating a 'critical mass' will remain unfulfilled. Tables 7.1 and 7.2 illustrate these points well. Women's representation in decision-making forums in political parties remains low, with numbers in central working committees varying between 2.7 per cent and 11.2 per cent.

Table 7.1 Female Members in the Party Hierarchy of Major Parties in Bangladesh

Committee	*AL*	*BNP*	*Jatiya Party*	*JSD*	*Workers' Party*	*Communist Party*	*Gonoforum*
Presidium and Secretariat	5 (36)	—	—	—	—	—	—
Central Working Committee	8 (71)	11 (148)	10 (346)	4 (112)	2 (53)	4 (45)	6 (100)
Percentage	11.2	7.4	2.8	3.5	3.78	8.8	6

Source: (Mohsin 2009: 48).

The Exercise of Voting Rights

Although women's participation in the political domain is low, an increasing number of women have participated in successive elections, which indicates their interest in engaging with democratic decision-making processes. The percentage of women voters have increased from 48.42 per cent out of a total voter list of 75 million in 2001, to 50.87 per cent out of a voter list of 81.05 million in 2008. Women voters have significantly increased from 27.95 million in 1996 to 41.23 million in 2008 (Figure 7.1). However, no sex-disaggregated data is available to discern the voting pattern of women. Women members of political parties have been very active in house-to-house campaigns, and in addressing political meetings. The role of media in projecting women's voice and concerns has also been critical in the 2008 elections. In the last general election held in 2018, women constituted 49.57 per cent of the total voters, and at least 103 out of 300 electoral areas had more female voters than male (Mondal 2018).

Again, the Cabinet, which is the highest level of the executive branch of the government, has traditionally witnessed marginal representation, or at times, no representation of women. In the past, three things were noteworthy: first, the number of women with full ministerial status had never reached more than two in a cabinet of 40 or 60 ministers. Second, women ministers, Deputy Ministers and Ministers of State were mainly allocated portfolios that were not regarded as important, and were often associated with the term 'feminine' ministries. These include Women and Children Affairs,

Figure 7.1 Trends of Women Voters in Bangladesh, 1979–2008

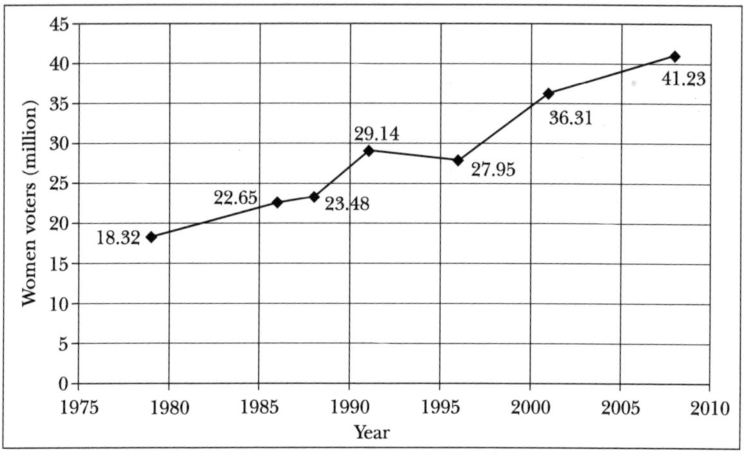

Note: Data for the figure is based on the author's compilation.
Source: Mohsin (2009).

Table 7.2 Women in Cabinet

Period	*Total Minister*	*Female Minister*	*Percentage of Women Minister*
1972–75 (Awami League)	50	2	4.0
1976–82 (BNP)	101	6	5.9
1982–90 (Jatiya Party)	133	4	3.0
1991–1996 (BNP)	39	3	7.7
1996–2001 (Awami League)	42	4	9.5
2001–2006 (BNP-led Coalition Government)	60	3	5.0
2009 (Awami League-led Mohajote)	32	5	15.62
2014 (Awami League-led Mohajote)	50	5	10
2019 (Awami League-led Mohajote)	47	4	8.51

Note: Data for the table is based on the author's compilation.
Source: Mohsin (2009).

Social Welfare, Cultural Affairs, Primary Education, etc. Third, most such ministers were not elected directly, and hence, lacked the political strength to exercise authority in the Cabinet. The last Cabinet was a major exception and departure from the past, where important ministries like Foreign Affairs and Home Ministry, were held by women who are elected as Members of Parliament (MP). The present Cabinet has a woman Education Minister, a woman Deputy Minister for the Ministry of Environment, Forest and Climate Change, and a woman State Minister for the Ministry of Labour and Employment.

The appointment of women who had been directly elected into these positions with full ministerial ranks is indeed a major departure and an important factor in the process of empowerment of women. It will be interesting to watch if these inductions would result in, or at the minimum, start the process of deconstructing the binaries of private and public, and transform the State into a gender-sensitive system.

The Economic Domain

Work is a domain where women are constantly undervalued. Men are traditionally looked upon as the breadwinners, while women's household work, which contributes substantially towards the maintenance of the household economy, remains invisible. It is interesting to look at the concept of the household, where men are considered the 'breadwinners', the epithet 'winners'; this appears to suggest a competitive sphere from where one wins the bread. The notions of winning and competition are linked to a masculine understanding of the world. This point is being made here to underline the patriarchy embedded in our thought processes and language, which is key for the construction of societal norms. According to a UN report, women performed two-thirds of the world's work and received only 10 per cent of the total income, and owned only 1 per cent of the means of production (Costa and Bose 1993). The pervasive idea that men are the primary earners led to the formulation of development strategies and a plan that excluded or diminished women's work. Women were regarded as passive dependents and were relegated to reproductive rather than productive roles, thereby resulting in their being confined to domestic spheres. This further shrunk the spaces for women. Women's activism and feminist scholarship stepped in to correct the situation. They challenged the existing notions of work and development. Ester Boserup's 1970 work, *Women's Role in Economic Development*, was a pathbreaker in this respect. She empirically established the vital role of women in agricultural economies, and also documented the negative impact of development on women and their lives. It was argued that the costs of modernisation were largely borne by women.

The development policies of the State have also added to the insecurity of women in many instances, especially those of the marginalised sections of the population. Agriculture is the mainstay of the economy of Bangladesh, and women have traditionally been a part of agriculture. The introduction of mechanised means into this sector has displaced the rural poor women. They have been deprived from their main means of livelihood. This has increased their economic and social vulnerability. It is common knowledge that there is a linkage between poverty and violence against women; an increase in one leads to an increase in the other as well. The mechanisation of agriculture also affects men. Many of them have migrated to urban areas in search of jobs. This further increases the vulnerability of women, who are left alone to look after the family. Women have often become victims of sexual harassment and violations by the village 'leaders' in this situation. Many young women have also migrated to towns in search of jobs. In a lot of instances, they have ended up in brothels or have become victims of the women trafficking chains. It has been reported that women and children of all ages are being trafficked to India, mostly from Jashore, Satkhira, Khulna, Bagerhat, Kushtia and southern districts. They are also sold to various brothels or pimps in Kolkata, Mumbai, Goa and Pune, among other Indian cities (Zaman 2017).

Women of minority communities have also been affected by the development paradigms of the State. For instance, the Garo women in the bordering area of Birishiri are victims of poverty. Eighty per cent of the Garo families in the area are dependent upon forest resources for their survival. But most of the forests have been taken over by the State as Reserved Forests. The insurgency in the Chittagong Hill Tracts (CHT) also affected the livelihood of the Hill people (Mohsin 2003). As forests were being cut down in the name of counter-insurgency, many of the hill people dependent upon *jhum* (swidden) cultivation lost their only means of livelihood. The Forest Department also declared large tracts of forest land as Reserve Forests. Entry into the forest was declared a criminal act. This placed many of the hill communities, particularly the numerically smaller ones, in the most vulnerable position. Women, who are an integral part of the subsistence economy system, become doubly marginalised due to such paradigms of the State.

The readymade garments (RMG) sector is often regarded as a case of successful women's empowerment in Bangladesh, as about 85 per cent of the RMG-employed workers were women. This has led to the feminisation of labour. This number, however, has come down recently. According to a recent survey carried out by the Centre for Policy Dialogue (CPD), Bangladesh, there are 3,596 active RMG factories in Bangladesh, with 3.5 million workers. Women constitute 60.8 per cent of this labour pool, while 39.2 per cent are men. In an earlier survey carried out in 2015 by the CPD, 64 per cent of workers in the RMG sector were female. The recent CPD survey revealed that only about 0.5 per cent of managers in the RMG sector is female and about 9.3 per cent of Human Resources (HR) managers in the RMG sector is female (Uddin 2018). The study found that despite the scope to do tailoring jobs, female workers remain helpers, since they find it difficult to take time off from their domestic chores, or do overtime if an urgent order comes and deliveries need to be made urgently (ibid.). In other words, upward mobility of women is stunted, owing to structural factors. It is argued here that despite much ado about women and empowerment through the RMG sector, the strategic gender needs of women remain unaddressed. The decline in the women labour force in the RMG sector has been associated with job cuts due to automation, wage increases, and safety and eco-friendly measures that had to be taken due to buyers' pressure on improving the working conditions and building safety measures for workers after the Rana Plaza tragedy in 2013, which killed 1,134 people. It is ironic that safety for workers' conditions at work and the introduction of technology at the workplace is happening at the cost of women workers, where they are losing their jobs. There is a dearth of research on the existing conditions of the women labour force that has lost its jobs. This research is important in order to answer the empowerment paradigm that is linked to the RMG sector.

However, there is no denying that on the surface, the employment of a large number of women in a vital employment sector like the RMG is a positive trend. It has made women visible in an otherwise traditional society where *purdah* is regarded as an important aspect of women's chastity, and is also linked to her family's honour. It needs to be emphasised that women belonging to the bottom strata of society have traditionally been working outside their homes, and thus, there is a class dimension to the concept of *purdah* as well.

The Structural Adjustment Programs (SAP) uprooted many women from their traditional agricultural work, forcing them to migrate to urban areas in search of work. The RMG provided them with a niche, and perhaps the only option. While the notion of option may be debated (Hossain, Jahan and Sobhan 1990), there is also no denying that for most young women, migrating to Dhaka garment factories remains the locus of employment. Kabeer's work on Bangladeshi garment workers makes the point that despite exploitative conditions, individual women are able to exercise a certain degree of autonomy and choice in their lives (Kabeer 2002). Petra Dannecker reiterates the same argument. According to her, women do exercise a certain degree of individual and collective agency, and cannot be regarded as a manipulated mass (Dannecker 2002).

Nonetheless, the RMG sector is infested with human insecurities. Human insecurity includes both physical and psychological insecurities. Job satisfaction is an important component of the psychological well-being of the workers. A study conducted by Pratima Paul Majumdar (Majumdar 2001) found a wide gap between the female worker's expectations and the actual realisations in the garments sector, with negative consequences for their mental health. Women are mostly employed in low-skilled and hazardous jobs like those of operators and helpers. The CPD survey referred to earlier attests to the same. Women also suffer from extreme bodily insecurity. Fear of sexual harassment, rape and teasing is common. A recent study by *Actionaid* reveals that 80 per cent of garment workers in Bangladesh have either experienced or have witnessed sexual violence or harassment at the workplace (*Actionaid* 2019).

Employment in the garments sector may bring temporary relief or material well-being to women and their families, but its long-term implications are quite dire. One may also suggest that women take up these jobs for the sake of survival rather than as a matter of choice, given the lack of options. They leave the jobs after three to four years, with physical impairments and little future job prospects due to their physical conditions (Mohsin, pers. comm. 2005). The notion of empowerment of women through employment in the RMG sector therefore needs critical examination within the matrix of its long-term implications and the options available to the women.

Apart from the RMG sector, empowerment of women via entrepreneurship is encouraged by the government. The Bangladesh government has adopted measures to incorporate women in the economic process and has given incentives for self-employment in the Five-Year Plans. Skill development programmes, credit-based programmes, etc., were initiated by both the State and the non-governmental organisations (NGOs) (Karim 2001). Small cottage industry and the production of handcrafted products, food processing works, jewelleries and beauty products, clothing and boutique shops, home appliances and artefacts are the major sectors where women invest and make profit. In recent years, access to the Internet and social media has greatly helped businesswomen. Online shopping has created a window of opportunity for women to work from home. Most of the owners of business pages on Facebook in Bangladesh are women.

According to the Labour Force Survey 2016–17, the unemployment rate of women in Bangladesh is higher; in fact, it is higher than the unemployment rate of men in Bangladesh (Bangladesh Bureau of Statistics [BBS] 2016–17). It is notable that among the unemployed women, the percentage of women with higher secondary and tertiary education is relatively high. Women mostly rely on their social ties to look for jobs rather than visit workplaces. According to the Report, the main concern for development policy is that 81.1 per cent of women do not seek jobs because of their family roles and duties. This summarises the plight of women in the economic domain in Bangladesh, and indicates the long road ahead towards achieving development and empowerment of women in the country.

EDUCATION

Education is a major arena of human development and empowerment. In the context of Bangladesh, a positive correlation has been found between women's education and the household (BBS 2016–17). Arguably, education can bring about positive changes in the strategic as well as the practical gender needs of women. Bangladesh achieved remarkable success in girls' and boys' enrolment at the primary and secondary levels of education. Enrolment of girls is higher than that of boys at the primary level, and the rate of passing for girls for the primary education completion (PEC) exam was more than that of boys. Dropout percentage is also higher among boys than among girls. Poverty, child labour and lack of interest are the major reasons for dropout in the case of boys and for girls, poverty, early marriage and parents' lack of interest are the dominant factors. With early marriage of women, comes the health hazards of early pregnancy. Besides, it is also a major impediment in the path to the empowerment of women. It also strengthens the patriarchal structures of society.

At the secondary level, girls are ahead of the boys in terms of enrolment, but have a lower completion rate than boys. The main reasons for dropout of girls here are their involvement in domestic chores, poverty, labour, distance of school from home, and parents' lack of interest (BBS, UCEP Bangladesh, Diakonia Bangladesh 2017). When a girl reaches the secondary level of education, it is also the time when she enters the adolescent stage. In traditional cultures like Bangladesh, at this stage, the reproductive role of women as well as the maintenance of *purdah* are considered more important than a girl going to a far-away school for education.

Enrolment in the tertiary level education is low for both boys and girls, with girls falling further behind. Gross enrolment rate for girls at the tertiary level is 14.48 per cent against 20.63 per cent for boys in 2017 (United Nations Educational, Scientific and Cultural Organization [UNESCO], Bangladesh Website). Thirty-three of the total students enrolled in universities are female

(Bangladesh Education Statistics 2015: 30). Child/early marriage, social constraints, and violence against women are major causes for female dropout and their inability to pursue higher studies. Women's enrolment in Technical and Vocation Training Institutes was 27 per cent of the total students (Asian Development Bank [ADB] 2017: 88–89).

Urbanisation and Women

Modernisation, economic growth and industrialisation, interpreted as development have contributed to rapid urbanisation. Today, half of the world population, that is, 54 per cent, live in urban areas (Bangladesh Education Statistics 2015: 30). In Bangladesh, with the increasing urbanisation rate, urban population is on the rise (*The Daily Star* 2015). The urban population is rapidly growing owing to internal migration from the rural areas. Unemployment, natural disasters, and poverty drive these huge populations to the cities (Bangladesh Education Statistics 2015: 30). According to the Bangladesh Bureau of Statistics, female population in urban areas is slightly higher than male population (specifically, female population is 0.2 million higher than male population) (BBS 2018: 25). Studies conducted in the urban setting have revealed that women face hardships in urban areas due to the paucity of basic needs and services for survival (ADB 2017; Ahmed and Ahmed 2015). A small number of women come to the cities for education. Poor women who have migrated mostly find residence in slums. Slums in Dhaka city lack proper living standards (Tanni, Hasan, Azad, et al. 2015). Unplanned urbanisation and the mushrooming of slums have led to ghettoisation of the human population, and these are often looked upon as crime zones. Police raids are common in these areas. Women often become dependent upon local thugs or *mastans* to have a 'safe' living in the slums (Mohsin, pers. comm. 2016–19). Violence against women is a critical issue in urban areas. Communication and transport system in the cities is also a point of concern for women. A recent study conducted by BRAC[2] showed that 94 per cent of women experience sexual harassment in public transports (Kabir 2018).

The question of whether urbanisation has any impact on women's empowerment is a complex one. The connection between these two concepts is not clearly defined. Most of the surveys and research works, which tried to explore women's empowerment in Bangladesh, have dealt with urbanisation as a demographic issue, to create spatial dynamics. Urbanisation has created opportunities for women in terms of employment, mobility, education, as well as other aspects of life such as health and living. Many studies show that urban women contribute to the household decision-making process more than rural women (Haque, Towfiqua, Islam, et al. 2011). Mobility has also increased in urban areas, mostly among married women. Control and share in household decision-making and control over own earnings—the two main indicators of empowerment—are also higher among urban women (Bangladesh Demographic and Health Survey 2014).

However, unplanned urbanisation has its limits, which hinder the process of women's empowerment (Kelly 2012). A majority of the poor migrant women live in the slum areas in sub-standard living conditions. Scarcity of basic resources and facilities are the characteristics of urban slums in Bangladesh (ADB 2017). Studies show that the collection and management of scarce resources take a good number of working hours away from women's hands, or put extra burden on the working-class poor living in the slum areas (Momsen 2001). Also, violence against women in the slum areas is a prominent issue. Several studies show that domestic violence and spousal violence are prevalent in the slum areas (Chowdhury, Rahman, Morium, et al. 2018). Female-headed households suffer from a severe lack of security in the slums.

The unplanned and rapid growth of urbanisation creates difficulties for women in more ways than for men (Silbaugh 2007). Most urban areas across the world, including Bangladesh, have adopted a plan to separate industrial areas from residential areas. These regions are linked with transport networks that are not women-friendly and are time consuming due to excessive traffic jams. Time management for public and private work (care-work) is difficult for women living in the city (Shefali 2000). Due to the double burden on women, unplanned or sprawled city without consideration of the time and distance, coupled with social relation between men and women, are a serious risk to women's empowerment.

The Personal Domain

The Constitution of Bangladesh, on the one hand, gives equality to women, and on the other hand, curtails it through personal laws. Women's rights activists have insisted that the personal is political. Discrimination starts at home; power relations and roles are played out within the private domain, supposedly the domain of women. Discussed below are the issues related to Muslim marriage and inheritance—the two critical areas of security for women in a society like Bangladesh.

Marriage

A marriage under Muslim law is a contract between a man and a woman. This is a civil contract, it requires mutual consent, and is formed by the participation of two equal parties. However, an examination of marriages shows that women in most instances appear to be secondary. The Muslim Marriages and Divorces (Registration) Act, 1974, prescribes a form called *Kabinnama*. It includes conditions such as the amount of *dower*,[3] the mode of its payment, the form of divorce, the custody of children, and all other conditions, which the spouses want to stipulate. Section 5 of this form mentions whether the bride is a virgin, a widow or a divorcee, but no such query is made regarding the man. While polyandry is absolutely prohibited, polygamy of up to four wives is permitted in marriage.

However, this is modified by the Muslim Family Laws Ordinance, 1961. This Ordinance necessitates the permission of the Arbitration Council in writing, along with an application stating the reasons for the proposed marriage, and the consent of the existing wife or wives. Although the Ordinance is an improvement to the extent that it brings about changes in the arbitrary practice of polygamy, the permission of existing wife/wives is often acquired through coercion, threats and physical torture. Muslim law allows the parties to separate from one another if every attempt to maintain the marriage fails. Divorce is referred to as *talaq*. It is a power available exclusively to the husband, although he may delegate the power to his wife, or even to a third person who can pronounce *talaq* on the wife on his behalf if the husband, for some reason, is unable to do so. There are different forms of divorce (Pereira 2002). Even in the case of judicial divorce, disparity exists between Muslim men and women with regard to the right to divorce. A man can obtain a divorce under any circumstance by pronouncing *talaq*, giving a notice to the Arbitration Council and waiting for 90 days for it to take effect. A woman, on the other hand, who has not been delegated the right to obtain a divorce, has to take recourse to a court and prove one or more of the grounds for divorce that are set out by the Dissolution of the Muslim Marriage Act, 1939.

A Muslim man may validly marry a *Kitabiya* (a Christian or Jewish woman), but a Muslim woman may marry only a Muslim man. Even if a Muslim man did marry a non-*Kitabiya*, the marriage would not be void but irregular, that is, the children from the marriage would be legitimate, but the parties would not inherit from each other. However, a Sunni Muslim woman is not allowed to marry a non-Muslim man, *Kitabiya* or non-*Kitabiya* (ibid.). Under Muslim law, a mother is not the legal guardian of her children in terms of right. Being the primary caregiver, she has the first claim of custody, in the case of a male child till the age of seven, and in the case of a girl child till the attainment of puberty. The father, however, continues to be the legal guardian and maintainer of the child. After his death, guardianship falls on the paternal side of the children.

Inheritance

The Quran designated 12 people, including eight women, as heirs: the wife, mother, daughter, sister (full, uterine and consanguine), son's daughter and grandmother. But they cannot all inherit concurrently. Depending upon the priority, one excludes the other. The Quran does not lay down any specific share for a son, but a text specifies that a son's share should be twice that of a daughter. Widows receive one-eighth of the husband's share. Husbands receive one-fourth of the wife's estate.

The continued existence of family laws, specially the provisions on inheritance and child custody rights, marginalises women, both of the Muslim and Hindu communities. The latter do not even have any rights of divorce, as Hindu marriages are not registered. It is important to bear in mind that Bangladesh is a signatory to the CEDAW, and thereby, the persistence of family laws is not only a violation of the above, but it also strengthens and privileges the patriarchal system (Sobhan 2004: 50–51).

Concluding Remarks

In summary, this chapter argues that development and empowerment are complex and multi-layered processes. A change in the masculine notion of power, which prescribes domination and 'control over' and power relations between the sexes, the social construction of gender, gender roles and gender spaces are at the core of breaking through the ceiling of patriarchy—the primary factor behind women's subordination. While Bangladesh has made remarkable strides in terms of narrowing the gender gaps in different arenas—women have become visible in the political and economic arenas—the cultural and societal norms of patriarchy remain quite entrenched. Women's organisations and women's rights movements through their advocacies and feminist scholarship have consistently called for equality, justice and well-being, which constitute the core of development and empowerment.

In order to attain these, multi-pronged interventions at the State and societal levels are required. To begin with, the State needs to move towards a uniform family law; if the 'personal' is secured by the law for woman, it is expected that pathways to public arenas will open. Gender-sensitive academic curriculum, civil spaces and transportation systems are also called for. Decision-making is an important component of empowerment. Mere visibility of women in the political and economic realm is insufficient to ensure this, and thus, the State needs to take this visibility to the community-level for it to gain meaningful traction. In the age of globalisation, challenges are many, but opportunities are in abundance. What is critical is the opening of spaces, both cognitive and physical, by men as well as women to create an equal, just system.

Notes

1. On 18 December 1979, the CEDAW was adopted by the UN General Assembly. The Convention was the culmination of more than 30 years of work by the UN Commission on the Status of Women, a body established in 1946 to monitor the situation of women and to promote women's rights. The Convention establishes not only an international Bill of Rights for women, but also an agenda for action by countries to guarantee the enjoyment of these rights. For details, see The Office of the High Commissioner for Human Rights (CEDAW 1979).
2. BRAC, or Building Resources Across Communities, previously known as Bangladesh Rehabilitation Assistance Committee, and initially known as Bangladesh Rural Advancement Committee, is an international development organisation based in Bangladesh and the largest NGO in the world. It was established in 1972 by Fazle Hasan Abed.
3. Dower or *mehr* is a sum of money payable to the wife by the husband in consideration of marriage. Sura 4, Ayat 4 requires this. It is an essential condition of Muslim law. Marriage can be prompt or deferred.

References

'80 Per Cent of Garment Workers in Bangladesh have Experienced or Witnessed Sexual Violence and Harassment at Work', *Actionaid*, 10 June 2019. Available at https://actionaid.org/news/2019/80-garment-workers-bangladesh-have-experienced-or-witnessed-sexual-violence-and (accessed 16 June 2019).

ADB. 2017. 'Bangladesh Gender Equality Diagnostic of Selected Sectors', pp. 88–89. Available at https://www.adb.org/sites/default/files/institutional-document/395641/bangladesh-gender-equality-diagnostic.pdf (accessed 13 June 2019).

Ahmed, N., and F. Ahmed. 2015. 'Problems and Challenges of Deserted Women in Bangladesh: An Observational Study', *Journal of International Social Issues* 3(1): 5–10.

Ahmed Karim, Nilufer. 2001. 'Gender and Small Enterprises in Bangladesh: Factors Affecting Women Entrepreneurs in Small and Cottage Industries in Bangladesh', No. 993467103402676. International Labour Organization (ILO). Available at https://www.

ilo.org/wcmsp5/groups/public/—ed_emp/-emp_ent/documents/publication/wcms_113774.pdf (accessed 13 June 2019).

BANBEIS, Bangladesh Education Statistics. 2015. Available at http://data.banbeis.gov.bd/Survey2015.pdf (accessed 13 June 2019).

'Bangladesh Demographic and Health Survey 2014'. Available at https://dhsprogram.com/pubs/pdf/FR311/FR311.pdf (accessed 13 June 2019).

'Bangladesh's Urban Population Rising Fast', *The Daily Star*, 20 December 2015. Available at https://www.thedailystar.net/country/bangladeshs-urban-population-rising-fast-190063 (accessed 13 June 2019).

BBS. 2018. 'Labor Force Survey 2016–17'. Available at http://203.112.218.65:8008/WebTestApplication/userfiles/Image/LatestReports/LFS_2016-17.pdf (accessed 13 June 2019).

BBS, UCEP Bangladesh, Diakonia Bangladesh. 2017. 'Education Scenario in Bangladesh: Gender Perspective', pp. 22–44. Available at http://bbs.portal.gov.bd/sites/default/files/files/bbs.portal.gov.bd/page/4c7eb0f0_e780_4686_b546_b4fa0a8889a5/BDcountry%20project_final%20draft_010317.pdf (accessed 13 June 2019).

Boserup, Ester. 1970. *Women's Role in Economic Development.* New York: Allen and Unwin.

CEDAW. 1979. 'Convention on the Elimination of All Forms of Discrimination against Women New York, 18 December 1979'. Available at https://www.ohchr.org/Documents/ProfessionalInterest/cedaw.pdf (accessed 25 August 2019).

Chatterjee, Partha. 1989. 'The Nationalist Resolution of the Women's Question', in Kumkum Sangari and Sudesh Vaid (eds), *Recasting Women: Essays in Colonial History*, pp. 233–53. New Delhi: Kali for Women.

Chowdhury, Mohiuddin Ahsanul Kabir, Ahmed Ehsanur Rahman, Salma Morium, et al., 'Domestic Violence Against Women in Urban Slums of Bangladesh: A Cross-Sectional Survey', *Journal of Interpersonal Violence*, 24 August 2018.

Costa, Edna Belen, and Christine E. Bose. 1993. 'From Structural Subordination to Empowerment: Women and Development in Third World Contexts', *Gender and Society* 4(3): 305.

Dannecker, Petra. 2002. *Between Conformity and Resistance: Women Garment Workers in Bangladesh.* Dhaka: The University Press Limited.

Fukuda, Sakiko Parr. 2003. 'The Human Development Paradigm: Operationalizing Sen's Ideas on Capabilities', *Feminist Economics* 9(2/3): 301–17.

Haque, Md. Morshedul, Mahfuza Towfiqua, Tareque Islam, et al. 2011. 'Women Empowerment or Autonomy: A Comparative View in Bangladesh Context', *Bangladesh e-Journal of Sociology* 8(2): 25–28.

Hossain, Hameeda, Rowshan Jahan, and Salma Sobhan. 1990. *No Better Option? Industrial Women Workers in Bangladesh*. Dhaka: The University Press Limited.

'How Small Businesses Use Facebook to Promote Products and Services', *The Dhaka Tribune*, 9 January 2018. Available at https://www.dhakatribune.com/business/2018/01/09/small-businesses-use-facebook-promote-products-services (accessed 13 June 2019).

Kabeer, Naila. 1999. 'Resources, Agency, Achievements: Reflections on the Measurement of Women's Empowerment', *Development and Change* 30(3): 435–64.

———. 2002. *The Power to Choose: Bangladeshi Garment Workers in London and Dhaka*. New York: Verso.

Kabir, R. 'Study: 94 per cent Women Victims of Sexual Harassment in Public Transport', *The Dhaka Tribune*, 7 March 2018, Available at https://www.dhakatribune.com/bangladesh/crime/2018/03/07/study-94-women-victims-sexual-harassment-public-transport (accessed 13 June 2019).

Kelly, A. 'Urbanisation in Bangladesh Proves a Double-edged Sword for Women', *The Guardian*, 5 November 2012. Available at https://www.theguardian.com/global-development/2012/nov/05/urbanisation-bangladesh-women (accessed 13 June 2019)

Mohsin, Amena. 2003. *The Chittagong Hill Tracts Bangladesh: On the Difficult Road to Peace*. New York: International Peace Academy.

———. 2005. Personal Communication with Garment Workers Working in a Factory at Elephant Road.

———. 2009. 'Gendering the Nation and Endangering Gender: Bangladesh National Regimes', *BIISS Journal* 30(3): 239–70.

———. 2010. 'Coming out of the Private: Women Forging Voices in Bangladesh', in Firdous Azim and Maheen Sultan (eds), *Mapping Women's Empowerment: Experiences from Bangladesh, India and Pakistan*, pp. 11–34. Dhaka: The University Press Limited.

———. 2016. 'The History of Sexual Violence, Impunity and Conflict: The Bangladesh Context', in Hameeda Hossain and Amena Mohsin (eds), *Of The Nation Born*. New Delhi: Zubaan Books.

———. 2016–19. Personal Communication with Slum Dwellers of Kurile in Dhaka.

Momsen, Janet Henshall. 2001. 'Backlash: Or How to Snatch Failure from the Jaws of Success in Gender and Development', *Progress in Development Studies* 1(1): 51–56.

Mondal, Shishir, 'More Women Voters in 103 Seats (103 Ashon e Nari Voter Beshi)', *Prothom Alo*, 14 December 2018. Available at https://www.prothomalo.com/bangladesh/article/1570550 (accessed 13 June 2019).

Paul Majumdar, Pratima. 2001. 'Occupational Hazards and Health Consequences of the Growth of Garment Industry in Bangladesh', in Pratima Paul Majumdar and Binayak Sen (eds), *Growth of Garment Industry in Bangladesh: Economic and Social Dimensions*, pp. 72–207. Dhaka: Bangladesh Institute of Development Studies; Oxfam GB.

Pereira, Faustina. 2002. *The Fractured Scales, The Search for a Uniform Personal Code*. Dhaka: The University Press Limited.

Shefali, Mashuda. 2000. 'Study on Gender Dimension in Dhaka Urban Transport Project', Washington, D.C.: The World Bank. Available at http://siteresources.worldbank.org/INTGENDERTRANSPORT/Resources/bangurbantransport.pdf (accessed 13 June 2019).

Silbaugh, Katharine B. 2007. 'Women's Place: Urban Planning, Housing Design, and Work-Family Balance', *Fordham Law Review* 76(1797): 1811–25. Available at http://ir.lawnet.fordham.edu/flr/vol76/iss3/18 (accessed 13 June 2019).

Sobhan, Salma. 2004. 'Women, Religion and the Law', in Imtiaz Ahmed (ed.), *Women Bangladesh and International Security: Methods, Discourses and Policies*, pp. 50–51. Dhaka: Bangladesh Freedom Foundation; The University Press Limited.

Tanni, T. T., M. J. Hasan, A. K. Azad, and B. Bakali. 2015. 'State of the Environment in Slum Area: A Case Study on Khora Slum, Khulna', *Journal of Environmental Science and Natural Resources* 7(1): 297–301,

Uddin, Mostafiz, 'How Technology affects Women', *Dhaka Tribune*, 7 June 2018.

UNDP, Human Development Reports. 2018. 'Human Development Indices and Indicators: 2018 Statistical Update'. Available at http://hdr.undp.org/en/countries/profiles/BGD (accessed 13 June 2019).

UNESCO, Bangladesh. Available at http://uis.unesco.org/country/BD (accessed 13 June 2019).

World Bank. 2018. 'Labor Force Participation Rate, Female (Percentage of Female Population ages 15+) (modelled ILO Estimate). Available at https://data.worldbank.org/indicator/SL.TLF.CACT.FE.ZS (accessed 25 August 2019).

World Economic Forum. 2018. 'The Global Gender Gap Report 2018'. Available at http://www3.weforum.org/docs/WEF_GGGR_2018.pdf (accessed 25 August 2019).

Zaman, Sheikh Shahriar, 'Growing Number of Bangladeshi Women in Indian Brothels', *Dhaka Tribune*, 29 June 2017.

8

Militancy in Bangladesh*

AMIT RANJAN and ROSHNI KAPUR

In most literature, terrorism and militancy are used synonymously, which, however, they are not. They are two different terms, both politically and etymologically. Since 1972, the United Nations (UN) has tried to define the term 'terrorism', but it has not been able to provide a universally accepted definition. Hence, the 1987 resolution of the UN General Assembly on terrorism still remains a standard reference (UN Website, General Assembly 1987). For a number of scholars and commentators, terrorism is the 'deliberate and illegal use of violence against civilians by non-state actors in order to advance political objectives' (Scribner 2015: 12). In contrast, the term 'militancy', as Scribner uses, 'refer[s] to individuals or groups engaged in acts of political resistance, both symbolic and armed' (ibid.).

This chapter deals with militancy in Bangladesh, whose roots can be traced to the country's Liberation War in 1971 and the existing debates around it. In East Pakistan (present-day Bangladesh), several Urdu-speaking people were against its separation from the Western part and sided with the Pakistani establishment. The members of the Bangladesh Jamaat-e-Islami (BJI), popularly known as Jamaat, comprising mostly non-Bengali Urdu-speakers, unleashed violence against ethnic Bengalis. The group was led by Professor Ghulam Azam, the then leader of Jamaat-e-Islami (Sikand 2013). A similar group, Al-Badr, was launched by the Islami Chhatra Sangha,[1] the student wing of the Jamaat-e-Islami. The Muslim League set up its own armed group, Al-Shams, for similar reasons (ibid.).

---

* This is a revised version of a paper published at the Institute of South Asian Studies (ISAS), National University of Singapore (Ranjan and Kapur 2018).

In the liberated country, the ethnic differences between the Urdu- and Bengali-speaking population remained, and violence ensued. Soon after the Liberation War, lawlessness saw an increase in the incidences of abduction and sexual violence of women, along with other acts of robbery, murder, etc. (Raunaq 1975). At the same time, many of the military personnel were not happy with the first President of Bangladesh, Sheikh Mujibur Rehman. In 1975, Rehman was assassinated by a group of military officers. The successive Heads of State, including military rulers General Ziaur Rahman (1977–81) and General Hussain Mohammed Ershad (1983–90), could not address the situation. Instead, as discussed in this chapter, Islamisation was promoted from above, that is, the leaders sought the support of the Muslim religious groups and clergy and allowed them greater space in the polity. In other words, Islamisation did not occur due to popular demand. The social and political conditions did not change even after the return of democratic rule in Bangladesh in 1991. Also, militancy evolved in Bangladesh mainly due to the prevailing socio-political structures present in the country. A few external developments certainly influenced many militant groups to carry out their activities within the country and beyond. We argue in this chapter that the ethnic differences, the spread of the radical version of Islam, as well as the existing social and political violence in the country provided favourable conditions for militancy in Bangladesh.

Political and Social Changes in Bangladesh

After the 1971 Bangladesh Liberation War, Sheikh Mujibur Rahman became the first President of the country. To provide justice to those against whom violence was committed, the government put the collaborators and members of the Pakistan army on trial. The government also enacted the Bangladesh Collaborators (Special Tribunals) Order, 1972, and the International Crimes (Tribunals) Act, 1973. Around 37,000 local collaborators were sent to jail, and some of them even faced life-term imprisonment after the trials (Ahmed 2009). Rahman also banned the Jamaat-e-Islami and the other groups that had collaborated with the Pakistan army during the Liberation War. The paramilitary force, Jatiya Rakkhi Bahini, set up by Rahman, was associated with arbitrary terrorising tactics, and acted as an instrument to quash any resistance against the regime (Schendel 2009). The government argued that the Jatiya Rakkhi Bahini was created to fight against the Marxist dissident group, Gono Bahini, but the targets were mainly dissenters, who were killed in large numbers by the cadres of the Jatiya Rakkhi Bahini.

Along with political violence, the way in which identity was defined by the 1972 Constitution also became a reason for political tension. The Constitution defined everyone as 'Bengali'. In the Constituent Assembly, the Chakma leader, Manabendra Narayan Larma, objected to this imposition of identity. He was against incorporation into the majority community (Siddiqi 2018). Later, when Rahman visited the Chittagong Hill Tracts, where the population comprises non-Muslims and non-Bengalis, he asked them 'to become Bengalis, to forget the colonial past and join the mainstream of Bengali culture' (Schendel 2009: 185). However, Rahman's 'Bengaliness' had more Islamic elements. For example, he resorted to using Islamic salutations. Also, despite being opposed by Pakistan, the religious identity made Rahman seek membership for Bangladesh to the Organisation of Islamic Countries (OIC) in 1974. On 15 August 1975, Rahman was assassinated by his opponents, along with 21 members of his family and close associates. After his assassination, Khondaker Mostaq Ahmad was appointed as the President of the country for a short stint (15 August 1975–6 November 1975). He was then succeeded by Justice Abu Sadat Mohammad Sayam (November 1975–April 1977).[2] During this period, out of the total number of accused men, around 26,000 were granted general amnesty by the government, and 11,000 were released after the Collaborators Act was scrapped on 31 December 1975 (Ahmed 2009).

In April 1977, General Ziaur Rahman became the head of the State. During his term in power, General Rahman faced three coup attempts and several rebellions organised by both political Right and Centre-Left forces (Riaz 2016). To quell the unrest, General Rahman attempted to appease the religious groups by enacting the Political Party Regulation Act, which cleared the way for JI and other like-minded groups to participate in the country's political system. A series of amendments were made in the Constitution to change the nature of the Bangladeshi State. The word 'secularism' was deleted from the Preamble and from Article 8 of the Constitution. A sentence, that 'absolute trust and faith in the Almighty Allah' should be 'the basis of all actions', was inserted through the Second Proclamation Order Number 1 in 1977. The words 'Bismillah-ar-Rahman-ar-Rahim' ('In the name of Allah, the Beneficent, the Merciful') were also inserted above the Preamble to the Constitution (Majumder 2016). He also facilitated the return of Ghulam Azam from his exile.

General Rahman was assassinated during his visit to Chittagong in 1981. He was succeeded by General H. M. Ershad, who used Islamic symbols and contacts with Islamic clergy to embed his authority. To please the Islamists, he amended the Constitution and replaced secularism with Islam as the religion of the State. He also made *Islamiat* (Islamic religious studies) a mandatory subject for students from grades three to ten.

As politics and society are inextricable in Bangladesh, the impact of developments in either of them affects the other. In the late-1970s and 1980s, religion gained ascendance over all other identities worn by the Bangladeshis. A new version of Islam (mainly Wahhabism) started passively replacing the centuries-old Sufistic Islam (Chowdhury 2016), practised by the majority of the Bangladeshis. This new brand of Islam was vernacular in nature. Soon after its introduction, it became popular in the rural areas, especially among the lower-middle class and people living below them (Schendel 2009).

Once radical Islam found acceptance among several Bangladeshis, many men and women started giving up their 'Bengaliness' and were drawn towards the 'pure' Islamic dresses and culture (Schendel 2009). Since then, the changes brought on by this 'new Islam' have been visible on the streets of many Bangladeshi cities and villages. Many women wear *burka* (veil) over their *sarees,*[3] and *lungi*-tied men[4] are easily spotted with a skull cap on their heads (ibid.). After the return of democracy in 1991, the spread of radical Islam yielded electoral dividends to the Islamists, and it was also being used by the political parties.

Ali Riaz divides the Islamist political parties into five categories: pragmatists, idealists, *pir*s (preachers of Islam), *mazar*s (shrines)-centric, urban elite-centric and 'jihadists'. Of these five categories, the first four, as Riaz observes, operate openly, while the fifth one is clandestine, and some groups representing such political ideologies have been proscribed (Riaz 2016: 165–66).

Most active among the Islamist parties in Bangladesh is the BJI. In the general elections of 1991, the BJI contested in 221 of the 300 seats that were open for direct elections. It won 18 seats and secured 12 per cent of the popular votes (Rehman 2013). Due to its tactical alliance with the Bangladesh Nationalist Party (BNP), the BJI gained two additional seats from the 30 indirectly elected seats for women. In 1996, the BJI won three seats and eight per cent of the total polled votes. In the 2001 elections, it secured four per cent of the votes and won 17 seats (ibid.). Years later, before the 2014 general elections, due to its ideology, the BJI was banned by the Election Commission of Bangladesh from contesting the polls.

During the years 2001–06, the BJI, while in power through an alliance with the BNP, occupied the country's social welfare ministry. This ministry controls the activities of many well-funded non-governmental organisations (NGOs) in Bangladesh. This period also witnessed the rise of the Islamic Bank as the third-largest bank of Bangladesh. Most of the members of the bank were affiliated to the BJI (ibid.).

In 2006, after the end of the BNP's term in the government, a Caretaker Government (CG)[5] assumed power in the country. This government was supposed to hold general elections in the country. However, the situation became tense between the CG and the political leaders. To establish peace in the country, a state of emergency was declared by the government. During the emergency, most of the political leaders, including Sheikh Hasina, leader of the Awami League, were imprisoned. In 2008, there was political reconciliation between the leadership of the country and the military. As a part of that reconciliation, a general election was held in 2009. The Awami League-led alliance won and formed the government. The party also won the successive general election in 2014.

Since 2009, the government of Bangladesh, under Prime Minister Sheikh Hasina, has taken steps to tackle the menace of militancy in the country. One such measure was the implementation of the Anti-Terrorist Act and the Anti-Money Laundering Act in 2009. Furthermore, the setting up of the Counter-Terrorism and Transnational Crime (CTTC) unit under the Dhaka Metropolitan

Police in 2016 to counter the militants' operations and to arrest them proved to be an effective measure as well. As a result of such acts and operations, there has been a decline in the number of militant attacks in Bangladesh. For example, in 2016, 30 militant attacks took place (South Asia Terrorism Portal),[6] while in 2017, the number of such attacks declined to twelve (ibid.).

Nevertheless, the Awami League has made use of Islamist political groups to win elections. Between 1991 and 1996, the Awami League had developed a close relationship with the BJI (Riaz 2016: 164). Awami League leaders publicly affirmed their belief in Islam and presented themselves as the custodians of Islamic values in the country. They also did not shy away from highlighting their founder Rahman's contribution in enhancing Islamic education in the country, establishing the Islamic foundation, and making Bangladesh a member of the OIC (ibid.). Despite such campaigns, the party lost the 1991 elections. However, its tilt towards the Right helped the party to gain victory in the 1996 elections. In recent times, as Sheikh Hasina faced severe criticisms from the opposition over her visit to India in April 2017 and the signing of 22 agreements, including a crucial $4.5 billion concessionary line of credit to finance development projects and defence purchases, she tried to please Hifazat-e-Islam, an Islamist pressure group of *madrasa* (an institution for Islamic teaching) teachers and students (Crispin 2017). Evidently, Sheikh Hasina's government, which was critical of the group in the past, had conceded to two of the group's key demands: government recognition of Qaumi *madrasa* degrees, which allow such graduates to compete for state jobs, and the removal of a Greek statue from the premises of the Supreme Court in Dhaka (ibid.). It is not that the Awami League adheres to Hifazat's religious ideology. However, given their social strength, the former needed the latter to win the elections.

Belief in the tenets of Islam per se, or the active presence of religious groups in the country do not lead to militancy, but the radicalisation of such beliefs and the presence of extremist elements in these groups do provide a favourable space to the militants. Like many other militancy-affected countries in the world, Bangladesh, too, is struggling to find a long-term and robust plan to deal with the militants. Many countries such as Malaysia, Singapore and

Saudi Arabia have deradicalisation programmes in which detained terrorists go through rigorous counselling sessions conducted by religious leaders to counter their ideological misconceptions. The final goal is to get the detainees to cut their ties with militant groups and reintegrate back into society.

Although Bangladesh has a few deradicalisation programmes, they are sporadic in nature, which have either been discontinued due to coordination issues or have not achieved substantial results. In 2019, the Religious Affairs Ministry started an anti-militancy awareness project that was conducted using ICT. In 2017, a book titled *Misinterpretation of Verses by Militants and the Right Interpretation of the Qu'ran and Hadith* was published and distributed across the country to spread awareness about the false narratives of militancy. From time to time, the government requests *imams* (a religious leader who leads prayers in a mosque) to deliver a pre-sermon speech during the Friday prayers to delegitimise militant organisations that use religion to justify their violent narratives. While these efforts were launched with good intent, their impact has been relatively negligible. Other countries such as Singapore and Malaysia have more successful deradicalisation programmes, given that they are mixed societies that do not have a history of violence. In contrast, Bangladesh's independence originated in violence, which has, in turn, become embedded in its society.

More than deradicalisation, Bangladesh's emphasis is on counter-terrorism where measures include the cancellation of the BJI's registration to participate in the 2019 general elections. Hasina's government has struck hard on the BJI for its hardline religiosity and political subversion. Most of its senior leaders have been executed after being implicated in the Liberation War for crimes against humanity and mass atrocities (*The New Indian Express*, Press Trust of India [PTI] 2018). The imprisonment of BNP leader Khaleda Zia and political opponents in corruption cases have also become a talking point. Perhaps this explains why the government has seen a plunge in the Economist Intelligence Unit's Democracy Index. While in 2006, it was ranked a flawed democracy (6.11), in 2017, it was listed as a hybrid regime (5.43).[7]

However, the BNP is continuing to echo its support for the BJI through a power-sharing deal, despite pressures to cut its ties with the BJI. One of the reasons for the persistence could be their strong historical and political relations that continue to remain intact. Moreover, the BNP may want to leverage the BJI's vote bank to boost its chances of winning the national elections (Antara 2018). On the other hand, the Awami League is making a conscious effort to reach out to other Islamist groups. It announced in November 2018 that 560 mosques and an Islamic university will be built with external funding from Saudi Arabia. A legislative bill was also passed to give the Dawra-e-Hadith degree the same recognition as a post-graduate degree in Arabic and Islamic Studies (*Hindustan Times*, PTI 2018). The move indicates that Islamists are an important vote bank in the country's electoral system.

Tactics Used by the Militant Groups

A number of militant groups are currently active in Bangladesh. Some of the prominent groups are Jama'atul Mujahideen Bangladesh (JMB), Jagrata Muslim Janata Bangladesh (JMJB), Harkat-ul-Jihad-Islami Bangladesh, Hizb-ut-Tahrir, Hefazet-e-Islam, Jund At-Tawheed Wal Khilafah and the Ansarullah Bangla Team. Besides, there are less prominent groups, too, such as Jaish-e-Muhammad, Jadid al Qaeda and Shahadat-e Al-Hikma.

Harkat-ul-Jihad-Islami Bangladesh was formed in 1992 by Bangladeshis returning after fighting against the former Soviet army in Afghanistan in the 1980s (Ali 2010: 290). This group was formed by Maulana Abdus Salam. After its formation, the group established contacts with Pakistan-based militant groups (Bashar 2015). In later years, the Afghan Taliban became its source of guidance.

JMB was founded in 1998 by Abdur Rahman. The group's objective is to impose an extremist interpretation of Islamic law on Bangladesh. It was banned in February 2005. Soon after the ban, it carried out a well-coordinated bomb blast in August 2005. The base of that operation was in Jamalpur district in Mymensingh province of the country (Bashar 2015). Following the blasts, arrests were made, and a new legislation was enacted by the government, which led to the execution of six convicts. Unlike most of the other militant groups, JMB recruits not only the youth, but also the entire family, including women members (International Crisis Group 2018).

For all militant groups, the targets are secular and liberal individuals who are critical of Islamic fundamentalism. Politically, they target the Awami League leadership because of the party's political ideology. An early attempt to assassinate Sheikh Hasina was made in 1989 by the members of the now defunct Bangladesh Freedom Party (*NDTV*, PTI 2017). They tried to carry out the attack at her family residence. In 1999, the liberal poet, Shamsur Rahman, was attacked by members belonging to the Harkat-ul-Jihad-Islami Bangladesh. In 2000, Sheikh Hasina was the target of members of the Harkat-ul-Jihad-Islami. Attacks were also carried out on people celebrating cultural festivals not sanctioned by the Islamists. For example, in 2001, a bomb exploded amidst a crowd celebrating the Bengali New Year. The programme was organised by a cultural organisation called Chhayanot (Schendel 2009: 208).

In recent years, there has been a shift in the militant groups' targets. Instead of targetting popular personalities of Bangladesh, they are attacking ordinary citizens who promote or support liberal values. On 27 February 2015, an atheist blogger, Avijit Roy, was hacked to death in Dhaka. Roy was a Bangladesh-born citizen of the United States (US) and the founder of a blog, *Mukto Mona* ('Liberated People'). On 30 March 2015, a second blogger, Washiqur Rahman, was stabbed to death for his progressive blogs. Niladri Chattopadhyay, who was a Gonojagron Manch (Platform for Popular Uprising) activist, was another blogger hacked to death in Dhaka in August 2015. Ansar al-Islam (Helpers of Islam) took responsibility for Niladri's murder. Then, in 2016, lesbian, gay, bisexual and transgender rights activists Xulhaz Mannan and Mahbub Rabby Tonoy were hacked to death. Many secular bloggers are now living in fear of greater attacks, while some have already left the country.

The militant groups have also targetted foreign citizens working or on tour of Bangladesh. In 2015, an Italian citizen, Cesare Tavella, was killed in Dhaka. A few days after Tavella, Hoshi Kunio, a Japanese citizen, was shot at in Rangpur on 3 October 2015. Both attacks attracted the attention of the international community towards the increasing occurrence of militancy incidents in Bangladesh. The law enforcement agencies have not done their part in arresting the perpetrators, leading to the criticism that there is a growing culture of impunity for militants. At times, the officials have even placed some of the blame on the activism and writings of the victims (Minority Rights Group International 2016: 13).

However, the most daring and deadly operation carried out by the militants in Bangladesh was on 1 July 2016, when seven fully armed militants stormed into Dhaka's popular eatery, Holey Artisan Bakery, and took about 60 people as hostages, mostly foreigners. The area was cleared after a joint operation launched by commandos from the Bangladeshi army, navy, special weapons and tactics teams, the elite Rapid Action Battalion, and the paramilitary Border Guards Bangladesh. In this operation, two policemen and six militants were killed, and one militant was captured. The militants killed nine Italians, seven Japanese, three Bangladeshis and an Indian hostage (Roy 2016). In a follow-up operation to the hostage crisis, it is believed that Bangladesh security officials killed about six to eight militant leaders between July and December 2016 (Bhaumik 2017). After the July attacks, the Bangladeshi security officials have begun using the term 'new-Jamaat-ul-Mujahideen (new JMB)' for the obscure members of the Islamic State (IS), which they believe are active in the country (International Crisis Group 2018). The 'new JMB' emerged in 2014.

Soon after the July 2016 attack, debates over the indulgence of home-grown militants or those from outside of Bangladesh raged on media portals across the world. Later, it was found that the two local militant groups, Ansar-al-Islam and JMB, which were involved in that attack, had external connections. Ansar-al-Islam is believed to owe allegiance to Al Qaeda and Jamaat JMB claims to be a representative of the IS in Bangladesh (*The Daily Star* 2016).

Another area of concern is the growing involvement of women in militant groups. This is a fairly new trend in the country's militancy. Three women from JMB were arrested in 2017 after their failed attempt to carry out a suicide bombing. One of them, the wife of acting JMB chief, Ayyub Bachchu, was even caught wearing a suicide bomb vest (*The Straits Times* 2017).

There are a number of reasons for women to engage in militancy in the country. First, wives of militants may get influenced or swayed by their husbands towards the 'jihadist' ideology. Many of their husbands hold powerful positions and have been involved in militancy for a long time. Second, some female fighters may feel that they will receive the same recognition and reward as their male counterparts if they take up roles as fighters and recruiters. A growing number of educated women from middle-class backgrounds are joining militant groups. They may view militancy as a platform for gender equality, emancipation and empowerment (Mohsina 2017: 8–9). According to an estimate, over 66 per cent of female terror suspects in Bangladesh, who were believed to be involved in militancy, were influenced by their family members, mostly their husbands (*The Daily Star*, Staff Correspondent 2019). On their association with the militant groups, according to an estimate of the CTTC unit officials, out of the majority of suspected women militants, about 63 per cent are linked to the 'new JMB', while 23 per cent have links with JMB, and 5 per cent are linked to Hizb ut-Tahrir (ibid.).

Militants' Support Base

The identity-based ethnic differences between the Bengali and non-Bengali exist even after more than 48 years of the country's liberation. A large number of the Urdu-speaking Bangladeshis still live in squalid camps. They are regarded as stranded Pakistanis living in Bangladesh. Only in 2008, after they won a legal battle in the High Court, were around 1,40,000 Bihari Muslims, as the Urdu speakers are called, who were born in Bangladesh, granted citizenship rights (Majumder 2008). However, they still face identity-related violence. One of the latest instances of violence against them was at Kalshi in 2014, when an ethnic Bengali leader from the Awami League, with the help of the local police, led an attack against the non-Bengali population of the area. Nine people were killed in this attack.

The setting up of the International Crimes Tribunal-2 in 2009[8] under the International Crimes (Tribunal) Act No. XIX of 1973 has aggravated tensions between those who support different narrations of the Liberation War of Bangladesh. The Tribunal was set up to try the perpetrators of violence during the Liberation War. Ghulam Azam was the first to be charged by the Tribunal for running and orchestrating pro-Pakistan militias during the Liberation War

(BBC News 2016). He was sentenced to 90 years of imprisonment. However, he died of a heart attack in 2014. Another high-profile conviction was that of Abdul Quader Molla in 2013, who was initially sentenced to life-term imprisonment for killing 344 civilians, among other crimes (ibid.). His sentence, in particular, did not satisfy a large number of Bangladeshis. A protest started against the judgment delivered by the Tribunal. People's furore, including the demand to ban the BJI, grew into what is popularly known as the Shahbagh Movement. The rallying cry of the protesters was '*fanshi chai*' ('we demand hanging') (Riaz 2016: 185). Under the pressure of the movement, on 17 February 2013, the Bangladesh parliament passed a bill to amend the International Crimes (Tribunal) Act of 1973. This amendment has a provision to appeal against the order of an acquittal or sentencing by the Tribunal in the Supreme Court of Bangladesh. Under the amended law, the government made an appeal against the life-sentence given to Abdul Quader Molla. On 17 September 2013, the Supreme Court accepted the appeal and sentenced him to death. A series of judgments against war criminals by the Tribunal has widened the divisions between the Bengali and non-Bengali ethnic groups.

Militancy and the militant groups cannot remain active without the support of a section of the local population. In Bangladesh, the majority do not support acts of militancy, but a substantive number of individuals have extended their support to their political objectives and views. According to a survey by Resolve Network, conducted by C. Christine Fair and Wahid Abdallah in April 2017, 'higher income groups tended to support JMJB [Jagrata Muslim Janata Bangladesh] and Da'esh [IS] for the implementation of Sharia globally' (Fair and Abdallah 2017: 11). The survey also showed that the 'the respondents in the subset with more education were more likely to support the assassination tactics employed by Ansarullah Bangla Team against the noted publisher' (ibid.: 12). Surprisingly, the number of women respondents supporting the militant groups were greater than the percentage of male respondents. The survey unveiled that '47 per cent of women from this [the] subset of respondents expressed support for the [militant] group's goal to implement Sharia; only 17 per cent of men took the same position. Female respondents were also more likely to support the violent means of the attack' (ibid.: 10). A total of 4,067 respondents participated in this survey (ibid.).

It is often alleged that almost all of the militants in Bangladesh have been taught in madrasas. This cannot be generalised because some of these militants are highly educated. However, in some of the madrasas, the extremists have managed to spread their presence and networks. There are two types of madrasas: Aliya (or Aaliyah, which means 'the highest' in Arabic) and Qawmi (the public). Aliya is run by the State and is modelled after the Calcutta Madrasa (which later came to be known as the Calcutta Aliya Madrasa) in colonial India. The Qawmi Madrasas are supported through private donations, and are not regulated by the Bangladesh Madrasa Education Board. They are modelled after the Deoband Madrasa. Often, many of these madrasas, especially those under the latter category, come under the scanner for disseminating radical religious ideologies. In 2005, when 450 bombs were exploded in sequence, the intelligence agencies of the country identified 233 madrasas where military training took place (Islam 2011). At the university level, the Islami Chhatra Shibir[9] has its presence in both public and private universities of Bangladesh.

To support its cadre, get weapons, and for other activities, several militant groups depend on external support for funds. In its study, the US Senate committee found that two Bangladesh-based banks, the Islami Bank Bangladesh Ltd (IBBL) and the Social Islami Bank Ltd (SIBL), were lenders to various terrorist activities. The report found that the Hong Kong and Shanghai Banking Corporation had supplied US dollars to IBBL and SIBL. Saudi Arabia's Al Rajhi Bank was also involved in the suspicious transactions. It was found that Lajnat-al-Birr-al-Islam, also known as the Benevolence International Foundation, is a contributor to the terror-related activities (Roy Chaudhary 2015). In order to check such financial transactions, Bangladesh promulgated the Money Laundering Prevention Act, 2012. Under this Act, an Anti-Money Laundering Department was established at Bangladesh Bank. The Act also set up the Bangladesh Financial Intelligence Unit to check money laundering and other illegal financial transactions (*Bangladesh Gazette* 2012).

More than banks, it is the support from charity groups which provides life to militant organisations. This form of support is both from within and outside the country. In the past, many charity organisations, such as the Jeddah-based International Islamic Relief Organisation, Al-Haramain Islamic Foundation and the Kuwait-based Revival of Islamic Heritage Society, have funded Bangladeshi militant groups and their operations (Riaz and Bastian 2011). The militant groups receive money through the *hawala* banking system (Cochrane 2009). This *hawala* system, which does not require any form of licensing or registration, has been misused for money laundering and running financial operations by the militant groups (Looney 2003).

Besides domestic factors, many of the militant groups are influenced by developments in other parts of the world. This is mainly because they see themselves as representatives of Islam, and hence, are ready to defend the cause of the religion at any cost. The US military activities in Afghanistan and in other countries in the Middle East are viewed as an attack on their religion. In this region, the Bangladesh military is a part of the Islamic Military Alliance. This alliance was formed in December 2015 to fight against the Islamic radicals in the Middle East. Entry into such an alliance has not been supported by the militant groups, who see it as an attack on Islam. For this, almost all of them held Sheikh Hasina responsible.

Regional Ramifications of Militancy in Bangladesh

The rise of extremism and militancy in Bangladesh is not limited within the country, but it also has ramifications for the bordering countries. There have been instances when Bangladeshi citizens have been implicated for their involvement in acts of militancy in other parts of the world. In Bangladesh, many militant groups are believed to have developed networks with terrorist groups, such as the Al Qaeda in the Indian Sub-continent (AQIS) and Islamic State (IS). These international terrorist outfits may see Bangladesh as a launch pad for Jihad in South Asia. Bangladesh is seen as strategically located, given that it shares its border with India and Myanmar. The porous borders of the region are scattered with mountains, forests, rivers and hills, which not only enable militant groups to cross over easily, but also make the task of patrolling extremely challenging.

India's concerns regarding the spilling over of militancy and fundamentalism from across Bangladesh international borders are legitimate. Soon after the 2016 Dhaka terror attack, the Border Security Force (BSF) that is deployed along the India–Bangladesh border was put on high alert to prevent terrorists from entering India (Bhattacharjee 2016). New Delhi fears that the rise in militancy in Bangladesh could undermine communal harmony in the sensitive areas of the north-east, such as Assam. Militancy across the borders may cause greater disruption in Assam, which has been facing insurgency for decades. Moreover, the JMB has made inroads into some of the border states of India. The militant outfit has been accused of orchestrating attacks such as the one in West Bengal in 2014 (Acharyya 2016).

In March 2018, Bangladeshi authorities managed to confiscate a consignment of arms that was being sent to India through the eastern border. The weapons were reportedly being sent to support the activities of insurgent groups in the north-east in India. Some of them are sourcing for arms and weapons outside of India (Siyech 2018).

Another area of concern is the radicalisation of Rohingyas in the squalid refugee camps in Cox's Bazar in Bangladesh. As of December 2017, there were 8,58,590 Rohingyas in the refugee camps in Bangladesh (Inter Sector Coordination Group 2007). The refugees in these camps face alienation, lack of education and employment, harassment from locals, and fear of forced repatriation. According to Magnus Ranstorp, the combination of these factors can be found in the processes of political radicalisation (RAN Centre of Excellence 2016: 3). In retrospect, international terrorist groups would recruit Rohingyas on a rare or occasional basis. These camps have now become breeding grounds for militancy and extremism. It has renewed pro-Rohingya jihadist sentiments that will have wider security implications in the region.

There is also anxiety surrounding the radicalisation of Bangladeshis living abroad. In June 2016, eight Bangladeshi workers residing in Singapore were convicted for planning to carry out attacks in Bangladesh to topple the Awami League government. They confessed that they had aspirations to join the Islamic State of Iraq and Syria, the Islamic State of Iraq and Levant or the

Islamic State. Their goal was to form an Islamic state in Bangladesh that will join the Caliphate of the IS. The media has also reported that Bangladeshis have joined the IS in the Middle East. It is believed that most of the Bangladeshi fighters in the Middle East have come to the region after being radicalised through online propaganda by the radical networks (ibid.).

It seems that the IS is now targeting South Asia to increase its foothold in the region. The local group, National Towheeth Jamath (NTJ), which carried out the 2019 Easter bombings in Sri Lanka, pledged its allegiance to the IS. The presence of the IS and use of local groups as proxies is turning into a regional issue. After the Easter bombings, a poster by Al-Mursalat Media, featuring a photo of five militants who carried out an attack in 2016 at a cafe in the diplomatic enclave of Bangladesh's capital, Dhaka, appeared in the city. The poster has a picture of the smiling militants carrying rifles, and the text states that the 'soldiers of the *khilafah* [or caliphate]' in Bangladesh and India have not been 'silenced', and that 'the anger of the mujahideen will suddenly bring destruction upon you' (*South China Morning Post*, Associated Press 2019). Although the security officials did not take the poster seriously, the threat remains due to the presence of a number of Islamists and militants in Bangladesh. It is worth mentioning here that security officials in Bangladesh are divided on the issue of the presence of the IS in the country.

Concluding Remarks

As discussed in this chapter, radicalisation does not take place in a vacuum. Militant and extremist ideas play a big role in radicalising individuals, who can then carry out acts of violence. Bangladesh's biggest problem is the narration of 1971, over which ethnic groups are divided. In retrospect, there were limited platforms to spread militant efforts; but in the age of technology, the means have broadened, changed and become more effective. As a result, a section of the Bangladeshi population has become intolerant towards other religions.

Social media has become a platform to express public ire against those who believe in a different religion; this often threatens the minorities of the country. In recent times, one such case happened in 2015, when the Bangladesh national team cricketer, Liton Das, received several online hate messages after uploading a photo of the Hindu goddess Durga on his Facebook page. Correspondingly, the role of religious channels is under question for the spread of radicalism in the country. After the July 2016 attacks in Dhaka, the Bangladesh government feared that hard-line views aired on the channel, Peace TV would radicalise the youth in Bangladesh. Hence, it took proactive measures to ban the Islamic television channel.

This chapter has also explored the influence of certain international developments, which have directly or indirectly aided the militant groups. Some of the militant groups have successfully built linkages and networks with international terrorist groups. Bangladeshi citizens have also engaged in militant activities in the bordering countries. To address this situation, a concerted action is needed at the regional level. At the bilateral level, Bangladesh is cooperating with India, but a lot has to be done to tackle the menace of militancy in the country, and across the borders.

Finally, as discussed in this chapter, Sheikh Hasina's government has taken many measures to deradicalise the youth and check the spread of militancy in the country. However, given the socio-political order in Bangladesh, and the use of religious groups to win elections, it is difficult to conclude that the government would be very effective in meeting its objectives.

Notes

1. The Islami Chhatra Sangha is the predecessor of the Islami Chhatra Shibir. The latter was formed in 1977.
2. After the assassination of Rahman, the Bangladesh military took charge of Bangladesh. For a brief period, they ruled from behind the curtains.
3. A female garment worn by women from the Indian subcontinent.
4. A long fabric wrapped around the waist. This is used by a large number of males in the Indian subcontinent, as well as in Indonesia and Malaysia.
5. In 2011, the Bangladesh parliament passed the fifteenth amendment to the Constitution. This abolished the need for a CG to hold free and fair elections in the country.

6. Data has been compiled by Roshni Kapur.
7. The Democracy Index by the Economist Intelligence Unit provides a brief summary of the state of democracy for 165 sovereign countries and two territories. Based on five categories: electoral process and pluralism; the functioning of government; political culture; civil liberties; and political participation, each country is categorised into one of the four types of regimes: full democracy, flawed democracy, hybrid regime and authoritarian regime (The Economist Intelligence Unit's Democracy Index).
8. The first tribunal to look into the war crimes was constituted in 1973. Tribunal-2 has remained non-functioning since 15 September 2015 (International Crimes Tribunal-1, Bangladesh).
9. It is a student organisation of the BJI. The members of this organisation have participated in almost all violent processions carried out by the Jamaat.

References

'63 Pc Female Terror Suspects Linked to "Neo JMB": CTTC', *The Daily Star*, 19 April 2019. Available at https://www.thedailystar.net/city/news/63pc-female-terror-suspects-linked-neo-jmb-cttc-1731865 (accessed 22 April 2019).

'8 Bangladeshi Men Detained under Singapore's ISA for Planning Terror Attacks Back Home', Zakir Hussain, *The Straits Times*, 3 May 2016. Available at http://www.straitstimes.com/singapore/8-bangladeshi-men-detained-under-singapores-isa-for-planning-terror-attacks-back-home/ (accessed 17 April 2018).

Acharyya, Kangkan, 'Well-educated Women Jihadists Recruited by Bangladeshi Terror Groups Pose Serious Threat', *Firstpost*, 20 August 2016. Available at https://www.firstpost.com/world/well-educated-women-jihadists-recruited-by-bangladeshi-terror-groups-pose-serious-threat-2967048.html (accessed 12 December 2018).

Ahmed, Imtiaz. 2009. *Historicizing 1971 Genocide: State versus Person*. Dhaka: The University Press Limited.

Ali, S. Mahmud. 2010. *Understanding Bangladesh*. New Delhi: Foundation Books.

Antara, Nawaz Farhin, 'Will BNP Maintain Ties with Jamaat?', *Dhaka Tribune*, 28 August 2018. Available at https://www.dhakatribune.com/bangladesh/politics/2018/08/28/will-bnp-maintain-ties-with-jamaat (accessed 10 December 2018).

Associated Press, 'Does Sri Lanka Attack Show Islamic State is Targeting South Asia? Indian and Bangladeshi Security Experts Play Down Threat', *South China Morning Post*, 2 May 2019. Available at https://www.scmp.com/news/asia/south-asia/article/3008518/does-sri-lanka-attack-show-islamic-state-targeting-south-asia (accessed 24 July 2019).

'Bangladesh Arrests Three Female Mlitants', *The Straits Times*, 3 July 2017. Available at https://www.straitstimes.com/asia/bangladesh-arrests-three-female-militants (accessed 10 December 2018).

'Bangladesh Timeline—Year 2016', South Asia Terrorism Portal. Available at http://www.satp.org/satporgtp/countries/ bangladesh/timeline/2016.htm/ (accessed 26 June 2018).

'Bangladesh Timeline—Year 2017', South Asia Terrorism Portal. Available at http://www.satp.org/satporgtp/countries/ bangladesh/timeline/2017.htm (accessed 30 July 2018).

'Bangladesh War Crimes Trial: Key Accused', *BBC*, 4 September 2016. Available at http://www.bbc.co.uk/news/world-asia-20970123 (accessed 20 April 2018).

Bashar, Iftekharul. 2015. 'India's Key Role and South Asia's Security Concerns'. In Rohan Gunaratna and Douglas Woodall (eds), *Afghanistan after the Western Drawdown*, pp. 51–62. London: Rowman and Littlefield.

Bhattacharjee, Rupak, 'Militancy in Bangladesh: Regional and International Dimensions', *Bdnews24.com*, 21 July 2016. Available at https://opinion.bdnews24.com/2016/07/21/militancy-in-bangladesh-regional-and-international-dimensions/ (accessed 11 December 2018).

Bhaumik, Subir, 'Is Bangladesh Winning the War against Militants?', *BBC*, 4 April 2017.

'Bloody End to Dhaka Hostage Crisis', *The Daily Star*, 2 July 2016. Available at http://www.thedailystar.net/online/security-forces-begin-offensive-end-hostage-crisis-1249219 (accessed 22 April 2018).

Chowdhury, Iftekhar Ahmed, 'Terror in Dhaka: Fundamentalism Spreads its Deadly Wings', 4 July 2016, *ISAS Brief No 439*, 4 July 2016. Available at https://www.isas.nus.edu.sg/wp-content/uploads/media/isas_papers/ISAS%20Brief% 20No.%20439%20-%20Terror%20in%20Dhaka%20-%20Fundamentalism%20Spreads%20its%20Deadly% 20Wings.pdf (accessed 7 May 2018).

Cochrane, Paul. 2009. 'The Funding Methods of Bangladeshi Terrorist Groups', *Combating Terrorism Center* 2(5), n.p.

'Countering Jihadist Militancy in Bangladesh', *International Crisis Group*, 28 February 2018. Available at Error! Hyperlink reference not valid. (accessed 11 May 2018).

Crispin, Shawn, 'Hasina, Under Political Duress, Looks to the Right', *Asia Times*, 21 April 2017. Available at https://cms.ati.ms/2017/04/hasina-political-duress-looks-right/ (accessed 24 July 2019).

Fair, Christin, and Wahid Abdallah, 'Islamist Militancy in Bangladesh Public Awareness and Attitudes', *Resolve Network*, Brief No. 4, September 2017. Available at https://resolvenet.org/system/files/2017-09/RSVE_ 04BangladeshBrief_MilitantSupport2017.pdf (accessed 7 June 2018).

International Crimes Tribunal-1, Bangladesh. 'About ICT BD'. Available at http://www.ict-bd.org/ict1/ (accessed 6 June 2018).

Islam, Md. Shamsul. 2011. 'Political Violence in Bangladesh'. In Ali Riaz and Christine C. Fair (eds), *Fair Political Islam and Governance in Bangladesh*, pp. 27–45. Oxon; New York: Routledge.

Jahan, Raunaq. 1975. 'Women in Bangladesh'. In Women for Women Research and Study Group, pp. 1–30. Dhaka: The University Press Limited.

Looney, Robert. 2003. 'Hawala: The Terrorist's Informal Financial Mechanism', *Middle East Policy Council* X(1), n.p.

Majumder, Azad, 'Bangladesh Citizenship Rights Divide Biharis', *Reuters*, 20 May 2008. Available at https://www.reuters.com/article/idINIndia-33670320080520 (accessed 30 July 2018).

Majumder, Shantanu. 2016. 'Secularism and anti-Secularism'. In Ali Riaz and Mohammad Sajjadur Rahman, *Routledge Handbook of Contemporary Bangladesh*, pp. 40–51. Oxon; New York: Routledge.

Mohsina, Nazneen. 2017. 'Growing Trends of Female "Jihadism" in Bangladesh', *Counter-Terrorist Trends and Analyses* 9(8): 7–11.

'Money Laundering Prevention Act', *Bangladesh Gazette*, 7 June 2012. Available at http://www.satp.org/satporgtp/countries/bangladesh/document/papers/Money_Laundering_Prevention_Act_2012.pdf (accessed 31 May 2017).

PTI, Bangladesh Election Commission Scraps Fundamentalist Jamaat-e-Islami's Registration', *The Indian Express*, 29 October 2018. Available at http://www.newindianexpress.com/world/2018/oct/29/bangladesh-election-commission-scraps-fundamentalist-jamaat-e-islamis-registration-1891604.html (accessed 9 December 2018).

———, 'Ahead of Polls, Sheikh Hasina Announces to Build 560 Model Mosques, Islamic University in Bangladesh', *Hindustan Times*, 4 November 2018. Available at https://www.hindustantimes.com/world-news/ahead-of-polls-sheikh-hasina-announces-to-build-560-model-mosques-islamic-university-in-bangladesh/story-028L84Dt9UZBFQtsKpcs0K.html (accessed 11 December 2018).

———, '11 Jailed for Assassination Attempt on Bangladesh PM Sheikh Hasina', *NDTV*, 29 October 2017. Available at https://www.ndtv.com/world-news/11-jailed-for-assassination-attempt-on-bangladesh-pm-sheikh-hasina-1768580 (accessed 18 April 2018).

Ranjan, Amit, and Roshni Kapur, 'Militancy in Bangladesh', *ISAS Working Paper* no. 304, 31 July 2018. Available at https://www.isas.nus.edu.sg/wp-content/uploads/2018/08/ISAS-Working-Paper-No.-304-Militancy-in-Bangladesh.pdf (accessed 18 April 2018).

Riaz, Ali. 2016. *Bangladesh: A Political History since Independence.* London; New York: I. B. Tauris.

Riaz, Ali, and Bastian Jessica. 2011. 'Islamist Militancy in Bangladesh'. In Ali Riaz and C. Christine Fair (eds), *Political Islam and Governance in Bangladesh*, pp. 153–66. New York: Routledge.

Roy Chaudhary, Dipanjan, 'Islamic Banking and Terror Financing in Bangladesh', *Pakistan Defence*, 18 October 2015. Available at http://defence.pk/threads/islamic-banking-and-terror-financing-in-bangladesh.208395/ (accessed 24 May 2016).

Roy, Shubhajit, 'Bangladesh Café Attack: Indian among 20 Killed in Dhaka's Night of Terror', *The Indian Express,* 3 July 2016. Available at http://indianexpress.com/article/world/world-news/bangladesh-cafe-attack-indian-among-20-killed-in-dhakas-night-of-terror-2890521/ (accessed 5 July 2016).

Schendel, William Van. 2009. *A History of Bangladesh.* Cambridge: Cambridge University Press.

Scribner, Charity. 2015. *After the Red Army Faction: Gender, Culture and Militancy.* Columbia: Columbia University Press.

Siddiqi, Dina M. 2018. 'Secular Quests, National Others: Revisiting Bangladesh's Constituent Assembly Debates', *Asian Affairs* XLIX(2): 238–58.

Sikand, Yoginder S. 2013. 'The Tablighi Jama'at'. In Meghna Guhathakurta and Willem van Schendel (eds), *The Bangladesh Reader: History, Culture, Politics*, pp. 336–44. London; Durham: Duke University Press.

'Situation Update: Rohingya Refugee Crisis', Inter-Sector Coordination Group, 7 December 2017. Available at https://reliefweb.int/sites/

reliefweb.int/files/resources/171207_iscg_sitrep_one_pager_final.pdf (accessed 10 December 2018).

Siyech, Mohammed Sinan, 'Crime–Terror Nexus Along India's Eastern Border', *RSIS*, 12 April 2018. Available at https://www.rsis.edu.sg/rsis-publication/icpvtr/co18068-crime-terror-nexus-along-indias-eastern-border/#.XBDkStszaUk (accessed 11 December 2018).

'The Economist Intelligence Unit's Democracy Index'. Available at https://infographics.economist.com/2018/DemocracyIndex/ (accessed 10 December 2018).

'The Jamaat Factor in Bangladesh Politics', Jyoti Rehman. *Kafila,* 13 March 2013. Available at http://kafila.org/2013/03/13/the-jamaat-factor-in-bangladesh-politics-jyoti-rehman/ (accessed 23 December 2014).

'The Root Causes of Violent Extremism', Ran Centre of Excellence, 4 January 2016. Available at https://ec.europa.eu/home-affairs/sites/homeaffairs/files/what-we-do/networks/radicalisation_awareness_network/ran-papers/docs/issue_paper_root-causes_jan2016_en.pdf (accessed 10 December 2018).

'Under Threat: The Challenges Facing Religious Minorities in Bangladesh', Minority Rights Group, 2016. Available at https://minorityrights.org/wp-content/uploads/2016/11/MRG_Rep_Ban_Oct16_ONLINE.pdf (accessed 4 Dencember 2018).

UN Website, General Assembly, 'A/RES/42/159, 94th Plenary Meeting', 7 December 1987. Available at https://www.law.kuleuven.be/iir/nl/onderwijs/terrorisme/GAres42e159.htm (accessed 5 June 2019).

9

Energy and Development

Issues of Sustainability

S. NARAYAN and SARIN PARAPARAKATH

Bangladesh, with an estimated population of 162 million in 2016, has been consistently growing at a rate of over 6 per cent since 2010. The World Bank (2019) has categorised the country as one of the five fastest-growing economies of the world. The Gross Domestic Product (GDP) of Bangladesh in 2018–19 was estimated at $274 billion (current price), with an impressive growth rate of 7.3 per cent (constant price). The sectoral share of the industrial sector increased from 26–30 per cent over the same period (2018–19), with the manufacturing sector's share increasing from 16–19 per cent in 2017–18. The substantial increase in the growth of GDP is on account of the sectoral shift from the agricultural sector to the services and industry sector.

Bangladesh aims at becoming a high-income country by 2041. Guided step-by-step by its 'Vision 2021', the country aims to become a middle-income country (MIC) by 2021, upper middle-income country (UMIC) by 2030, and high-income country (HIC) by 2041. In order to achieve the targets of Vision 2041, the country must continue to grow at over 7 per cent annually (Alam 2019).

Economic growth in Bangladesh has mainly been powered by the textiles and garments industry, which is labour-intensive. It is the largest industry in the manufacturing sector and accounts for approximately 60 per cent of the total value added in the sector. In order to achieve a sustained growth rate of over 7 per cent annually to become an HIC, dependence on such labour-intensive industries to propel growth may not help. A structural change in the economy, especially in the manufacturing sector, with a shift towards high value-added, non-labour-intensive (use of more machines instead of labour) industries would be required to achieve this vision.

ENERGY CONSUMPTION IN BANGLADESH

The primary energy supply in Bangladesh increased from 5 millions of tonnes of oil equivalent (Mtoe) in 1971 to 47 Mtoe in 2017–18. During the past 10 years, the primary energy supply has increased by over 82 per cent, growing at over 6 per cent per annum (see Table 9.1 and Figure 9.1).

Table 9.1 Energy Supply in Bangladesh, 2017–18

Fuel	*Mtoe*
POL	6.9
LPG	0.5
Natural Gas	22.3
Coal—Imported	2.1
Coal—Domestic	0.6
Renewable Hydro	0.2
Renewable Solar	0.3
Electricity Imported	0.5
Biomass	13.6
Total	**47.0**

Source: Ministry of Power, Energy and Mineral Resources (2019a).

Figure 9.1 Growth of Primary Energy Supply in Bangladesh, 1971–2017

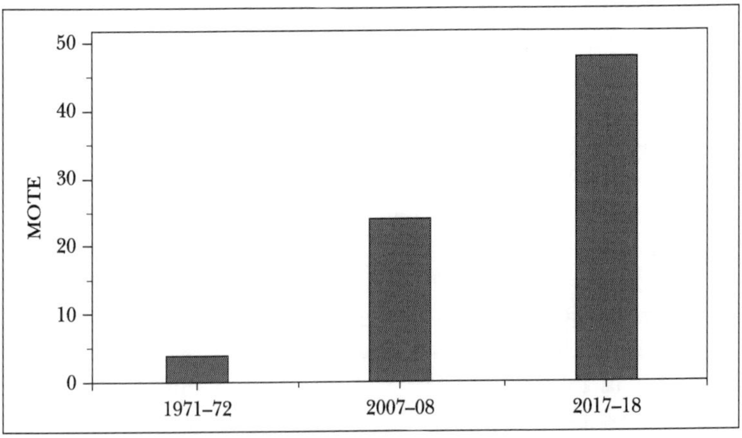

Source: Ministry of Power, Energy and Mineral Resources (2019b).

Energy sources in Bangladesh are categorised into commercial energy and primary energy. Commercial energy sources include indigenous natural gas, coal, imported oil, Liquefied Petroleum Gas (LPG), imported Liquefied Natural Gas (LNG), imported electricity and hydro-electricity. In 2017–18, commercial energy sources accounted for 71 per cent of the total energy supplied. Primary energy, which is mainly biomass, accounted for 29 per cent of the total energy supply.

Natural gas is the largest source of energy in Bangladesh, accounting for 68 per cent of the commercial energy and 47 per cent of the primary energy supplied in Bangladesh. The entire supply of natural gas is domestically produced; however, the reserves are depleting quickly. Imported oil, including crude, refined products and LPG account for the second-largest source of commercial energy, accounting for 6.9 millions tonnes of oil equivalent (Mtoe) or 14 per cent of the primary energy supplied. Although the country has a large reserve of coal, only about a million tonnes of coal are mined and used as an energy source. Energy demand is also being met by importing electricity from India.

Although the use of renewables to meet the energy demand has increased in the country, it accounts for under 1 per cent of the total energy supplied. However, various initiatives have been implemented, such as including solar home systems, solar irrigation systems, etc., to increase renewables uptake.

An analysis of the total primary energy supply in Bangladesh indicates that natural gas is the primary energy source in the country. Reliance on natural gas increased from around 50 per cent in 2006–07 to over 60 per cent in 2016–17, of the total commercial energy sources. The share of biomass or waste as a source of energy reduced from 33 per cent in 2006–07 to around 23 per cent in 2016–17, owing to an increased electricity coverage and LPG availability to replace biomass as a fuel source. Figure 9.2 shows the historical trend of primary energy supply, sector-wise, between 2000 and 2016.

The total consumption of energy for 2016–17 in the country was estimated at 28,773 kilotonnes of oil equivalent (Ktoe), compared to 15,163 Ktoe in 2000–01. Given the increased economic activity in the country, the share of industry and transport has been increasing gradually. The share of energy consumption in 2016–17 for the

Figure 9.2 Total Final Energy Consumption in Ktoe: 2000 Versus 2016

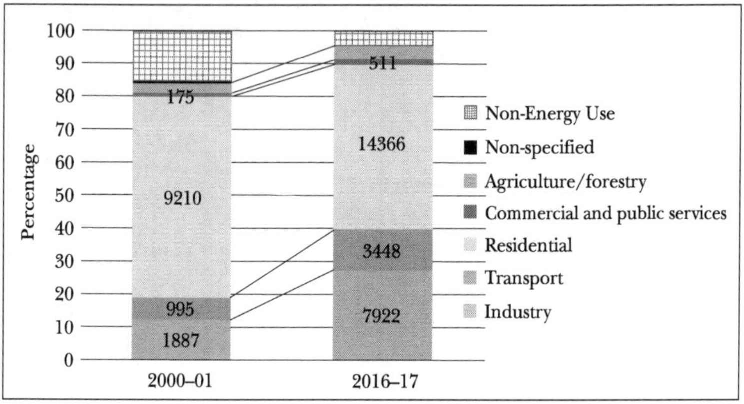

Source: International Energy Agency (IEA) (2018).

industry sector stood at 27 per cent, and that of the transport sector stood at 12 per cent, compared to 12 per cent and 6 per cent, respectively, in 2000–01. The percentage share for the two sectors not only increased two-fold, but the energy consumption in absolute terms increased by over three times in 2016–17.

In 2016–17, as per the latest estimates available with the IEA, the residential sector was the largest consumer of energy, and it accounts for over 50 per cent of the energy consumed. This is mainly on account of the biofuel and waste that is exclusively consumed by the residential sector. However, modernisation of energy supply, and the shift to electricity and gas in the residential sector is resulting in the gradual decrease of the share of the biomass and the overall consumption of energy by this sector (see Table 9.2).

Demand and Supply for Energy in Bangladesh

In order to achieve the targets of Vision 2041, a sustained economic growth of 7 per cent is required. A structural change in the economy would be required, where the share of agriculture is expected to reduce to around 10 per cent, the share of the industrial sector is expected to increase to around 37 per cent, and the service sector is to remain at around 53 per cent by 2041.

Table 9.2 Total Final Consumption of Energy, 2016–17

(In Ktoe)	*Coal**	*Oil Products*	*Natural Gas*	*Biofuels and Waste*	*Electricity*	*Total (Sector-wise)*
Industry	1,419	265	3,703	0	2,534	7,921
Transport	0	2,344	1,104	0	0	3,448
Residential	0	250	3,317	9,262	1,537	14,366
Commercial and public services	0	0	214	0	298	512
Agriculture/forestry	0	976	21	0	135	1,132
Non-specified	0	0	0	0	49	49
Non-energy use	0	96	1,249	0	0	1,345
Total (Fuel source-wise)	1,419	3,931	9,608	9,262	4,553	28,773

Source: IEA, Data and Statistics 2018.

Dependence on traditional industries such as textiles, garments, and leather industry will need to gradually decrease, followed by growth in new industries, such as light engineering products, processed foods and pharmaceutical products, if this target is to be achieved. To further continue the momentum, upgrading of the industrial sector to adopt to higher value-added industries and products such as electronics, information and technology/software, automobile parts, machinery and shipbuilding, would be required. With the anticipated structural change and the change in the industrial sector from a labour-intensive sector to an energy-intensive sector, energy consumption by the industrial sector is expected to increase rapidly.

In addition to the industrial sector, the share of final energy consumption by the transport sector is expected to increase rapidly. Vehicle ownership in Bangladesh is among the lowest in the world, with only 3.4 million vehicles for a population of 162 million. With increased economic activity, growth in per capita income, and changes in standard of living and vehicle ownership are expected to increase exponentially. Furthermore, it is expected that the movement of goods transported by road will increase from the current 80 per cent, owing to improvements in the road and bridge network. As a result, energy consumption by the transport sector is expected to be among the highest.

Based on the expected growth in the economy and the transformation in the industrial and transport sector, the Power and Energy Sector Master Plan (PSMP), 2016 of the Ministry of Power, Energy and Mineral Resources, Government of Bangladesh, has estimated two scenarios for total final energy consumption in Bangladesh until 2041. The two scenarios include:

- Projection of Final Energy Consumption under the business-as-usual scenario; and
- Projection of Final Energy Consumption under the Energy Efficiency Scenario (see Table 9.3).

As per the business-as-usual scenario, the total final energy consumption in the country is expected to increase from 38,753 Ktoe in 2021–22 to over 1,36,645 Ktoe by 2041–42. It is estimated that the total final energy consumption will grow at around 6.3 per cent between 2021 and 2041. The industrial and transport sectors are expected to be the largest consumers of energy in Bangladesh from 2030 onwards.

Under the energy efficiency scenario, it was assumed that the policies and measures of the 'Energy Efficiency and Conservation Master Plan up to 2030', formulated in 2015, would be implemented, resulting in the reduction of the total energy consumption per unit of GDP. As a result of the energy efficiency measure, final energy consumption will increase from 36,688 Ktoe in 2021–22 to 98,071 Ktoe in 2041–42. Under this scenario as well, industrial and transport sectors are expected to be the largest consumers of energy.

Based on the expected final energy consumption, and projecting under a base case scenario for the power sector, the PSMP, 2016 of the Ministry of Power, Energy and Mineral Resources, Government of Bangladesh, has estimated the Primary Energy Supply for Bangladesh at 48,207 Ktoe in 2021–22 and 130,827 Ktoe in 2041–42 (Tables 9.4, 9.5 and 9.6). Under the energy efficiency scenario, the average annual primary energy supply is expected to increase at the rate of 4.8 per cent up to 2041.

The challenge for Bangladesh is to find reliable long-term sources of fuels that will enable this demand to be catered to. The

Table 9.3 Projection of Final Energy Consumption

Final energy consumption under the business-as-usual scenario (in Ktoe)				*Final energy consumption under the energy efficiency scenario (in Ktoe)*			
	2021–22	*2030–31*	*2041–42*		*2021–22*	*2030–31*	*2041–42*
Residential	14,880	18,227	22,797	Residential	13,987	14,399	15,958
Industrial	13,732	30,386	54,524	Industrial	13,045	25,828	40,893
Commercial and public service	782	1,475	2,368	Commercial and Public Service	743	1,217	1,776
Transport	5,919	22,523	51,187	Transport	5,528	18,807	34,295
Agriculture	1,860	3,072	4,198	Agriculture	1,804	2,749	3,568
Others	47	47	47	Others	47	47	47
Non-energy use	1,534	1,534	1,534	Non-energy use	1,534	1,534	1,534
Total	**38,753**	**77,263**	**136,654**	**Total**	**36,688**	**64,581**	**98,071**

Source: Japan International Cooperation Agency (JICA) Library, PSMP (2016), p. 42.

Table 9.4 Energy Supply and Demand Balances, 2021–22

	Coal	*Crude oil*	*Oil products*	*Natural gas*	*Nuclear*	*Hydro, renewables*	*Biofuel and waste*	*Electricity*	*Total (Ktoe)*
Total Primary Energy Supply	**9,723**	**1,361**	**5,625**	**21,925**	**0**	**36**	**8,030**	**1,507**	**48,207**
Electricity Plants	–8,281	0	–49	–8,378	0	–36	0	8,811	–7,933
Oil refineries		–1,361	1,320						–41
Own use, loss, etc.	–26		–72	–346			–144	–1,450	–2,038
Total final Consumption	**1,416**	**0**	**6,825**	**13,201**	**0**	**0**	**7,885**	**7,361**	**36,688**
Industry	1,416		330	6,958				4,341	13,045
Transport			3,756	1,769				3	5,528
Residential			1,028	2,654			7885	2,420	13,987
Commercial and public service			0	350				394	743
Agriculture			1,619	28				157	1,804
Not specified			1	0				46	47
Non-energy use			92	1,442				0	1,534

Source: JICA Library, PSMP (2016), p. 42.

Table 9.5 Energy Supply and Demand Balances, 2031–32

	Coal	*Crude oil*	*Oil products*	*Natural gas*	*Nuclear*	*Hydro and renewables*	*Biofuel and waste*	*Electricity*	*Total (Ktoe)*
Total Primary Energy Supply	**16,637**	**1,361**	**17,448**	**33,119**	**7,953**	**172**	**6,009**	**3,390**	**86,090**
Electricity plants	–13,782	0	–365	–8,234	–7,953	–172	0	15,967	–14,539
Oil refineries		–1,361	1,320						–41
Own use, loss, etc.	52		–124	–627			–108	–2,627	–3,538
Total final consumption	**2,803**	**0**	**18,280**	**24,259**	0	0	5,901	13,340	64,582
Industry	2,803		653	13,777				8,596	25,828
Transport			12,776	6,019				12	18,807
Residential			2,291	2,406			5,901	3,801	14,399
Commercial			0	572				645	1,217
Agriculture			2,406	42				240	2,749
Not specified			1	0				46	47
Non-energy use			92	1,442				0	1,534

Source: JICA Library, PSMP (2016), p. 43.

Table 9.6 Energy Supply and Demand Balances, 2041–42

	Coal	*Crude oil*	*Oil products*	*Natural gas*	*Nuclear*	*Hydro and renewables*	*Biofuel and waste*	*Electricity*	*Total (Ktoe)*
Total Primary Energy Supply	**26,273**	**1,361**	**30,792**	**50,149**	**11,942**	**197**	**4,086**	**6,027**	**1,30,827**
Electricity plants	–21,752	0	–1	–11,803	–11,942	–197	0	24,333	–21,362
Oil refineries		–1,361	1,320						–41
Own use, loss, etc.			–210	–955			73	–4,004	–5,326
Total final consumption	**4,438**	**0**	**31,900**	**37,391**	**0**	**0**	**4,013**	**20,330**	**98,071**
Industry	4,438		1,033	21,813				13,609	40,893
Transport			23,298	10,976				21	34,295
Residential			4,274	2,271			4013	5,401	15,958
Commercial and public service			0	835				941	1,776
Agriculture			3,202	54				311	3,568
Non-specified			1	0				46	47
Non-energy use			92	1,442				0	1,534

Source: JICA Library, PSMP (2016), p. 43.

ensuing paragraphs attempt to describe the availability of different types of fuel, and whether they would be adequate to meet this demand.

Natural Gas

Natural gas is the largest source of energy in Bangladesh, accounting for over 47 per cent of the total primary energy supplied in 2017–18. However, the amount of gas available is limited and is not expected to last beyond two decades. Natural gas was first discovered in the country in 1955. As of 2017–18, 26 gas fields (24 onshore and two offshore) have been discovered in Bangladesh, with an estimated proven-plus-probable recoverable reserve of 28.69 trillion cubic feet (tcf).

Presently, only 19 gas fields are in production. One offshore gas field has depleted, and the remaining six gas fields are unviable for production, owing to small reserves. As of 2018, a total of 15.96 tcf of natural gas has already been produced, with a recoverable reserve of only 12.72 tcf in the proven-plus-probable category.

Given that over 40 per cent of the gas produced is supplied for power production, it results in the production of over 66 per cent of the grid power supplied. The availability of natural gas, and favourable prices for the same have helped industrial growth in the country, and is also used in captive power and heating. All the seven fertiliser plants in Bangladesh use fertiliser as a feedstock, accounting for around five per cent of the natural gas consumption. Natural gas is also supplied for domestic consumption through piped supply to over 7 per cent of the population. With Compressed Natural Gas (CNG) being adopted at a rapid pace, especially in Dhaka to combat pollution, over 0.25 million cars run on CNG (see Figure 9.3).

In order to meet the energy demands in the country, it is expected that the supply of natural gas would require 6,199 MMSCFD of capacity. Currently, the entire demand for natural gas is being met through domestic sources. However, the reliance on imports would increase substantially to over 68 per cent of the total natural gas requirement in the country (see Table 9.7).

Figure 9.3 Projected Supply of Natural Gas Million Million Standard Cubic Feet Per Day (MMSCFD), 2018–41

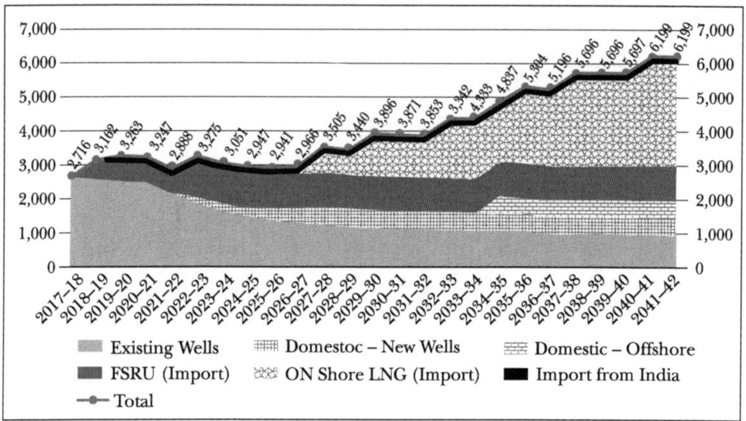

Source: JICA Library, PSMP (2016).

Table 9.7 Assumptions for Natural Gas Supply Scenario until 2041

1. The primary supply scenario is based on the existing gas production profile by Petro Bangla	
2. Ninety-five per cent discount factor is introduced based on the assessment by PSMP 2016	
3. Assuming new onshore gas fields are developed as follows:	• 2022 and After: Supply of 170 MMSCFD by Bangladesh Petroleum Exploration and Production Company Limited (BAPEX) as shown in the Petro Bangla Five-Year Plan • 2024 and after: 30 MMSCFD from a new gas field • 2025 and after: 100 MMSCFD from a new gas field • 2026 and after: 100 MMSCFD from a new gas field • 2027 and after: 100 MMSCFD from a new gas field
4. Assuming new domestic offshore gas fields are developed as follows:	• 2034 and after: 500 MMSCFD from a new gas field

Table 9.7 Contd.

Table 9.7 Contd.

5. Floating Storage Regasification Unit (FSRU) project	• 2018 and after: 500 MMSCFD is supplied by FSRU Phase 1 • 2022 and after: additional 500 MMSCFD is supplied by FSRU Phase 2
6. Onshore LNG terminal	• 2027 and after: 500 MMSCFD at the initial phase with 3 × 180,000 kl tanks • By 2041, Capacity is increased to 3,000 MMSCFD Introduction from abroad
7. Gas Introduction from abroad	• 2019 and after: 200 MMSCFD from India

Source: JICA Library, PSMP (2016), p. 25.

PETROLEUM, OIL AND LUBRICANTS (POL)

Petroleum, Oil and Lubricants (POL) account for about 6.9 Mtoe of energy supplied in Bangladesh, translating to around 15 per cent of the total primary supply, and about 22 per cent of the commercial energy supply in the country. The country consumed over 6.95 million metric tonnes (MT) of POL in 2017–18 (see Table 9.8).

Table 9.8 Consumption of POL in 2017

Total consumption of POL	69.48 Lac MT
Import of refined oil	55.42 Lac MT
Import of crude oil	11.73 Lac MT
Import of furnace oil	13.99 Lac MT
Domestic production of LPG	15,936 MT
Production of LPG under private	5,37,686 MT
The demand for POL in FY 2018–19	76 Lac MT

Source: Ministry of Power, Energy and Mineral Resources (2019c).

Bangladesh also produces POL domestically. The natural gas fields produce a small portion of condensates, amounting to about 4.3 million barrel or 6 per cent of total petroleum products. These condensates produce LPG, petrol, diesel and kerosene. The remaining 94 per cent of the oil demand in Bangladesh is met through imports from foreign countries. In 2017–18, Bangladesh imported over 1.2 million MT of crude oil and 5.5 million MT of refined petroleum products.

Demand for petroleum products in Bangladesh has grown at a Compound Annual Growth Rate (CAGR) of over 5.2 per cent between 2010 and 2017. In the past two years, however, demand for petroleum products has increased by 15 per cent (see Figure 9.4). The demand for petroleum products in the country is driven mainly by the transport sector, which roughly accounts for half of the total consumption. The power sector accounts for around 27 per cent, followed by the agriculture sector at 16 per cent.

Figure 9.4 Share of POL Products, 2017–18

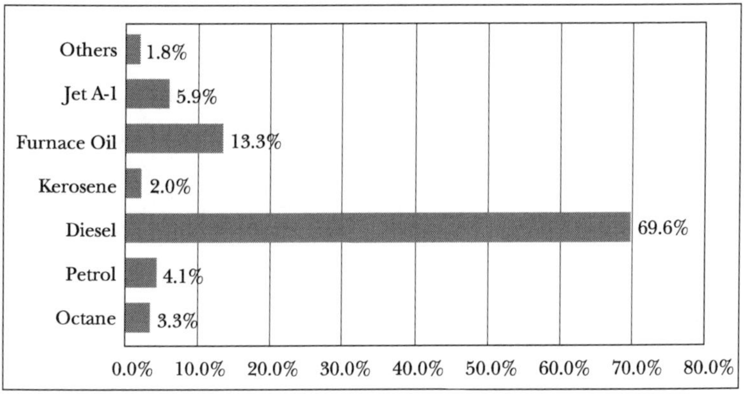

Source: Ministry of Power, Energy and Mineral Resources (2019c).

With regard to the consumption share of POL products, it may be noted that diesel oil accounts for around 70 per cent of the total petroleum products consumed in the country. This can be attributed to its extensive use in transportation, power, industry and agricultural sectors. Furnace oil accounts for 13 per cent of the total consumption and is widely used in the industrial sector. Only four per cent of the total petroleum products is consumed as petrol, given the low motorisation in the country and the fact that it is still in the early stages of private car ownership. The country is among those with the lowest car per capita, at four per 1,000 people in the world. The total number of cars registered in Bangladesh in

2017–18 stood at 3.4 million, with 1.9 million having been added since 2010.

With an expected increase in economic activity, followed by growth in per capita income and changes in standard of living, ownership of vehicles is expected to increase exponentially. In addition to increased growth in the vehicles, movement of goods by land is expected to increase from the current 80 per cent, owing to improvement in the road-and-bridge network. As a result, energy consumption by the transport sector is expected to be among the highest, resulting in an increased demand for petroleum products. Demand for POL is expected to increase to about 31,900 Ktoe by 2041–42.

It is expected that POL will be supplied from the following sources, to meet the increase in demand for petroleum products in the country:

- The existing Eastern Refinery Limited, which has a capacity of around 1.5 million tons per year;
- Expansion of the Unit-2 Project of ERL with a capacity of 3.0 million MT of crude oil processing capacity;
- Proposed Kuwait Petroleum Corporation (KPC) refining and petrochemical complex in Maheshkhali Island in southern Chittagong. KPC has plans to set up 8.0 million tonnes of crude oil proceesing capacity;
- To meet the remaining demand, it is expected that the finished oil products will be imported into the country (see Figure 9.5).

Power Sector Overview in Bangladesh

As per the data available from the Ministry of Power, Energy and Mineral Resources, the total installed capacity of power in Bangladesh stood at 18,876 megawatt (MW) in April 2019. However, 20 per cent of the capacity is under maintenance and forced outage (see Figure 9.6).

Given the country's reliance on natural gas, gas-based power plants account for the largest share, that is, over 53 per cent, of the total installed capacity available among various fuel types in Bangladesh. Petroleum product-based power plants, including diesel and furnace

Figure 9.5 Total Oil Demand and Supply Projection from 2014–41

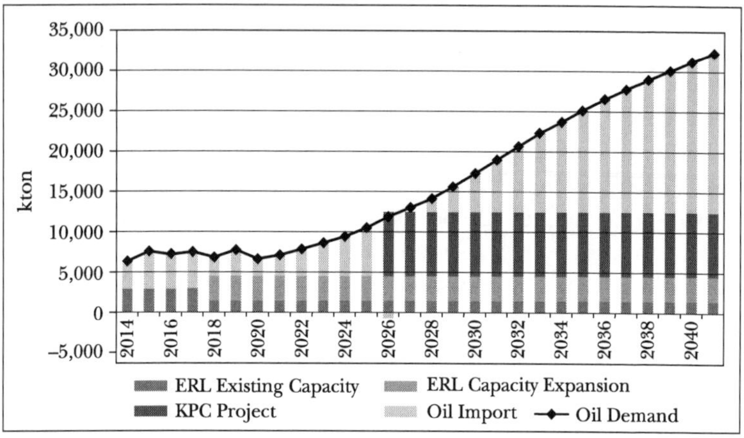

Source: JICA Library, PSMP (2016).

Figure 9.6 Fuel Type-wise Electricity Generation (in gigawatt hours [GWH]) and Percentage Share, 2017–18

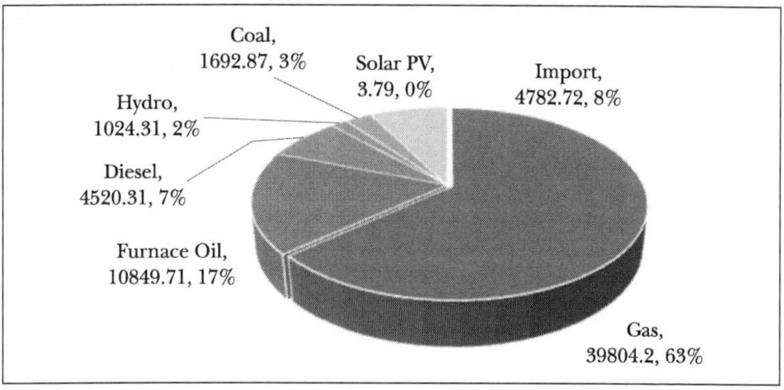

Source: JICA Library, PSMP (2016), p. 15.

oil, account for 36 per cent of the installed capacity available. Despite having large reserves of coal, Bangladesh's dependence on it for power generation is only around 3 per cent of the total installed capacity. To meet the power demand of the country, Bangladesh also imports 1,160 MW from India as cross-border energy trade. The maximum peak generation in 2018–19 was 12,893 MW, an

11 per cent increase compared to 2017–18. Lower peak generation is on account of operation and maintenance, lower efficiency on account of aging power plants, and gas shortages.

Of the total generation capacity, around 50 per cent is owned by the public sector, 44 per cent is owned by the private sector, while the remaining 6 per cent of the available capacity is imported from India. The dependence on imported fuel and imported power to supply electricity accounted for 32 per cent of the total energy generated (imported diesel, furnace oil, and electricity import from India). Cross-border energy trade between Bangladesh and India started in 2013, with an import of 660 MW, and it increased to 1,160 MW in 2018. This amount is expected to increase further in the future.

Net electricity generation in the country in 2017–18 stood at 62,678 GWH with a per capita generation of 464 kilowatt hours (KWH). Electricity coverage in Bangladesh stood at 88 per cent in 2017–18, with 100 per cent coverage in urban areas and 81 per cent coverage in rural areas.

The World Bank has identified Bangladesh as one of the countries with the largest number of people with no access to electricity. Since 2010, electricity coverage in the country has been growing at over 8 per cent per annum, resulting in improved electricity coverage at 50 per cent in 2010–11 to 88 per cent in 2017–18. Similarly, electricity generation has been increasing at a CAGR of over 10 per cent between 2010–11 and 2017–18 (see Figure 9.7).

The domestic sector is the largest electricity consumer in the country, accounting for over 52 per cent of the electricity consumed. Given the increased electricity coverage and the fact that 12 per cent is yet to be covered, the share of the domestic consumer is expected to increase further in future.

Renewable Energy

Renewable energy resources used in Bangladesh are classified into three categories: traditional biomass fuels, conventional hydropower and new-renewable resources, for example, solar photovoltaic [PV], wind, biogas, etc. (see Table 9.9).

Figure 9.7 Net Electricity Generation (2005–2018) in GWH

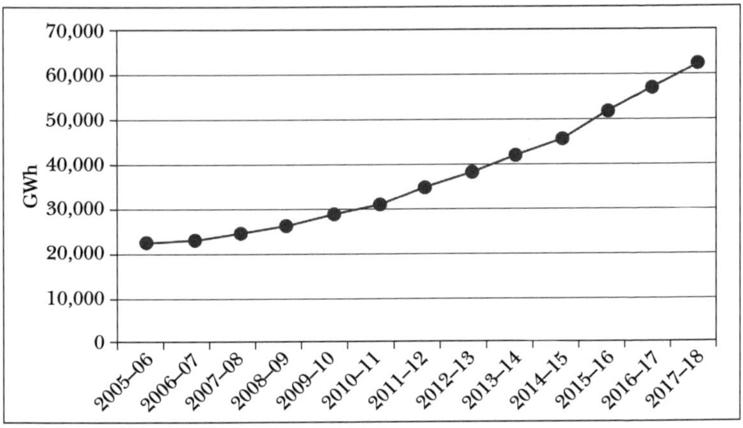

Source: Ministry of Power, Energy and Mineral Resources (2019d: 23).

Table 9.9 Installed Renewable Capacity as in March 2019

Technology	*Off-Grid*	*On-Grid*	*Total*
Solar	295.63	55.11	350.74
Wind	2	0.9	2.9
Hydro	—	230	230
Biogas to electricity	0.68	—	0.68
Biomass to electricity	0.4	—	0.4
Total	**298.71**	**286.01**	**584.72**

Source: Sustainable and Renewable Energy Development Authority (SREDA) (2019).

Deployment of renewable energy in Bangladesh is a key priority in energy security, while reducing the country's dependence on imported fuel and complementing its goal of providing electricity to all by 2021 through off-grid rural electrification. Bangladesh is among the most vulnerable countries, owing to a rise in sea level. Hence, the adoption of renewable energy is critical as a mitigation strategy for countering the impact of climate change. Owing to this necessity, the Ministry of Power, Energy and Mineral Resources, in their Renewable Energy Policy, 2008, set a goal to increase renewable energy share to 5 per cent by 2015 and 10 per cent by 2020.

Total generation from renewable energy, including hydropower, off-grid and captive, was 584.72 MW in 2017–18. Most of the on-grid renewable energy was on account of the 230 MW hydropower project.

For the Bangladesh economy to grow at over 7 per cent, its power generating capacity must be 24,000 MW by 2021. Renewable energy will need to account for 10 per cent of the electricity produced by 2020, resulting in an installed capacity of over 2,000 MW of renewables by 2020. By 2041, Bangladesh's expected installed capacity requirement and installed renewable energy capacity requirement must be 56,000 MW and 3,864 MW, respectively. If Bangladesh intends to extend the 10 per cent renewable energy target by 2041, it would require 5,600 MW renewable energy capacity. However, Bangladesh also submitted its Nationally Determined Contribution (NDC) to the Paris Climate Agreement. The NDC for the power sectors is set at adding 1,000 MW of solar PV and 400 MW of wind power generation by 2030, which is very conservative compared to the 2041 target. Regardless of the differing targets, it can be considered a progress towards renewables, given the limited progress in renewable energy deployment (see Table 9.10).

Table 9.10 Renewable Potential in Bangladesh

Solar parks	1,400*
Solar rooftops	635
Solar home systems	100
Solar irrigation	545
Wind park	637**
Biomass	275
Biogas	10
Municipal waste	1
Mini hydro	60
Mini grid, micro grid	3***
Total	**3,666**

Notes: * Case 1 (agricultural land excluded) estimate.
** Case 1 (flood-prone land excluded) estimate.
****Based on planned projects only, not a theoretical maximum potential, because there is potential overlap with off-grid solar systems. Either could be used to serve off-grid demand.*

Source: Ministry of Power, Energy and Mineral Resources (2019e).

SREDA was established in 2014 to promote renewable energy and energy efficiency. The renewable energy policy of the government promotes both public and private-sector investment in renewable energy projects to substitute indigenous non-renewable energy supplies and scale up contributions of existing renewable energy-based electricity production.

The renewable energy potential in Bangladesh is significant. The Bangladesh Climate Investment Funds Scaling Up Renewable Energy Program (CIF-SREP) investment plan has estimated that Bangladesh has a potential of 3,666 MW of renewable energy capacity. The CIF-SREP investment plan's estimate of the total potential for ground-mounted solar, wind and the solar rooftop is about 2,600 MW. It should be noted that 3,666 MW is a tentative number and has the potential to be updated. Furthermore, Bangladesh has a regulation on land usage for utility-scale solar PV (as they require vast areas of land). The policy prohibits private projects from using agriculture or cultivable land for a utility-scale solar PV project. According to SREDA, utility-scale solar PV potential is estimated at 1,400 MW with land-usage regulation, while 19,000 MW is the estimated potential for utility-scale solar in the absence of regulation.

As per the Renewable Energy Year-Based Plan of SREDA, the country is expected to achieve a total of around 2,360 MW of renewables by 2021–22. Most of the capacity is planned from solar (1,150 MW) and wind (953 MW).

Given the renewable potential and the planned targets, it may be difficult for Bangladesh to meet its target domestically. To address this, cross-border power import from hydropower generation is counted as renewable energy that could address this problem and easily meet the potential policy target.

Long-term Generation Plan

PSMP 2016 accounts for the long-term electricity generation against the demand up to 2041. As per the long-term plan, expected installed capacity requirement by 2035 will be 40,459 MW, against a peak demand of 36,400 MW, and installed capacity in 2041 will be 56,634 MW, against a peak demand of 47,800 MW. Both coal-based (20,195 MW) and gas-based (20,177 MW) power will account for 35 per cent of total installed capacity, with imported power accounting for 15 per cent or 9,000 MW. The long-term power plan also estimated that nuclear plants will contribute to 7,032 MW of the total installed capacity by 2041 (see Figure 9.8).

Coal

Coal in Bangladesh currently accounts for 2.7 Mtoe or 6 per cent of the total energy requirement in Bangladesh. Although Bangladesh is estimated to have a reserve of over 31 billion tonnes of coal with a mineable reserve of 438 million tonnes in 2017–18, only 0.92 million tonnes of coal was locally produced, while 3.35 million tonnes was imported into the country.

As per the estimates of PSMP 2016, the demand for coal in Bangladesh is expected to increase substantially to meet the growing needs of power generation and industrial use. Coal-based power plants are expected to increase to 5,873 MW by 2020 and 20,195 MW by 2041. Owing to this, the demand for coal in the country is expected to increase to over 52 million tonnes by 2041 (see Table 9.11).

To meet such a high demand in future, it is expected that the production of domestic coal will be increased substantially.

Figure 9.8 Summary of Power Development Plan (Base Case 2020–41)

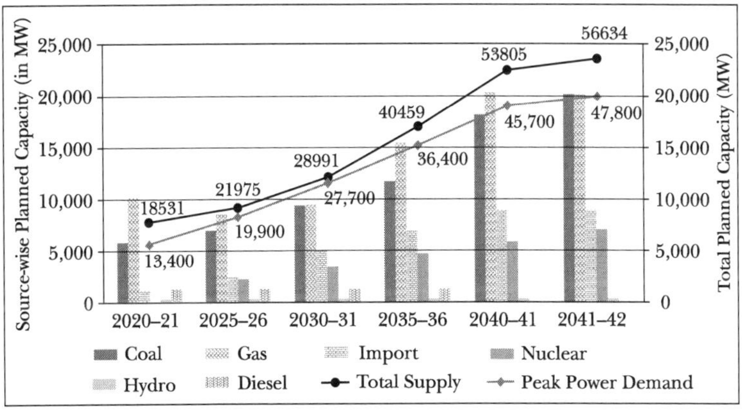

Source: JICA Library, PSMP (2016), pp. 33–36.

Table 9.11 Coal Demand and Supply Forecast

In Million Tonnes	*2020–21*	*2025–26*	*2030–31*	*2035–36*	*2040–41*	*2041–42*
Domestic	1.1	2.1	6.2	8.2	11.2	11.2
Import	17.9	21.3	25.3	29.7	38.0	41.0
Total Supply	**19.0**	**23.4**	**31.5**	**37.9**	**49.2**	**52.2**
Power	16.3	19.5	26.1	30.9	40.5	43.1
Non-power	2.7	3.9	5.4	7.1	8.8	9.1
Total Demand	**19.0**	**23.4**	**31.5**	**37.9**	**49.2**	**52.2**

Source: JICA Library, PSMP (2016), p. 16.

As demand for thermal coal is expected to considerably increase in Asia owing to demand from China and India, there exists an uncertainty as to whether Bangladesh will be able to import overseas coal at reasonable prices, given that globally, there is an aversion to increase in coal production.

Nuclear Power

Currently, no energy is supplied through a nuclear source in Bangladesh. However, given the growing energy demand in the country and the expected increased reliance on fossil fuel in future, the Bangladesh government signed an agreement with Russia in 2015 for the construction and commissioning of the first nuclear plant in the country. The proposed nuclear plant in Rooppur will have an installed capacity of 2×1200 MW, with an estimated cost of \$12.65 billion.

To further meet the electricity demand in the country, a second nuclear plant is also being considered by the Bangladesh Atomic Energy Commission (BAEC), for which suitable sites are being evaluated.

Concluding Remarks

It is clear from this chapter that energy demand in Bangladesh is set to rise substantially over the next decade, as Bangladesh transitions to a middle-income economy. The estimates of individual energy source demands indicate that there would be considerable dependence on imports of coal, petroleum and natural gas. There are opportunities for import of power as well from India and Bhutan.

The concerns with import dependency for energy are obvious. First, there is the need to secure long-term contracts and to fix availability. For petroleum and natural gas, there are short- and medium-term options, as it is a dynamic market, with new players and new prices emerging periodically, depending on the demand–supply situation. Coal contracts must be entered into for a longer term, as the output from coal mines is usually contracted for longer periods.

This leads to the second issue, that of logistics. Imports of fossil fuels, gas and coal require the development of infrastructure and logistics. Not only must there be vessels that are owned or contracted to deliver the fuels, but there should also be the port infrastructure to unload the fuels as well as the transportation infrastructure to carry the fuel inwards to consuming centres. In Bangladesh, given the flat, flood-prone landscape, the construction of heavy road and rail infrastructure is particularly difficult and time-consuming. Thus, there is a need to invest in ports, and rail and road infrastructure.

Third, this investment requires capacity, both manufacturing and technical. Bangladesh does not have the infrastructure and the manufacturing and technical capacity to undertake these infrastructure projects; there is little evidence of planning or project-planning, or programme conceptualisation for these investments. There is also a need to create refining and processing capacity, as well as new power stations, to meet the growing demand.

Fourth, and most important, is the ability to finance these investments. The current account balance is positive largely due to exports from the textile and garment sector and worker remittances. However, textile exports are likely to face headwinds as the preferred access to Bangladesh products decreases, and this industry must reinvent itself. The external balances by themselves would be inadequate to take care of energy imports in the long term. Internal budgetary resources are constrained by a low tax base, and a habit of tax avoidance, which is keeping governmental revenues low. The options for financing such a large infrastructure commitment and energy imports would be limited to external borrowings or project related aid, both of which may prove difficult as sustainable alternatives.

Fifth, there is a possibility of inter-regional cooperation, especially for the import of power. It is possible to enter into bilateral agreements with neighbouring countries, especially Nepal, India and Bhutan for the import of power. This would be concomitant with the development of new generation in these countries, which could be locally or internationally financed, with a clear agreement on purchase or pay contracts. Once again, the financial ability to service these contracts needs to be delved into.

Sixth, there is the need to invest in the domestic production of energy sources. There are existing reserves of coal that could be mined to increase production from the current low of one million tonnes per annum. There are reserves of natural gas that have not been exploited, as the exploration for new fields has been at a very slow pace. It is important to revitalise these areas through domestic or external funding, to create new domestic capacity, especially in coal and natural gas.

Finally, there is the issue of supply. The question of where Bangladesh would access long-term, reliable sources of supply for its crude oil, natural gas and coal needs is not clear. Neither has there been an attempt to enter into any special relationship with oil-producing countries, nor any long-term coal supply agreement with coal producers. For some reason, this aspect of policy is not getting adequate attention in Bangladesh, and is likely to turn into a stumbling block for continued growth.

Bangladesh is at an inflection point in terms of its energy sustainability (World Bank 2019). Hitherto, growth has been managed by ad hoc additions to capacity and to imports. However, with energy demand set to grow significantly, these measures need to be replaced by a well-thought out energy sustainability plan that needs to be implemented. Otherwise, energy availability would remain a very vulnerable limitation to the growth story of Bangladesh.

References

Alam, Shamsul. 'Bangladesh: Vision 2041: Alignment with Other Macro Plans', *South Asia Journal*, 7 April 2019. Available at http://southasiajournal.net/bangladesh-vision-2041-alignment-with-other-macro-plans (accessed 3 December 2019).

IEA. 2018. Power and Energy Sector Master Plan 2016. Available at https://www.iea.org/statistics/?country=BANGLADESH&year=2016&category=Energy%20consumption&indicator=TFCShareBySector&mode=table&dataTable=BALANCES (accessed 3 December 2019).

IEA, Data and Statistics. 2018. *Bangladesh: Balances for 2016, IEA World Energy Balances 2018.* Available at https://www.iea.org/statistics/?country=BANGLADESH&year=2016&category=Energy%20consumption&indicator=TFCShareBySector&mode=table&dataTable=BALANCES (accessed 3 December 2019).

JICA, PSMP 2016. Available at http://open_jicareport.jica.go.jp/pdf/12269759_01.pdf (accessed 3 December 2019).

Ministry of Power, Energy and Mineral Resources. 2019a. *Energy Scenario Bangladesh: 2017–18.*

———. 2019b. International Energy Agency. Available at https://www.iea.org/statistics/?country=BANGLADESH&year=2016&category=Energy%20consumption&indicator=TFCShareBySector&mode=table&dataTable=BALANCES (accessed 3 December 2019).

———. 2019c. *Energy Sector Scenario Bangladesh: 2017–18.*

———. 2019d. Available at http://hcu.portal.gov.bd/sites/default/files/files/hcu.portal.gov.bd/publications/b84e0d36_2355_4581_a4b3_b8d5abbf9fdd/25102018%20Energy%20Scenario%202017-18_Final.pdf (accessed 3 December 2019).

———. 2019e. Available at https://www.climateinvestmentfunds.org/sites/cif_enc/files/bangladesh_srep_ip_final.pdf (accessed 3 December 2019).

SREDA. 2019. Available at http://www.sreda.gov.bd/index.php/site/re_present_status/16 (accessed 3 December 2019).

10

Five Decades of Bangladesh–India Relations

SHAMSHER M. CHOWDHURY

In trying to analyse the various aspects of the bilateral relations between Bangladesh and India as it has traversed over the past nearly five decades, it would be relevant to trace the historical context that led to the emergence of Bangladesh as an independent State in 1971.

This came about after Bangladesh's nearly two-and-a-half decades of uneasy existence as East Pakistan, the final break following a bloody nine-month-long armed War of Liberation in which India had played a major role, if not a decisive one.

THE PAINFUL PASSAGE TO FREEDOM

Noted author Salman Rushdie, in his 1983 book, *Shame*, describes Pakistan as it was created, '... that a country divided into two Wings a thousand miles apart, that fantastic bird of a place, two Wings without a body, sundered by the land-mass of its greatest foe, joined by nothing but God ... ' (Rushdie 1983: 178). Sceptics of the creation of Pakistan called it a geographical, social and political absurdity. The sceptics were proven right.

The disparity between the two wings was visible in almost every area: economic, social and political. Very few East Pakistanis made it to the top echelons of the civil service, and even less to the military. Politically, it was as if the Bengalis did not matter. The degree to which the Pakistani establishment chose to ignore the security vulnerability of East Pakistan was most glaringly exposed during the Pakistan–India War of 1965. As Pakistan's Prime Minister, the late Zulfiqar Ali Bhutto said, as Foreign Minister, in a speech in

1965, 'There were three considerations that prevented India from attacking East Pakistan—God, monsoon and the ultimatum from China' (Bhutto 2010: 65).

The outcome of the 1970 Parliamentary elections of Pakistan, in which the Awami League, under the charismatic leadership of Sheikh Mujibur Rahman, had won a clear mandate to govern Pakistan, revealed the deep divide between the democracy-loving *Bangali* in the East and Pakistan's political and military leadership in the West. Between the end of 1970 and early-1971, the rift between Pakistan's two wings continued to grow as talks between Sheikh Mujibur Rahman and Pakistan's military ruler, General Yahya Khan, to find a common ground for the transfer of power to the elected representatives failed to yield an acceptable outcome.

Among all these incidents, an incident of huge political significance involving India, took place. On 30 January 1971, two Kashmiri Muslims hijacked an Indian Airlines Fokker Friendship plane and diverted it to Lahore. In West Pakistan, this act of piracy was warmly welcomed as an act of valour and patriotism. Bhutto embraced the hijackers as heroes and demanded that they be given political asylum in Pakistan. India reacted by closing down any air corridor to Pakistani military flights and demanded the extradition of the hijackers to India, a formal apology from Pakistan, and compensation for the destroyed aircraft.

In East Pakistan, Sheikh Mujibur Rahman sensed political danger from the whole incident. He deplored the blowing up of the aircraft and sent a warning to the people that they should be fully alert to resist all attempts by vested quarters to exploit this occurrence. He felt this was necessary in order to create abnormal conditions, with the ulterior purpose of sabotaging the peaceful transfer of power to the people.

On 5 February 1971, General Yahya Khan spoke of a grave emergency following the hijacking incident. War preparations were immediately put in place, and a massive ferrying of troops to East Pakistan was set in motion. It culminated in the Pakistani military launching a brutal and genocidal military campaign on the *Bangali* population just after midnight of 25 March 1971.

The people of Bangladesh rose up in arms against the action of the Pakistani military, which led to the breakup of Pakistan and the eventual birth of independent Bangladesh nine months later, aided in a very large measure by the government and the armed forces of India. This armed resistance by the people of Bangladesh is what the world has come to know as the War of Liberation. The process, however, was not without massive deaths and wanton destruction.

Bangladesh's Journey as an Independent State

Bangladesh's early days were exceedingly difficult. *Bangabandhu* (Friend of Bengal) Sheikh Mujibur Rahman and his Awami League had taken the reins of the government with overwhelming public support, but had inherited a country in shambles, shattered physically, dysfunctional economically, the infrastructure and transport system damaged badly, and with severe law and order problems with armed gangs roaming the countryside. Six million homes were destroyed, and well over a million farmers had no tools or animals for their work. At the end of the war, the country lacked almost every resource it needed for recovery, let alone a rapid one.

For *Bangabandhu* and his government, there were major challenges on the international front as well. This was the Cold War era and the major players saw issues through the prism of a bipolar world, as it existed then. Although the United States (US), under President Richard Nixon, recognised Bangladesh very early on, it seemed unsure of its next moves. The major Arab countries, especially Saudi Arabia, refused to accept the breakup of Pakistan and refrained from recognising Bangladesh as an independent country. The same was the case with the People's Republic of China. It was not until 1974 that China withdrew its objection at the United Nations Security Council (UNSC) to Bangladesh becoming a full member of the UN, but formal diplomatic recognition was still not forthcoming. Bangladesh joined the Commonwealth in early 1972 and the Non-Aligned Movement (NAM) the following year.

The year 1974 was also when Prime Minister Sheikh Mujibur Rahman, in a bold and arguably his most dramatic diplomatic move, laced with political connotations, took Bangladesh to the centre of the Islamic world, when he accepted an invitation from key members of the Organisation of Islamic Cooperation (OIC), as it was called then, to attend the OIC Summit, ironically, in Lahore, Pakistan. His host was Pakistan's then Prime Minister, Zulfiqar Ali Bhutto. Reports indicate that the Lahore trip and joining the Islamic fold was apparently not seen favourably in Delhi, especially so soon after the traumatic events of the Liberation War. The decision of Prime Minister Sheikh Mujibur Rahman to join the OIC, and to do so by going to Pakistan, was seen by analysts at home and abroad as a calculated move on three counts. First, the formal recognition of Bangladesh as an independent State by Pakistan was a political necessity. Second, as Prime Minister of a sovereign country, Sheikh Mujibur Rahman, was keen to demonstrate a measure of autonomy in making the country's foreign policy choices. Third was giving vent to the demographic makeup of Bangladesh as a Muslim-majority country, which had a rightful place in this group. Whatever might have been the rationale, the move resonated well at home.

Both the People's Republic of China and the Kingdom of Saudi Arabia formally recognised Bangladesh on 17 August 1975, just two days after *Bangabandhu* Sheikh Mujibur Rahman was brutally killed, along with most of his family members, in a military putsch backed by some of his close associates in his own party.

Bangladesh–India Relations

The passage of Bangladesh's relations with India may be broadly divided into at least three major phases. The first phase is the period between 1972 and 1975, or the Awami League rule under *Bangabandhu* Sheikh Mujibur Rahman, first as the Prime Minister, and then briefly as the President. The second phase will be the long period between 1975 to 1990 when Bangladesh was under, at times directly and at times indirectly, military rule. The first one was under General Ziaur Rahman (1975–81), and the second one was under General Hussain Mohammad Ershad (1982–90). The third phase would be the post-1990 period till date, during which the country has been run by elected civilian governments, except for a brief two-year period, between 2007 and 2008, when a controversial military-backed unelected civilian administration was in charge.

Phase 1: 1972–75

The Early Days

Bilateral relations between Bangladesh and India are rooted in history and conditioned by geography. This is a relationship that is written in blood. India's direct role in Bangladesh's War of Liberation in 1971 is a fundamental element in the parameters that have shaped the relationship between the two South Asian neighbours. *Bangabandhu* Sheikh Mujibur Rahman assumed the office of Prime Minister of Bangladesh against the backdrop of this remarkable state of bilateral ties, which were more like a natural bonding between two peoples. The feeling of mutual goodwill was as real as it was pervasive.

On the bilateral front, three major events happened in this atmosphere of bonhomie between India and the newborn country. First, at the request of the Sheikh Mujibur Rahman, Indian Prime Minister Indira Gandhi, herself riding on a wave of popularity in India and goodwill in Bangladesh, agreed to withdraw all Indian military personnel from the territory of Bangladesh, and that, too, within the time frame asked for by Bangladesh. The event, loaded with political symbolism, happened as early as March 1972 during Prime Minister Indira Gandhi's official visit to Dhaka. *Bangabandhu*'s request to the Indian Prime Minister to withdraw the Indian troops from Bangladesh must have been driven by a realisation that the presence of a foreign military in its territory would be seen as an infringement on the sovereignty of Bangladesh. On the other hand, Prime Minister Indira Gandhi must have reasoned that to procrastinate would have risked losing the immense goodwill India and its military had earned with the people of Bangladesh for their role in the Liberation War of Bangladesh.

There are very few instances in history where the victorious military or the liberator (and in this instance, they were one and the same) agreed to withdraw itself from a territory that it has helped liberate. The Bangladesh–India case can therefore be cited as a study in contrast, and one of political wisdom and vision. The second was the signing of the 25-year treaty titled 'The India–Bangladesh Treaty of Friendship, Cooperation and Peace' in Dhaka on 19 March 1972, by Prime Ministers Indira Gandhi and Sheikh

Mujibur Rahman, on behalf of their respective governments. This treaty, however, did become a subject of controversy in Bangladesh, especially provisions (ix) and (x), which people saw as an unequal imposition of excessive Indian influence, undermining the sovereignty of Bangladesh. Not surprisingly, therefore, the treaty was not renewed after its expiry in 1997, even though *Bangabandhu*'s daughter, Sheikh Hasina, was the Prime Minister at that time.

The third event of significance was the signing of the India–Bangladesh Land Boundary Agreement (LBA) in 1974 by Prime Ministers Sheikh Mujibur Rahman and Indira Gandhi. The agreement was aimed at resolving once and for all the bizarre anomalies in the land boundaries between the two neighbours, which included the demarcation of sections of the boundary, the exchange of enclaves and lands in adverse possession in each other's territories, and legacies left behind by the departing British colonial rulers. Bangladesh, on its part, ratified the agreement and implemented its side of the deal in quick succession, handing South Berubari to India. India, on the other hand, held back on delivering its part of the deal for more than four decades, citing legal and constitutional complications, among others.

This was one of the two major issues that stood out as sore points, the other being the Farakkah Barrage. Importantly, while Bangladesh had agreed to a trial run of the barrage over the Ganges at Farakkah on the Indian side, there had not been any conclusive talks on a permanent arrangement for sharing the Ganges water that Bangladesh was entitled to receive as a lower riparian country. As seen subsequently, the effects of the Farakkah Barrage on the ecology and economy of Bangladesh was to emerge as a major issue of discord between the two neighbours. This, in a large measure, led to the gradual seeping in of words like 'trust deficit' into the lexicon of Bangladesh–India relations.

By the time *Bangabandhu* Sheikh Mujibur Rahman's government came to a tragic end in mid-1975, bilateral ties between Bangladesh and India stood on a balance. Publicly, both sides tried to demonstrate that the ties were stable. However, strains were discernible, and these were expressed by both governments behind closed doors. Former Indian Foreign Secretary and National Security Advisor, late J. N. Dixit, makes clear reference to this in his book, *Liberation and Beyond: Bangladesh–India Relations* (Dixit 1999). Incidentally, Dixit was the Deputy High Commissioner of India in Bangladesh until early 1975, and had a ringside view of things as they played out during that period.

Phase 2: 1975–90

2a: 1975–81

The Ziaur Rahman Government: With the coming to power of General Ziaur Rahman, a decorated hero of the Bangladesh Liberation War, in November 1975, following a series of coups and counter-coups that followed the assassination of *Bangabandhu*, the state of Bangladesh–India relations was initially characterised by mutual suspicion, although it remained far short of being hostile or estranged. India, on its part, reconciled to having to deal with the government of the day even when there was a military man in charge. Policymakers in Delhi knew little about the new government, except that it enjoyed a good measure of acceptance with the public in Bangladesh. General Ziaur Rahman followed a path of engagement with the Indian government by dispatching special envoys to Delhi at high political and foreign policymaker levels.

In November 1975, the unthinkable happened. A group of presumably ultra-Left extremist youths made an attempt on the life of Indian High Commissioner Samar Sen in Dhaka. The High Commissioner survived the gun attack, but he was seriously wounded. To say that Prime Minister Indira Gandhi was angry at this most unfortunate incident would be an understatement; she was furious. It took a direct communication from General Ziaur Rahman to the Indian Prime Minister to calm things down, but the stain remained.

The major element in General Ziaur Rahman's foreign relations domain was the jump-start of Bangladesh's bilateral political, economic and military relations with China, on the one hand, and with the Muslim world, especially, Saudi Arabia, on the other. This created an altogether new dynamic for Bangladesh. This manifested itself most visibly when Bangladesh was elected as a non-permanent member of the UNSC in 1978, defeating Japan in the process.

Bangladesh's relationship with both China and Saudi Arabia has grown exponentially stronger over time and with every successive government in Bangladesh, elected or otherwise. In the context of relations with India, the Farrakah issue was brought to the forefront by the Ziaur Rahman government very early on in its stint. This found strong resonance at home. In 1976, Bangladesh tried to up the ante by raising the issue at the UN General Assembly. The effort, however, failed to garner sufficient support, and Bangladesh had to revert to dealing with India bilaterally.

After the assumption of the office of Prime Minister by Morarji Desai and the Janata Party government in India in early-1977, a bilateral agreement on the sharing of the waters of the Ganges was signed in Dhaka, which satisfied both sides. This agreement was to be valid for five years, and could be renewed if both parties agreed.

Interestingly, the minister who signed this agreement for the Indian government was Jagjivan Ram, the very same person who, as the Minister for Water Resources under the former Congress government, had resisted it. Just prior to the Lok Sabha elections of 1977, Ram had switched allegiance and joined the Janata Party of Morarji Desai, and had retained his cabinet portfolio in the new government. This clearly demonstrated that at times, decisions on key bilateral issues were taken more on political considerations, and not always on the merits of the issue at hand.

With the return of the Indira Gandhi-led Congress (I) government in 1980, India opted not to renew the agreement. A series of short-term interim arrangements followed, but a permanent solution was not seen on the horizon. The other issue that generated great heat was the competing claims by Delhi and Dhaka over a piece of a small uninhabited offshore sandbar island in the Bay of Bengal, off the coast of the Ganges–Brahmaputra delta region. Bangladesh called this South Talpatty, while Indian records showed it as New Moore. This issue reached a head when both India and Bangladesh briefly deployed their respective naval assets in the area to establish their claims.

The dispute has since become academic as the sandbar island has submerged, apparently by rising sea water caused by global warming. Besides, the delimitation of the maritime boundary between Bangladesh and India, through international arbitration in July 2014, put an end to any dispute on this matter.

The form and content of the bilateral relations between India and Bangladesh during General Ziaur Rahman's five-year period, first as the Chief Martial Law Administrator and then as the President, is a mixed story. Trust deficit on both sides was perceptible, but this did not prevent either side from engaging with each other at various political and official levels. Delhi also recognised that Ziaur Rahman was a popular leader in Bangladesh. The relationship went on an upward curve between early 1977 and 1980, when Desai was the Prime Minister of India. The important features during this period were the signing of the Farrakah Agreement in mid-1977 and President Ziaur Rahman's high-profile official visit to Delhi in December in the same year. This visit was characterised by warmth and cordiality. President Ziaur Rahman again visited Delhi in 1980 and had extensive discussions with Prime Minister Indira Gandhi.

The concept of institutionalised regional economic cooperation among the countries of South Asia was first floated in 1980, when President Ziaur Rahman addressed formal letters to the Heads of State and Governments of the other South Asian countries, spelling out the logic behind such a concept. This introduced a new element in the domain of Bangladesh–India relations. The initiative eventually led to the formation of the South Asian Association for Regional Cooperation (SAARC), which was formally launched in Dhaka during a summit meeting of all the seven South Asian nations in 1985; it was the first time ever such that a gathering had taken place. India was represented at the summit by Prime Minister Rajiv Gandhi. General Ziaur Rahman was assassinated in another military putsch in May 1981.

2b: 1982–90

The Ershad Period: The period of General Hussain Muhammad Ershad's eight-year rule, again, first as the Chief Martial Law Administrator and then as the President, was unremarkable on almost every front. Coming to power through a military coup in 1982 by usurping an elected civilian government, General Ershad was haunted by a legitimacy crisis throughout his term of office.

On the international front, President Ershad could do little more than continue with what he had inherited, especially strengthening relations with China and the Arab countries. An abortive second attempt at gaining a non-permanent seat in the UNSC, losing comprehensively to Malaysia, was the manifestation of a directionless foreign policy. Similarly, in terms of bilateral relations with India, other than half-hearted attempts at finding some form of permanent arrangement on sharing the waters of the Ganges river, there were no other initiatives that could find special mention. General Ershad's government, however, did push forward on getting the South Asian countries to agree to institutionalised regional socio-economic cooperation. His major, perhaps only, achievement was to chair the first-ever SAARC Summit meeting in Dhaka in 1985.

Phase 3

3a: 1991–96

The Bangladesh Nationalist Party (BNP) Government: With the return of democracy in Bangladesh following the fall of General Ershad in December 1990, Bangladesh held its first fully participatory, free and fair Parliamentary election in February 1991. The Bangladesh Nationalist Party (BNP) won this election, and its leader Khaleda Zia, widow of President Ziaur Rahman, was sworn in as the Prime Minister on 20 March 1991. This outcome was against almost every pre-election prediction. Kris Srinivasan, in his book, *The Jamdani Revolution; Politics, Personalities and Civil Society in Bangladesh* (Srinivasan 2008), says that the outcome caught him by total surprise, as it was against all their calculations. One might even have noticed a tinge of disappointment with the outcome in what Srinivasan said in his book.

However, bilateral relations between Bangladesh and India started off on a positive note when India sent its Foreign Secretary, Muchkund Dubey, as a special envoy, with a message that Delhi was prepared to actively engage the newly elected government in Dhaka for furthering the bilateral ties. There was yet another event, albeit, due to tragic circumstances, which created the grounds for a positive state of relations. Prime Minister Khaleda Zia's decision to attend the funeral of former Prime Minister Rajiv Gandhi, who was assassinated by a suicide bomber of the Liberation Tigers of Tamil Eelam (LTTE) in May 1991, sent the right signals all around. The gesture was well-received in Delhi and was viewed positively in Bangladesh.

However, three issues came to the fore, which worked as impediments to building a healthy, mutually beneficial relationship. First was the lack of any progress and the differences between the two sides regarding the sharing of the waters of the Ganges. While Bangladesh wanted something close to the 1977 Farrakah Agreement, India's stance was that there was not enough water available at Farrakah to return to the 1977 formula. Second was the non-implementation of the LBA of 1974. Bangladesh pressed for early implementation, but Delhi's consistent response was that the process of making the necessary Constitutional Amendment in India was a complex one, and more time was needed to carry out this change. One, however, did not notice any sense of urgency on the part of India in its attempt at moving forward with this. The situation was made more complicated by litigations in India on the deal, which worked as impediments, or were seen as such, to any forward movement. The third issue was the sheltering of insurgents from the Chittagong Hill Tracts, called the Shanti *Bahini* (army), and their political leadership in India's Tripura state where, allegedly, the group was also receiving training and military equipment.

From the Indian side, two issues featured prominently in the discourse: first were the allegations of illegal infiltrations from Bangladesh, causing Delhi to adopt a policy of 'push back', and the second were reports of insurgents from India's north-east entering Bangladesh, and even finding shelter there. Such a combination of ingredients was not conducive to creating the right chemistry for strengthening the ties. This found reflection at Begum Khaleda Zia's official talks with Prime Minister Narasimha Rao during her visit to Delhi in 1992. There was one major positive outcome of this visit, which was the signing of the accord on the Teen Bigha Corridor, along with other agreements, to expand bilateral cooperation, on 27 May 1992. In hindsight, given the fact that this was a popularly elected government in Bangladesh, observers believe that a more positive outlook from Delhi would have been well-advised, especially on the issues of water-sharing and the implementation of the LBA.

3b: 1996–2001

The Awami League Government: However, the situation changed almost dramatically with the coming to office of the Awami League government led by Sheikh Hasina, following the Parliamentary election in mid-1996. Things were put on fast-track when a 30-year Ganges Water Treaty was signed in Delhi by Prime Ministers Sheikh Hasina and H. D. Deve Gowda in December 1996, which provided for a more permanent resolution to the highly sensitive issue of sharing of the water of the Ganges river. This was followed by the signing of a political agreement and a peace treaty in December 1997, called the Chittagong Hill Tracts Treaty, between the government of Bangladesh and the United People's Party of the Chittagong Hill Tracts, the political organisation that ran the so-called *Shanti Bahini*. The signing of this treaty enabled the insurgent group to disarm itself and return to Bangladesh. This removed yet another major irritant in the bilateral relations between the two countries. Within weeks, this was followed by the arrest of Anup Chetia, a wanted leader of the United Liberation Front of Assam (ULFA) in Dhaka, ostensibly, under the Foreigners Act and the Passports Act. Chetia was sentenced to seven years of imprisonment by a Bangladeshi court. Although the Bangladesh government did not extradite him to India straight away, his arrest further added to the spirit of positive intentions between Dhaka and Delhi. It was a combination of all this that the Awami League government, in its tenure between 1996 and 2001, saw as a tangible upgrading of political relations between the two countries, and the sense of cordiality was visible. The degree of trust at the highest political level was such that even the conscious decision of the Sheikh Hasina-led government to continue and strengthen its bilateral political, military and economic ties with China did not seem to disturb Delhi much.

An incident that caused major tension among all the positives was the killing of 16 Indian Border Security Force (BSF) personnel in the northern Kurigram district inside Bangladesh by the Bangladesh Rifles (BDR) in April 2001. According to claims from the BDR, 33 BSF men had entered the territory claimed by Bangladesh at the Roumari area of Kurigram, and had started indiscriminate mortar-shelling on the villagers. The BDR claimed that it had resorted to action in self-defence. Three BDR men were also killed in the incident. The situation was restored to a degree of normalcy after the Prime Ministers of Bangladesh and India, Sheikh Hasina and Atal Bihari Vajpayee, had a phone conversation and agreed to order a high-level investigation into the incident, and both sides promised to exercise restraint in future. Interestingly, the Indian government, angered as it might have been with the incident, avoided harsh criticisms of Sheikh Hasina; nor did India demand her apology.

3c: 2001–06

The BNP–Jamaat Coalition Government: With the return of the BNP government, with a two-third majority following the parliamentary election in 2001, bilateral relations between Bangladesh and India went on a perceptible downward trajectory. Jamaat-e-Islami as a coalition partner in the new government complicated things further because of the party's historically close links with Pakistan and its role during the 1971 Liberation War. Although the BNP-led government was critical of the Ganges Treaty as well as the Chittagong Hill Tracts peace deal, it did not make any move to scrap these either. However, heightened Indian complaints that insurgent groups from India's north-east were finding shelter inside Bangladesh added to the sense of tension prevailing then. The relationship hit a new low when the Bangladesh police and Coast Guard intercepted the loading of 10 trucks of arms and ammunition into the port city of Chattogram on the night of 1 April 2004, and seized extensive illegal arms and ammunition. Investigators believed that this delivery was intended for the ULFA. India was convinced that this established their claims that Indian insurgent groups were able to use Bangladesh territory as a transit for their arms supply. Attempts by Dhaka to convince Delhi otherwise met with little or no response. Paresh Barua, military-wing Chief of the group, then living in Dhaka, was among the 50 persons ultimately charged in the case. For India, this was like the proverbial final nail in the coffin. This was made known during Prime Minister Khaleda Zia's official visit to Delhi in 2006. In sum, there was no effective positive interaction between the two sides during the entire tenure of the BNP–Jamaat government in Bangladesh other than routine meetings at the working and political levels. Bilateral relations during this tenure remained far short of what had transpired during Begum Zia's first BNP government between 1991 and 1996.

3d: 2007–08

The Military-backed Government: Not much is publicly known about the contents of Indo-Bangladesh relations during this two-year period. The visit of the then Army Chief of Bangladesh, General Moin U. Ahmed, to India did draw some media attention, or what news was permissible under the circumstances, but did not go much beyond speculations. A book, more of a biography, by former President of India Pranab Mukherjee revealed some interactions between him and the Foreign Minister and the Bangladesh Army Chief, which touched on assurances given to the Army Chief by the Indian leader on a safe exit for him if the Awami League won the elections, which would follow the end of this controversial government. On substance, however, nothing much happened on the bilateral front that deserves special mention.

3e: 2009–14

Return of the Awami League: In the elections held in 2008, after a two-year military-backed civilian government interregnum, the Awami League under Sheikh Hasina returned to office with almost a three-fourth majority of seats in the Parliament. Much like her 1996–2001 term in office, the Prime Minister moved quickly to put the bilateral ties between Bangladesh and India back on a positive track. The high point of this period was the signing of the Framework Agreement on Cooperation for Development between the two governments, at the level of Prime Ministers, in September 2011, during the visit of Prime Minister Manmohan Singh to Bangladesh. The wide-ranging agreement was comprehensive and covered virtually all aspects of bilateral cooperation between Bangladesh and India. Much of what has followed since then can be attributed to what the two sides committed themselves to in the document. Promoting trade, investment and economic cooperation, including taking steps to narrow trade imbalances, progressively removing tariff and non-tariff barriers, was a primary focus of the agreement. Arrangements for cooperation in the generation, transmission and distribution of electricity, including electricity from renewable or other sources, added a new element within the ambit of bilateral cooperation. They also agreed to use power-grid connectivity to promote power exchanges for mutual economic advantage. The Framework Agreement was effectively a game changer in the overall bilateral relations between the two countries.

However, the non-signing of the Teesta deal during the visit in the face of stiff resistance from the Chief Minister of West Bengal left a bad taste and turned out to be a major media bite. As a follow-up to the new state of bilateral ties, security cooperation was heightened and Bangladesh addressed India's security concerns regarding the insurgents in the north-east by ensuring that they do not find any place on Bangladesh soil. This was very well-received in Delhi. Political interactions reached new heights, and a high-level exchange of visits served to cement the ties further. Bangladesh also allowed India transit facilities to move goods through Bangladesh territory from West Bengal to the north-eastern states, and vice versa. Connectivity was boosted through the establishment of bus and train services between Dhaka and Kolkata. With regard to bilateral trade, exports from Bangladesh to India rose significantly, including trade in energy. India also become increasingly involved in infrastructure development in Bangladesh.

3f: 2014–18

Awami League Returns the Second Consecutive Time: The Awami League under Sheikh Hasina returned to office after the parliamentary elections in Bangladesh in January 2014, which was boycotted by the BNP and most of the other political parties. The bilateral relations continued on their upward trajectory when the Bharatiya Janata Party (BJP) won the elections in India and Narendra Modi became Prime Minister in mid-2014. A number of events impacting positively on the bilateral relations followed.

The first such event was the verdict by the Permanent Court of Arbitration (PCA) at The Hague in July 2014, delimiting the maritime boundary between Bangladesh and India. The second was the eventual implementation of the LBA in June 2015 during the visit of Prime Minister Narendra Modi to Bangladesh after the Indian Parliament ratified the Agreement and passed the LBA Bill into Law, more than four decades after it was first signed. The resolution of these two highly critical issues contributed greatly to placing the bilateral ties on a firm footing. Greatly enhanced people-to-people contact and strong cultural exchanges provided important inputs in this very critically important bilateral relation. Bangladeshi Prime Minister Sheikh Hasina's high-profile visit to Delhi in April 2017 weighed more on the side of optimism. More than 20 deals covering a wide range of issues were signed, including memorandums of understanding (MOUs) on defence cooperation. Connectivity was boosted with new rail and road, and now river, connections. A credit line of $4.5 billion from India was signed to cover costs related to multifarious projects. Currently, the figure of the Indian credit line to Bangladesh was $8 billion—the highest that India has given to any country. Furthering the ongoing cooperation on combatting trans-boundary terrorism and violent extremism was also agreed upon. The Joint Statement issued following the talks said, *inter alia*, 'The two Prime Ministers affirmed that the relationship between India and Bangladesh was anchored in history, culture and language, one that goes far beyond a strategic partnership' (Bangladesh–India Joint Statement 2017). More recently, the relationship has been cited as a 'model between two neighbouring countries which needs to be showcased for a wider audience around the world'. The lack of any progress on the Teesta, however, continues to remain an issue for Bangladesh. One hopes that a common basin management approach for common rivers, as envisaged in the 2011 Framework Agreement, would help lead to a satisfactory resolution.

Concluding Remarks

The catalogue of facts stated above paints a clear picture of the path that the bilateral relations between the two South Asian neighbours has traversed over the last nearly five decades. There has also been a noticeable pattern in which the relations have fluctuated between visibly more convergence, when an Awami League government was in office, and less so, when a non-Awami League government was in charge in Bangladesh. Successive governments in India have also followed this pattern. The exception was the three years of the Morarji Desai-led Janata Party government between 1977 and 1980, when bilateral ties were warm even when a non-Awami League government was running affairs in Bangladesh.

It is perhaps pertinent to ask here why non-Awami League-led governments in Bangladesh did not find much convergence with successive governments and India while Awami League-led governments did. A combination of the elements of history, personal equations, intentions, shifting geo-politics, a heightened sense of nationalism and trust deficit can be attributed to the undulations in the journey of this relationship. It is precisely for this reason that the larger question of finding common grounds through a more inclusive approach acquires greater relevance if all sides were to chart the course for the days ahead for mutual benefit and with mutual respect.

Awami League governments have an inherent advantage *vis-à-vis* India. This is because of 1971, when the Bangladesh government in exile, led by the Awami League, was physically based in India. Links that were formed during this very critical period of history have endured over time. Importantly, the relationship that was forged by Sheikh Hasina personally with the Indian political establishment when she spent a large part of her period in exile in India after 15 August 1975 has served as an additional bonding and trust.

Governments led by others, primarily by the BNP, are products of the post-1975 period, and they have hence tended to look at the bilateral relations somewhat differently, less from a historical and emotional point of view, and more from a nationalistic perspective. The stance of the BNP-led government between 2001 and 2006, more often than not, verged on negativity.

Non-Awami League governments, more so the ones led by Begum Khaleda Zia's BNP, highlighted burning issues like water-sharing, the non-implementation of the LBA, and the killing of Bangladeshis on the border by the Indian BSF personnel as major contents in the bilateral discourse, but did not deliberate much on the broader context of the relationship. In the context of bilateral trade, for example, the BNP–Jamaat government focused only on the trade imbalance, but remained negative on potential investments from India or from Indian business houses. Even the talks of India importing natural gas from Myanmar through a pipeline that would run through parts of Bangladesh territory was stalled when Bangladesh insisted, without much logic, on linking the project with trade imbalance with India. There was also near-total disconnect on security cooperation and patrolling of the borders despite continued suggestions from Delhi. This only heightened Indian suspicions of Bangladesh providing shelter to Indian insurgent groups.

Consequently, with perceptions that India was biased towards the Awami League and was not being sensitive to genuine Bangladeshi concerns, a sense of deep-rooted distrust towards India was fermented. Playing the 'India card', therefore, played well with the public and paid political dividends for these governments at home. At the same time, fostering closer political, economic and military relations with China was also a calculated strategic move that was viewed as creating a necessary balance against India.

Smruti S. Pattanaik has tried to explain the mindset of governments in Bangladesh, more so of the non-Awami League governments, on forging closer strategic ties with China as a balancing act, in the following words,

> In the past, India was perceived as a threat to its sovereignty since its expansive security architecture included Bangladesh without Dhaka's consent which means Bangladesh's foreign and security policies have to cater to India's security needs. This, in other words, binds Bangladesh to India's security and even restrict it to follow an autonomous foreign policy that New Delhi may interpret as a threat. Therefore, to engage China which defeated India in 1962 war is seen as a hallmark of Bangladesh's independent policy and also a rejection of India's attempt to include Dhaka in its security framework (Pattanaik 2019, n.p.).

While there is merit in the comments quoted above, they refer to a period in the past. It is in that context that her views may be judged.

In a big neighbour–small neighbour scenario, as is the case with India and Bangladesh, suspicion by the smaller neighbour of the intentions of its larger neighbour is not unusual. The onus therefore falls on the bigger neighbour to comfort the smaller neighbour and relieve it of the fear factor. There is also a realisation on both sides that while Bangladesh, the smaller neighbour, may look for balance, which is an acceptable practice in diplomacy, approaching relations with India with a positive mind is of critical importance, and can be mutually beneficial. Dhaka and Delhi also recognise the need to be sensitive to each other's political and security concerns as well as interests, and to look for pragmatic ways to address issues on which they may have divergent views. India also recognises that the smaller countries of South Asia like Bangladesh are today in a position to demonstrate a good measure of autonomy in pursuing their foreign policy goals that protect their political, economic and security interests while balancing their strategic friendships.

The present is a changed scenario, one that is marked by positive intentions and actions. The resolution of contentious issues like the land and maritime boundaries, and the signing of the long-term water sharing agreement on the Ganges, has also played its part. Border killings have gone down, although it is yet to reach the zero-figure promised, and some incidents, of late, have again raised concerns that needs to be addressed. People-to-people contact and cultural exchanges have seen an exponential rise. This is the right way to nurture these relations for sustainability and healthy growth. While Dhaka must remain sensitive to India's concerns, Delhi, on its part, should be able to recognise that many of those concerns are common to both, and that they need to be addressed as such. Of late, for instance, India's perceived ambiguity on the ongoing Rohingya crisis has raised questions in Bangladesh. Here, Bangladesh would expect her closest neighbour and friend to recognise that the Rohingya refugee crisis is not just a bilateral humanitarian crisis between Bangladesh and Myanmar, but is also one that can have broader ramifications, potentially threatening security and stability, and therefore respond accordingly. Bangladesh expects that India would use its leverage and play a more proactive role in finding a solution acceptable to all sides. India's geo-political goals in the region must take the interest and concerns of Bangladesh into consideration, and not be at the cost of it.

Addressing the critical needs of a proven friendly neighbour and not subjecting them to domestic political considerations is vitally important to sustaining trust. The issue of sharing the waters of the common rivers is a strong case in point here. Similarly, political leaders on all sides of the spectrum in Bangladesh must accept the reality that broadening connectivity in every sector has to be seen as an area of common interest. Connectivity is about connecting people and nations that go beyond governments and politics. The element of inter-dependence and the spirit of mutual compromise must remain integral parts of the narrative.

Resorting to political rhetoric on both sides may serve narrow political gains in the short term, but in the long term it will not create a climate of mutual trust and confidence which, along with the mutuality of benefit, must be the foundations on which sound and stable bilateral relations need to be built. This is the path to building a relationship that has the elements of history and geography on its side. It is happening now and it needs to be sustained. It is important to note that in the parliamentary elections in Bangladesh in December 2018, the so-called 'India card' was conspicuous by its absence. This is a sign of changing times and of political maturity. This augurs well for the future of a relationship that both Bangladesh and India recognise is of vital importance to them bilaterally, as well as in the larger regional context.

References

Bangladesh–India Joint Statement, New Delhi, 8 April 2017.

Bhutto, F. 2010. *Songs of Blood and Sword.* London: Jonathan Cape.

Dixit, J. N. 1999. *Liberation and Beyond, Bangladesh–India Relations.* Dhaka: The University Press Limited.

Krishnan Srinivasan, F. I. 2008. *The Jamdani Revolution: Politics, Personalities and Civil Society in Bangladesh.* New Delhi: Har Anand Publications.

Pattanaik, S. S. 2019. 'Engaging the Asian Giants: India, China and Bangladesh's Crucial Balancing Act', *Issues and Studies: A Social Science Quarterly on China, Taiwan, and East Asian Affairs* 55(2), n.p.

Rushdie, S. 1983. *Shame.* London: Jonathan Cape.

11

Bangladesh's Foreign Policy

Acquiring New Relevance

SREERADHA DATTA

In this millennium, Prime Minister Sheikh Hasina will not only be one of the longest-serving female leaders in the world, but will also be known to have attracted the world's attention to Bangladesh. Given the projection of Bangladesh becoming one of the top 30 economies by 2030, there is significant international attention being riveted on this South Asian state. Given its traumatic beginning of 1971, the periodic political instability that ensued, and the recurring environmental and climate challenges it faces, this is no mean achievement.

Notwithstanding the critique of Hasina's domestic policies and the practice of undemocratic norms under her watch, Hasina has been able to establish her country's relevance to the international community as well as to all the major powers. Bangladesh has two of the largest Asian powers, India and China, as its wooing partners, and it manages a perfect balance of political and strategic ties with both of them. Apart from this, Bangladesh has established stable bilateral ties with nations spanning across America, Europe, and the Muslim world, and has been the front runner for regional groupings, having initiated the South Asia Association for Regional Cooperation (SAARC) in 1985. It is now also an active member in the Bay of Bengal Initiative for Multi-Sectoral Technical and Economic Cooperation (BIMSTEC) and other sub-regional groupings in the region. The only exception to this growing global engagement is Bangladesh's volatile relations with Pakistan. This bilateral discord remains embedded in the birth of Bangladesh.

The Liberation War provided Bangladesh with a direction that has continued to influence and steer Dhaka's relations with the outside world. This War remains an emotive issue and Bangladesh has chosen to view some of its bilateral relations through this prism. In fact, most of the time, Dhaka seems engaged in foreign ties and relations, and not so much in strategising a foreign policy. The struggle to create Bangladesh and the victory that emerged shaped the destiny of Bangladesh not only through its journey of difficult times, but also through its subsequent choices and decisions. Bangladesh's two main political parties, the Awami League and the Bangladesh Nationalist Party (BNP), standing at opposite ends of the spectrum, remain divided over this issue of the War. This political division invariably drives deep cleavages in the polity and tends to spill over into the political parties' foreign relations, too. It is not poised much differently even today.

In trying to understand Bangladesh's foreign policy, there are four distinct phases that can be delineated. Each phase has its distinctiveness, reflecting Bangladesh's ideological moorings and national interests of that particular period. The sharp domestic turnarounds that occurred in the first few decades, changing the national identity narrative and its search for recognition, had an impact on the foreign ties that were pursued by the successive political leaders. The domestic vacillation between electoral democracy (1971–75) and military regimes (1975–90), the return to multi-party democracy (1991–2006), the interregnum period (2006–08), and then, the return to democracy post-2008 (albeit a stilted one at present) has brought forth a continuation as well as a break from the past in Dhaka's foreign policy. As the years unfolded, and different leaders took over, it was evident that the domestic context within which Dhaka's foreign policy evolved had a direct imprint on how Bangladesh sought to navigate its foreign engagements.

Post the return to democracy in Bangladesh in 1991, the political landscape was dominated by four political parties, namely the Awami Legaue led by Sheikh Hasina, the BNP, led by Khaleda Zia, carrying forward the legacy of military ruler Ziaur Rahman, the Jatiya Party, led by Ershad, the military-general who took over the reins of Bangladesh post President Zia's death, and the Jamaat-e-Islami, a religious political party that resurfaced under the military rule. Of course, the international system that was evolving, moving from periods of the Cold War to post-Cold War, globalisation, and the rise of Asia, undeniably contributed and became a factor in Bangladesh's foreign policy-making. As has been argued, '[T]he means and methods of pursuing the foreign policy aspirations change over time and domestic inputs play crucial role in this regard' (Masud 2016: 264). Undoubtedly, the present international recognition of the country's strategic role is a reflection of its growing capacities and its ability to not only showcase, but also leverage its geographical position. With the Bay of Bengal assuming greater salience and the Indian Ocean becoming a focal point for jostling of major powers, Bangladesh's ability to effectively use its geographical position has contributed positively to its foreign policy decisions.

This chapter, while discussing Bangladesh's foreign polices spanning the four phases, shall also weave in some of the factors that influenced foreign policy-making in Bangladesh, and shall attempt to contextualise some of the decision-making processes. Thus, Bangladesh's initial search for recognition, its search for economic aid, its attempts at regionalism, providing leadership to the South Asian regional forum, becoming the largest contributor to the United Nations (UN) peacekeeping force, and also its willingness to provide humanitarian support for the Rohingya refugees who were forced to leave Myanmar form critical components to Bangladesh's present position, are some such factors. This chapter, while briefly touching upon Bangladesh's relation with India, shall also highlight the opening up to the Muslim world, mainly through the Organisation of Islamic Cooperation (OIC) platform, its increasing engagement with China, its troubled relation with Pakistan, and its engagement with Western democracies, namely the United States (US).

Bangladesh's foreign policy has been largely incumbent on its leaders and their policies. With greater political stability post the 1991 period, there has been some continuity in their foreign policy, with the exception of their policy towards India and Pakistan. China and India are two important bilateral partners, and while Sino-Bangladeshi bilateral relations have gathered strength with each phase, beginning from 1975, the significant betterment of the Indo-Bangladeshi relations in the last decade was largely possible due to Prime Minister Sheikh Hasina's initiative and interests, and her ability to address Indian core security concerns. Similarly, Hasina's ambition for Bangladesh has led her to become closer to other Asian powers.

POST-LIBERATION WAR PERIOD: INDO-CENTRIC POLICIES

The first phase is centred around the birth of Bangladesh. It was a short but a very critical phase, leading to serious consequences for the future and one that would continue to have an impact upon Bangladesh's policies both at home and with the outside world for the next few decades. Thus, recognition or non-recognition of the newly emerged State of Bangladesh became an issue, and indeed its close association with India also become a factor in its foreign policy trajectory.

Given the severe differences East Pakistan faced with West Pakistan, Bengali cultural identity played a dominant role in its origin. The revival of Bengali cultural identity became an essential factor for differentiating East Pakistan from West Pakistan. Post the partition of the sub-continent, Islam was unable to unify the culturally diverse communities. Thus, unlike in 1947 when battle lines were drawn between Muslim Bengalis and Hindu Bengalis of Eastern India, in 1971, the Bengalis of the East rebelled against the non-Bengalis of West Pakistan (Datta 2004: 17, 184). An inevitable alienation occurred with the Muslim world during this period. While Bhutan, India, Soviet Union, East Germany and Poland were the first few countries to recognise Bangladesh, many states close to Pakistan, including China, preferred to remain distant. American recognition, too, came by in April 1972, within a few months of the war coming to an end. Certainly, as Imtiaz Ahmed points out, '[T]he first phase could be considered as the diplomacy of recognition as the country had to struggle to build relationship with those countries which were against the Liberation War of Bangladesh with Pakistan' (Ahmed 2011: 208).

Given its critical role in the Liberation War, India assumed an importance unlike no other country during the first phase. Although Bangladesh's bilateral tie with India is not under review in this chapter, it still merits a mention, as India has been a determining factor in Bangladesh's foreign policies undertaken by all its leaders. As is explained succinctly by Bhumitra Chakma:

> Since 1971, Bangladesh–India relations have experienced ups and downs, but the 'India factor', as a positive force or a negative one, has remained constant and continued to affect Bangladesh's foreign policy behaviour. Indeed, Dhaka's foreign policy in the past four decades can be seen in a binary fashion: 'pro-India' or 'anti-India'. Such a distinction may seem arbitrary, but it helps to understand the extent of India's influence in Bangladesh's foreign policy. The general trend has been that when an AL government was in power in Bangladesh, it adopted an India-positive foreign policy, while non-AL governments generally maintained an attitude of mistrust towards New Delhi and pursued counterbalancing strategy vis-à-vis India (Chakma 2015: 45).

The Indira–Mujibur agreement of 1974, which laid the basis for Indo-Bangladeshi friendship, soon ran into heavy weather, with the sudden turn of events. Given the Indian influence, Bangladesh became a secular state, and all political parties with Islamic leanings were banned from the day the Awami League leaders assumed office in Dhaka. But gradually, when the excitement of being a new independent nation settled down, and grievances surrounding Sheikh Mujibur Rahman and some of his policies begin to raise their heads, the author notes that while the Bengali Muslims were earlier not particularly concerned about stressing a Muslim identity in Pakistani politics, they now 'seemed more anxious to do so in secular Bangladesh'. M. Rashiduzzaman further notes that the anti-Indian feelings and sympathy for Bangladesh's identity as a Muslim nation became so strong that even Mujibur Rahman began to modify his policy. To the surprise of the Indian government and even his close political associates, he accepted an invitation to attend the Islamic Conference held in Pakistan in the spring of 1974 (Rashiduzzaman 1977: 797). Foreign policy also interested Mujibur Rahman; he went on state visits to Yugoslavia and Japan, and attended the Commonwealth Conference in Ottawa, Canada.

The assassination of Mujibur Rahman drastically changed everything. Rapid political developments had an impact not only on the domestic political order, but also on how the international community perceived Bangladesh. The takeover by the military ushered in the second phase. Turbulent unstable times needed a new mantra. And Islam came in as a handy tool. Ziaur Rahman, who took over in 1977, reinvented the wheel fully and ushered in an era of military rule with far-reaching changes in the polity with the launching of the BNP in the following year.

II

THE SECOND PHASE

The second phase began with Ziaur Rahman making serious overtures to find common ground with many extra-regional states, including the Muslim world. This phase saw Bangladesh leverage its religious identity to establish bilateral cooperation and also to seek aid, which it needed urgently. The drastic domestic changes necessitated many of the new foreign policy initiatives. Having realised secession from West Pakistan in 1971, Bengali nationalism lost its relevance for Bangladesh. The dividing line once again moved back to religion. The emergence of a national identity of Bangladesh now depended upon its ability to differentiate itself from the Bengalis of West Bengal in India rather than the non-Bengali Muslims of erstwhile West Pakistan (Datta 2004: 17, 184). Moving away from the cultural factors that led to its breakaway from West Pakistan, Islam emerged as the primary national identity of Bangladesh, also reflecting the changing social moods. In fact, this shift had already begun to manifest in the politics and policies of Bangladesh's founder-leader, Mujibur Rahman. Despite his secular moorings and commitments, shortly after taking office as President of Bangladesh, he found it opportune to opt for Islamic symbolism. Mujibur Rahman resorted to symbolism such as using terms like *Allah, Insha Allah, Bismillah* (common Islamic terms) in his vocabulary, and also banning un-Islamic activities like horse-racing, etc. Dependence upon countries such as Saudi Arabia, whose economic aid polices are often linked to Islamic causes, provided an external incentive to Mujibur Rahman's 'political discovery' of Islam (ibid.). It has been pointed out that this change coincided with the widespread sympathy for Islamic identity in Bangladesh among the elites as well as the rural masses (Rashiduzzaman 1977: 797).

Ziaur Rahman Introduces New Elements to Domestic Politics and Foreign Relations

Under Ziaur Rahman, the 1977 Constitution replaced secularism, with 'absolute trust and faith in the almighty Allah'. This rightward shift was inevitable. For the post-Mujibur Rahman leaders, Islam emerged as a mobilising force, and the Islamic identity of the state became the focus and agenda of the leaders (Datta 2004: 21, 184). Significantly, the Collaborators Act, 1972, was repealed, which gave some legitimacy to those Muslim leaders who were alleged to have been supportive of Pakistan in the War of Liberation in 1971 (Rashiduzzaman 1977: 798). Membership to the OIC became the cornerstone for Bangladesh's existence, and it was essentially initiated by Mujibur Rahman.

Ironically, while Bangladesh today celebrates being nominated as the OIC city of tourism for the year 2021, its relation with the OIC began tenuously when it joined the organisation as a member in 1974. An interesting account by Arashad-uz Zaman reflects upon the first overture made by Bangladesh to join the Non-Aligned Group Summit in Algiers in 1973 (Zaman 2005). This was considered a major breakthrough for Bangladeshi diplomacy, as the Non-Aligned Summit assembled more than 100 heads of states and governments from Africa, Asia and Latin America. Very few of those states had, in fact, recognised Bangladesh. About OIC, Zaman further recalls that in February 1974, the Islamic countries, specifically, the Arab countries wished to join the OIC summit in Lahore. He describes the situation in the following account:

> Bangabandhu had taken a principled stand that for him to visit any foreign country, that state had to accord recognition to Bangladesh. Our Foreign Minister Dr. Kamal Hossain came to Algiers and had very important talks with his counterpart Abdel Aziz Bouteflika (currently the President of Algeria).... When the decks were cleared, a five-member OIC delegation led by Algeria came to Dhaka.... Pakistan announced recognition of Bangladesh and Bangladesh did likewise and with an aircraft provided by the authorities of Algeria, Bangabandhu and

> his delegation reached Lahore and joined the OIC deliberations amidst scenes of great emotional fervour (Zaman 2005).

Later in 1974, Mujibur Rahman visited Egypt, Kuwait and other Muslim nations to establish relations with them (Rashiduzzaman 1977: 798). The support of the OIC was critical for Bangladesh; this support lent it not only recognition, but also credibility in the Muslim world and gave the country a direction it sought fervently. This association proved fruitful as the governments of Turkey and Iran also granted their recognition on the same day (Shah Amran 2018).

Even in today's context, the OIC is extremely relevant to Bangladesh. The country is presently seeking OIC support for taking the case of the Rohingya refugees to the International Court of Justice. Interestingly, Bangladesh has been urging reforms within the OIC to include India, which has a large Muslim population.[1] The opening up with the Islamic world also brought in huge dividends in the later years. The OIC states are not only critical towards the political support Bangladesh receives, but also towards the remittance flowing from many of these countries and contributing to Bangladesh's economy, amounting to 18 per cent of its Gross Domestic Product (GDP) through the substantial contribution of $16.4 billion it received during 2018–19.[2] Most of the workers are located in Saudi Arabia, Kuwait, Qatar, United Arab Emirates (UAE), Bahrain and Oman. Much of Bangladesh remittances flow from the Middle East (Rashid 2019). The number of workers in the Middle East is usually over 300,000 Bangladeshis (Amin 2018).

This phase was not only about consolidation of its religious identity, but also about engaging with the Middle Eastern region, other Islamic countries, and the rapprochement with Pakistan. As evident, the second phase ushered in many friends for Dhaka, but one of the most stable partnerships Bangladesh built would be its relation with China.

China's Recognition of Bangladesh Opened up Vistas of Cooperation

The Sino-Bangladeshi relations formally took off with the visit of President Ziaur Rahman to China in 1977. Occurring within months after the Chinese recognition, this visit put the bilateral relations firmly in place, and both sides quietly buried the uneasy and unfriendly phase. The Chinese non-recognition of Bangladesh and its opposition to UN membership (in 1972) was explained away 'within' the Cold War context, and both sides began to expand and intensify their bilateral ties. Thus, Bangladesh presently enjoys the most comprehensive and robust ties with China, straddling a wide spectrum of areas, including political ties, economic cooperation and defence assistance (Datta 2014: 227). For China, befriending Bangladesh meant an opportunity to expand its sphere of influence in the South Asian region. Beginning with the first-ever visit by the Chinese leadership to Bangladesh in March 1978 and President Ziaur Rahman's return visit to China in August 1980, the tone and tenor for a strong bilateral relation was set.

For the post-Mujibur Rahman military junta, China served another purpose. Because *Bangabandhu* and his Awami League were close to India, the new leaders adopted a twin strategy. Indeed, Islamic identity became the centre of resistance against Indian predominance in Bangladesh politics and it provided a tool for the opposition against Mujibur Rahman's government (Rashiduzzaman 1977: 799). The two major political forces which ruled Bangladesh between 1975 and 1990, namely Mujibur Rahman's BNP and Hussain Muhamman Ershad's Jatiya Party, worked towards improving Bangladeshi–Chinese relations. Ershad, while in office, visited China as many as five times. Even Jamaat-e-Islami, known for its religious agenda, made friendly overtures towards China. Thus, by the time the first multi-party elections were held in 1991, Bangladesh–China relations had acquired a widespread national consensus.

The other break from the past during this period was Dhaka's official contact with Islamabad. Post-Mujibur Rahman and Zulfikar Ali Bhutto, relations between Pakistan and Bangladesh improved. To recall briefly in the aftermath of the War, the thorny issues revolved around the fate of the prisoners of war.[3] But it was only much later, during 1977, that two consecutive meetings between the two leaders would lead to a thawing in the bilateral ties.[4] Two main bilateral issues that remained now were, first, the question of the Bihari refugees in Bangladesh, and second, the resettlement of peoples' property and assets. After much discussion in 1986 between Bangladeshi President Ershad and Pakistani President Zia-ul-Haq, an agreement was arrived at about the repatriation of 250,000 Biharis. However, with the accidental death of Zia-ul-Haq in 1989, the repatriation decision remained unresolved (Shukla 2015). Khaleda Zia, post her being elected in 1991, also kept up the engagement with Pakistan, and as has been pointed out, 'BNP has always had better relations with Pakistan and in the past often used anti-Indian rhetoric to boost popular support' (Jahan 2003: 228).

III

The third phase, with the return of democracy, allowed for not only a robust relationship with China, but also with the Western democracies. But the growing ties with China was the high point during this period, and the Awami League also threw its weight behind improving Bangladesh–China ties.

China and Pakistan both Move Closer

Post-1991, both the Awami League and the BNP were comfortable working with China. Sheikh Hasina and Khaleda Zia visited China both as Prime Minister and as leaders of the opposition. Indeed, there was a subtle rivalry among mainstream parties to promote closer political and economic ties with Beijing. Correspondingly, China is not a battleground for the Awami–BNP rivalry, something that India has come to symbolise. Both Dhaka and Beijing have shown greater accommodation of each other's concerns and interests. Conscious of Chinese sensitivity, Dhaka has periodically reiterated its support for a 'One-China' policy (Datta 2008: 760). Despite economic advantages, Bangladesh was quick to close down the Taiwanese trade office following Chinese protests.

For Dhaka, which was deliberately moving away from India, it became important to engage with Pakistan. In August 1992, Bangladeshi Prime Minister Khaleda Zia visited Pakistan and held talks with her Pakistani counterpart, Nawaz Sharif, over a variety of issues, including the repatriation of Pakistani Biharis, and sharing of assets and liabilities. Sheikh Hasina, during her term as Prime Minister (1996–2001), also communicated the same to Nawaz Sharif, that the Biharis were unacceptable to Bangladesh. However, subsequently, Pakistani positions hardened, and they refused to accept that Biharis were Pakistani in any way. On the issue of division of assets, no progress could be made during the democratic interlude in Pakistan. It still remains an outstanding issue.

Khaleda Zia, in her second term (2001–06), visited Pakistan in February 2006 after a gap of a decade, signalling the subtle changes that drove the bilateral relations. Earlier in her term, Pervez Musharraf's July 2002 visit was portrayed as highly successful because of the fact that the Pakistani President, who was also the Chief of Army Staff, expressed his regret for the events of 1971. The opposition, Awami League, did not accept his speech as a formal and unconditional apology that they had expected, but more as an acknowledgement about the crimes and excesses against the innocent East Wing of Pakistan. This issue of apology remains deeply embedded in the Bangladesh psyche and is the source of anguish for many Bangladeshis (Datta 2006). Indeed, the resumption of the International Crime Tribunal that would finally bring to trial the collaborators who did not support Bangladesh's Liberation War caused another friction between Bangladesh and Pakistan. The Tribunal and the government of Bangladesh have accused Pakistan, in particular, its army, of war crimes in East Pakistan. Islamabad, in response, has actively denied these allegations and has expressed concern about the executions of senior politicians in Bangladesh (Shahab Ahmed and Zahoor 2019). For the Awami League, this issue was non-negotiable and highlighted their view of Pakistan. Given this history, there are no easy solutions; and with Sheikh Hasina at helm in Dhaka since 2008, Bangladesh's relations with Pakistan remain nearly hostile.

Democracy and Stability

Understandably, the return to multi-party democracy in 1991 not only opened up engagement with the Western democracies, namely the US, but also ushered in another opportunity in the form of Bangladesh providing the largest peacekeeping force to the UN. Bangladesh has deployed more than 0.15 million of its peacekeepers in 54 missions spread across 40 different countries (Rasul 2018). The higher earnings of $1,028 as compared to the starting salary for a Bangladeshi soldier, $193, as per 2015 estimates, is clearly worthwhile. As per some estimates, between 2001 and 2010, Bangladesh received $1.28 billion from the UN as compensation for its peacekeeping operations. It was also calculated that the earning from this contributed to nearly 1 per cent of the GDP (Gowan 2015). Apart from the economic benefit, this service has also earned Bangladesh international prestige, promoted a positive image of the country, and enabled the growth of democratic values (Uz Zaman and Biswas 2014). It has also enabled them to develop a well-trained professional military. But importantly, this has de-incentivised the military from interfering into domestic politics. In the past, the UN had warned that it 'will seriously consider withdrawing the Bangladesh peacekeepers from the UN missions' if Bangladesh army played any role in the political processes in Bangladesh (*The China Daily* 2007). This is possibly a strong reason for the military to remain in the background despite the periodic political instability in Bangladesh. As is well-known, the US has also been one of the main states trying to propagate democratic values through many of its aid programmes.

America has been a great supporter for introducing democratic norms, and it was in the forefront when advocating Bangladesh as a moderate Islam majority country; it also initiated computers and scientific subjects in the many state-funded *madrasas* during this period. In fact, although American President Bill Clinton's visit to Dhaka in 2000 for a day was very low-key, it sent a clear message about the critical importance of Bangladesh in US's South Asia policy. Their bilateral engagement has been robust, ranging from trade, aid and investment. Although Bangladesh strongly resisted US's attempt to commit troops to Iraq under a US-led force in 2004, Bangladesh's relationship with the US remained reasonably steady for years. However, outbursts of terror attacks in Bangladesh would be a cause for the American-voiced concern about the deteriorating law-and-order conditions. In spite of this, their partnership has grown with time, and US would be Bangladesh's single largest destination for exports, mainly $5.5 billion worth of products, primarily apparel and textiles, in 2018. The US is also one of the largest sources for foreign direct investment (FDI) in Bangladesh. At the end of 2017, the US accounted for 23 per cent of the stock of FDI in Bangladesh.[5]

Bangladesh went through a two-year hiatus during 2006–08, which saw the Caretaker Government (CG), with the support of the army, lead Bangladesh. Given the peculiar nature of the polity, several of the Western democracies urged for a return of democracy and parliamentary election. The fourth phase essentially began with the December 2008 elections, which brought Sheikh Hasina back to Dhaka with a huge majority.

IV

The fourth phase saw Sheikh Hasina's return to Dhaka in 2008 post the interregnum period, and also a growing presence of China and India. Sheikh Hasina's continued three terms in office has also provided continuity to the policies and states she has reposed faith in, namely India, China, US, a large number of other European nations, and other countries, too. Given the US goods imports of $6.1 billion from Bangladesh in 2018, an increase of 7.3 per cent ($416 million) from 2017 is estimated to support over 6,000 jobs in Dhaka (Office of the United States Trade Representative 2019). However, China has gained the position of a trusted partner in Bangladesh.

Consolidation of the Economy, and Partnership with India and China

The rapidly growing economy changed one of the critical components of Bangladesh's diplomatic engagement. For a long time, aid was one of most important factors in Bangladesh's foreign policies. As the economy grew, Bangladesh's dependency on aid has not only decreased, but its nature has also reversed from the earlier trends. From bilateral aid, Bangladesh has now has moved to over 65 per cent being covered by multilateral funds in 2018. Much of Bangladesh's outreach has been to garner aids and grants for its developing economy, and its dependence on aid has decreased over time. Net foreign assistance (gross inflows of grants and loans, net of repayments) has continued to rise gradually over the years. The amount of aid amounts to an average of 12 per cent of the total revenues since 2010–11 (Chattopadhyay 2018).

Figure 11.1 Total Grants and Loans (in Million $)

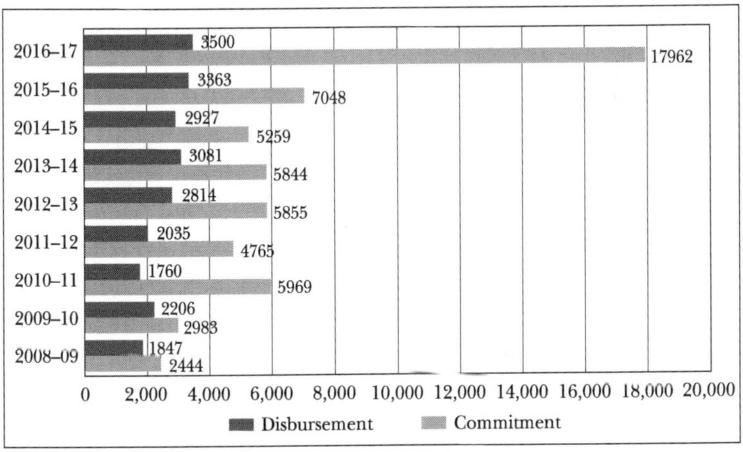

Source: Statistical Year Book Bangladesh 2018.

China, the US and India are three major economies to work closely with Bangladesh during this phase, although as it appears, China has become Bangladesh's top trading partner, knocking India out of the position it had held for 40 years (Anwar 2019). Chinese President Xi Jinping's visit to Bangladesh in 2016 after a gap of 30 years resulted in substantial agreements and decisions. Although the President's stopover at Dhaka lasted less than 24 hours, it resulted in the signing of 27 agreements and memorandums of understanding (MoUs) between the two governments, involving an amount of over $25 billion (HSBC 2017). There was also reporting about China waiving off $24 billion worth of loans for Bangladesh. The bilateral trade was soaring with each passing decade. It had stood at \$13.75 million in 1975, it touched \$918 million in 2001, \$1.14 billion in 2003–04, crossed \$3.4 billion in 2007, surpassed \$8 billion in 2012, and \$12.4 billion in 2017–18. During this same period, FDI from China reached \$506 million, with about 400 Chinese companies doing business in Bangladesh, including about 200 large companies and 200 other small and medium enterprises in the power sector, specifically coal-based power projects (Siddique 2019). It has also, for a long time, been involved in various infrastructural projects in Bangladesh, and 13 of these bilateral agreements covered infrastructure, construction, and energy and transportation. Sheikh Hasina and Xi Jinping's meeting in 2019 resulted in further agreements covering trade and defence. China's overwhelming role as Bangladesh's defence partner is evident. China has also emerged as the key supplier of Bangladesh's military procurement. China has supplied armoured personnel carriers, fighter aircraft and frigates to Bangladesh over the past few years (D'Costa 2012: 153).

Some of the equipments include:

- 44 Chinese MBT-2000 main battle tanks worth \$162 million in 2011;
- During 2012–15, five maritime patrol vessels, two submarines, 16 fighter jets, and 44 tanks, as well as anti-ship and surface-to-air missiles;
- In 2017, the Bangladesh Navy took the delivery of two Chinese submarines at a minimum price (Anwar 2019). It is reportedly also building bases for the three submarines.

Bangladesh is one of the three key countries that is expected to be the biggest beneficiary of the China-led \$1.5 trillion 'Belt and Road Initiative' (BRI), and is reportedly set to receive a total investment of \$38 billion, equivalent to 15 per cent of its 2017 GDP, under the Bangladesh–China–India–Myanmar (BCIM) Corridor, which is aimed at improving land, rail, water and air interconnectivity among the four countries (*The Financial Express* 2018). As economist Mustafizur Rahman notes, 'China's presence in Bangladesh as a trading partner, as an important FDI source and a key player in infrastructure development will likely increase in future' (Rahman

2019). Russia and India have also entered the defence arena recently. In 2011, Russia agreed to help construct two 1,000-megawatt (MW) nuclear reactors, including providing funding, fuel and training. It was further agreed in 2018 that India would also be part of this project, for the Rooppur nuclear power plant. This would be first initiative under an Indo-Russian deal to undertake atomic energy projects in other countries (*Livemint* 2018). The other significant move has been to focus on regional efforts.

Regionalism

As is well-known, the idea of a regional grouping in South Asia, the SAARC, was first mooted by Ziaur Rahman. This had received fulsome support from China. For its part, Bangladesh has been keen to have a Chinese presence in South Asia, and together with Nepal and Pakistan, it has worked towards Chinese admission into the SAARC as an 'observer' (Datta 2008: 762). While for political reasons, the SAARC did not really flourish, the idea of sub-regionalism within South Asia has found favour with Bangladesh. Bangladesh mooted the idea of a South Asian Task Force to contain terrorism in the region, but unfortunately, it did not find much appeal among its neighbours. But with the unveiling of the Indo-Bangladeshi Joint Communiqué of 2010, a new interest in sub-regionalism grew. The Bangladesh–Bhutan–India–Nepal (BBIN) grouping will essentially provide seamless movement across the nations through the Motor Vehicle Act for facilitating trade and commerce within the region and outside. As it stands now, and as it is being discussed, the BBIN will also dovetail into the BIMSTEC organisation where Bangladesh hosting the Secretariat plays a key role. The cobweb of cross-border transport networks that are being developed in the region will be the precursor to the growth of regionalism in the neighbourhood of Bangladesh, and given the country's pivotal geographical position, it is bound to have great strategic appeal in the region. Chinese interests in the development of the Mongla and Payra port in Bangladesh has been well-known. However, the Sri Lankan experience over the lease of Hambantota to China seems to have touched a nerve in Bangladesh, too. Certainly, Bangladesh seems to have avoided any similar debt crises issues vis-a-vis China, but given the sudden plethora of the unveiling of large infrastructural projects supported by Beijing, the uncertainty and the possibility of complications cannot be ruled out. Reportedly, China is seeking to convert $20 billion dollars of loan into commercial credits. As is evident in other regions where China has left an imprint, the viability of the projects, the loan terms and the conditions laid down, need greater transparency. Moreover, Dhaka will have to watch out for the threat of 'asset seizure' and ensure that the project collaborations bring dividends to Bangladesh, too. Bangladesh will be negotiating from a position of strength, given its present strong economy; and that augurs well for its future.

The Rohingya Preoccupation

Bangladesh's foreign policy has been intertwined with its domestic environment, and presently, it stands strong and vindicated. Given the sharp critique of many of its past issues, the fact that Bangladesh not only received international attention, but has become a critical South Asian region, and that all states, among which there are the most important states, are coveting to engage in it, speak of its success. In this journey, Bangladesh's humanitarian side has also been extremely evident. Sheikh Hasina's response to accommodate the 75,000 Rohingyas in the latest influx in 2017, who came across the Myanmar–Bangladesh borders, fleeing the attacks on them in the Rakhine homeland, has been lauded by the international community. These refugees have been coming from the mid-1990s, and 3 million of them are estimated to be housed in refugee camps across Bangladesh, spread over the Nayapara, Kutupalong camps in Cox's Bazar and Teknaf, Cox Bazar Sadar, Ramu and Ukhiya. Bangladesh and Myanmar had signed an MoU for repatriation of the refugees in 2018, and India also built 250 houses in the Rahine region to enable the same; but the ground situation remains unchanged.

The international community is unable to exert any influence to bring an amicable solution to this crisis except for economic sanctions; it seems strange but unfortunately true that no leverages appear available. The Myanmar government remains intransigent.

There are as yet no forthcoming assurances from the Tatmadaw about providing an enabling atmosphere in Myanmar for the Rohingyas to return. For Bangladesh, already struggling with its own huge population pressure and erosion of land with its sea levels rising, providing the Rohingyas support cannot be a tenable option indefinitely. Bangladesh is using all its good offices to solicit support and help to find justice for these large populations without a homeland. This issue has been Bangladesh's single-most important preoccupation in recent times and finds mention in many of Dhaka's interactions abroad. Given the depth of the problem, Sheikh Hasina is hoping to gather international support to resolve this problem.

Concluding Remarks

As has often been pointed put, Bangladeshi leaders have pursued foreign relations and not foreign policies. The 50-year journey of the country reflects its preoccupation with internal political and economic developments, which to some extent limited Bangladesh's strategic policies. Apart from amassing whatever support it could gather from leaders across the globe, in every phase through which it travelled, there was limited scope and space to plan and formulate ideas to enhance its foreign relations. Given the nature of its birth and the difficult circumstances emerging from one of the worst famines in history in 1974, which aggravated an already weak economy, the choices ahead in its foreign relations were expectedly based on existential reasons rather than any long-term strategic view.

Mujibur Rahman, the founding father, and undoubtedly one of the most popular leaders in Bangladesh, had many expectations to fulfil. The challenges were many, and ensuring internal stability was the expected priority. For understandable reasons, once again India was one of the main factors in Bangladesh's foreign relations. For the two consecutive military leaders, namely Ziaur Rahman and Ershad, nation-building not only meant consolidating their rule in a nation that had emerged by resisting military rule and many of its undemocratic policies, but also earning legitimacy to establish their writ. Thus, most of their foreign policies were rooted in the pursuit of strengthening their position. Quite ironically, Ziaur Rahman's dream of Bangladesh leading the region to regionalism seems to be taking shape again through Sheikh Hasina's many connectivity and transport corridors that she is building to connect Bangladesh with the neighbourhood. While India has been playing a key role in this, the BRI project initiated by China has also shown Bangladesh many prospects. Sheikh Hasina's three consecutive terms, from 2008 till the present, have allowed her the luxury of time to formulate and posture Bangladesh as never before. Bangladesh seems suitably poised to make a long-term contribution to global politics.

Notes

1. On 1 March 2019, India participated as the 'guest of honour' in the forty-sixth session of the Council of Foreign Ministers of the OIC held in Abu Dhabi.
2. It received $15.5 billion in 2017–18 and $13.5 billion during 2016–17.
3. The 1973 agreement provided for Bangladesh agreeing to the release of all but 195 Pakistani prisoners of war, and Pakistan agreed to let all Bengalis leave Pakistan, and to accept back a substantial number of Pakistani civilians and Biharis living in Bangladesh.
4. In August 1977, Tobarak Hussain, Foreign Secretary of Bangladesh, visited Pakistan, followed by a visit by Bangladeshi President Ziaur Rahman during December, and by a return visit by Pakistani President Zia-ul-Haq to Dhaka in 1985.
5. Chevron is the single largest foreign investor, producing some 55 per cent of Bangladesh's domestic natural gas. US companies are the largest foreign investors in Bangladesh, with $3.4 billion in investments as of 2018, which account for 20 per cent of the total FDI stock in Bangladesh. The vast majority of these investments are in the oil and gas, banking and insurance, and power generation sectors.

References

Ahmed, Imtiaz. 2011. 'Bangladesh Foreign Policy: Constraints, Compulsions and Choices', *BIISS Journal* 32(3): 20718.

Amin, Mehedi et al., 'Manpower Exports to Middle Eastern Countries Drop by 48 Per Cent', *Dhaka Tribune,* 3 October 2018. Available at https://www.dhakatribune.com/bangladesh/migration/2018/

10/03/manpower-exports-to-middle-eastern-countries-drops-by-48 (accessed 18 May 2018).

Anwar, Anu, 'How Bangladesh is Benefiting from the China–India Rivalry', *The Diplomat*, 12 July 2019. Available at https://thediplomat.com/2019/07/how-bangladesh-is-benefiting-from-the-china-india-rivalry/ (accessed 18 April 2019).

'Bangladesh, Malaysia, Pakistan to Gain Most from Belt and Road Initiative Project', *The Financial Express*, 19 April 2018. Available at https://thefinancialexpress.com.bd/economy/bangladesh/bangladesh-malaysia-pakistan-to-gain-most-from-belt-and-road-initiative-project-1524116263 (accessed 18 April 2019).

Chakma, Bhumitra. 2015. 'Sheikh Hasina Government's India Policy: A Three-level Game?', *Journal of Asian Security and International Affairs* 2(1): 27–51.

Chattopadhyay, Suvojit, 'Role of Foreign Aid in Bangladesh', *The Daily Star*, 12 July 2018. Available at https://www.thedailystar.net/business/role-foreign-aid-bangladesh-1603780 (accessed 18 April 2019).

Datta, Sreeradha. 2004. *Bangladesh: A Fragile Democracy*. New Delhi: Shipra Publications, 2004.

———, 'Khaleda's Pakistan Visit Shifts Focus to Economic Synergy', IDSA Comment, Manohar Parrikar Institute for Defence Studies and Analyses, 27 February 2006. Available at https://idsa.in/idsastra tcgiccomments/KhaledasPakistanvisitShiftsFocustoEconomicSynergy_SDatta_270206 (accessed 18 April 2019).

———. 2008. 'Bangladesh's Relations with China and India: A Comparative Study', *Strategic Analysis* 32(5): 755–72.

———. 2014. 'Bangladesh–China Growing Ties'. in Satish Kumar (ed.), *India's National Security*, pp. 226–35. New Delhi: Routledge.

D'Costa, Bina. 2012. 'Bangladesh in 2011: Weak State-building and Diffident Foreign Policy', *Asian Survey* 52(1): 147–56.

Gowan, Richard, 'Why 1 Small Nation Plays a Major Role in Peacekeeping', *Centre on International Cooperation*, 5 August 2015. Available at https://cic.nyu.edu/news_commentary/why-1-small-nation-plays-major-role-peacekeeping (accessed 16 November 2018).

'India, Russia, Bangladesh Sign Pact for Rooppur Atomic Plant', *Livemint*, 1 March 2018. Available at https://www.livemint.com/Industry/QD5ex7YkwRkooAmYgWPVHK/India-Russia-Bangladesh-sign-pact-for-Rooppur-atomic-plant.html (accessed 18 April 2019).

Jahan, Rounaq. 2003. 'Bangladesh in 2002: Imperiled Democracy', *Asian Survey* 43(1): 222–29.

Masud, Md. Rezwanul Haque. 2016. 'Inputs in Bangladesh Foreign Policy: A Critical Reappraisal', *Journal of the Asiatic Society of Bangladesh (Humanities)* 61(2): 259–81.

Office of the United States Trade Representative, US–Bangladesh Trade Facts', 20 September 2019. Available at https://ustr.gov/countries-regions/south-central-asia/bangladesh (accessed 18 February 2009).

Rahman, Mustafizur, 'Making the Most of Bangladesh–India Trade', *East Asia Forum*, 17 September 2019. Available at https://www.eastasiaforum.org/2019/09/17/making-the-most-of-bangladesh-india-trade/ (accessed 18 September 2019).

Rashid, Mamun, 'Bangladesh in the Middle East', *The Daily Star*, 6 March 2019. Available at /https://www.thedailystar.net/news-detail-78558 (accessed 18 May 2018).

Rashiduzzaman, M. 1977. 'Changing Political Patterns in Bangladesh: Internal Constraints and External Fears', *Asian Survey* 17(9): 793–808.

Rasul, Ilyas Iftekhar, 'Bangladesh in Peacekeeping: 30 Years of Service and Sacrifice', *The Daily Star*, 29 May 2018. Available at https://www.thedailystar.net/opinion/perspective/bangladesh-peacekeeping-30-years-service-and-sacrifice-1582756 (accessed 18 April 2019).

Report, 'Belt and Road Initiative: Opportunities for Bangladesh', *HSBC*, 6 December 2017. Available at https://www.about.hsbc.com.bd/news-and-media/belt-and-road-initiative-opportunities-for-bangladesh (accessed 18 April 2019).

Shahab Ahmed, Zahid, and Musharaf Zahoor, 2019. 'Bangladesh–Pakistan Relations: Hostage to a Traumatic Past', *Commonwealth and Comparative Politics* 57(1): 1466–2043.

Shah Amran, Syed, 'OIC and Bangladesh', *Prothom Alo*, 6 May 2018. Available at https://en.prothomalo.com/opinion/news/175124/OIC-and-Bangladesh (accessed 18 April 2019).

Shukla, Asish. 2015. 'Pakistan–Bangladesh Relations', *Himalayan and Central Asian Studies* 19(1–2): 210–35.

Siddique, Abu, 'Infrastructure and Energy Bind Bangladesh to China', *The Thirdpole.Net*, 13 *May* 2019. Available at https://www.thethirdpole.net/en/2019/05/13/infrastructure-and-energy-bind-bangladesh-to-china/ (accessed 18 April 2019).

Statistical Year Book Bangladesh. 2018. Available at bbs.gov.bd/site/page/29855dc1-f2b4-4dc0-9073-f692361112da/Statistical-Yearbook (accessed 18 April 2019).

'UN Suspends Technical Support to Electoral Process in Bangladesh', *The China Daily*, 11 January 2007. Available at english.peopledaily.com.

cn/200701/11/eng20070111_340278.html (accessed 18 February 2009).

Uz Zaman, Rashed, and Niloy Ranjan Biswas. 2014. 'Bangladesh's Participation in UN Peacekeeping Missions and Challenges for Civil–Military Relations: A Case for Concordance Theory', *International Peacekeeping* 21(3): 324–44.

Zaman, Arshad-uz, 'OIC and Bangladesh: Anniversary thoughts', *The Daily Star,* 9 July 2005. Available at http://archive.thedailystar.net/2005/07/09/d507091501105.htm (accessed 18 April 2019).

Notes on the Editors and Contributors

Salehuddin Ahmed is Former Governor, Bangladesh Bank (Central Bank), Dhaka, Bangladesh.

Shamsher M. Chowdhury is Career Diplomat, and Former Foreign Secretary, Bangladesh.

Sreeradha Datta is Centre Head, Neighbourhood Studies, and Senior Fellow, Vivekananda International Foundation, New Delhi, India.

Roshni Kapur is Research Analyst, Institute of South Asian Studies, National University of Singapore, Singapore.

Amena Mohsin is Professor, Department of International Relations, University of Dhaka, Dhaka, Bangladesh.

S. Narayan is Senior Research Fellow, Institute of South Asian Studies, National University of Singapore, Singapore.

Amitendu Palit is Senior Research Fellow and Research Lead, (Trade and Economic Policy), Institute of South Asian Studies, National University of Singapore, Singapore.

Sarin Paraparakath is Senior Vice-President, Guidance, Government of Tamil Nadu, India.

Mustafizur Rahman is Distinguished Fellow, Centre for Policy Dialogue (CPD), Dhaka, Bangladesh.

Selim Raihan is Professor, Department of Economics, University of Dhaka, Dhaka, Bangladesh.

Amit Ranjan is Research Fellow, Institute of South Asian Studies, National University of Singapore, Singapore.